DEBT TO SOCIETY

DEBT TO SOCIETY

Accounting for Life under Capitalism

MIRANDA JOSEPH

University of Minnesota Press
Minneapolis
London

Portions of chapters 1 and 2 were previously published as "A Debt to Society," in *The Seductions of Community: Emancipations, Oppressions, Quandaries,* edited by Gerald W. Creed (Santa Fe: School of American Research Press, 2006); reprinted by permission of SAR Press; all rights reserved. Portions of chapter 1 were published as "Theorizing Debt for Social Change: A Review of David Graeber's *Debt: The First 5,000 Years,*" at http://www.ephemerajournal.org. Chapter 4 was published as "Gender, Entrepreneurial Subjectivity, and Pathologies of Personal Finance," *Social Politics* 20, no. 2 (2013): 242–73; reprinted courtesy of Oxford University Press. An earlier version of chapter 5 was published as "Accounting for Interdisciplinarity," in *Interdisciplinarity and Social Justice: Revisioning Academic Accountability* (Binghamton, N.Y.: SUNY Press, 2010).

Published by the University of Minnesota Press
111 Third Avenue South, Suite 290
Minneapolis, MN 55401–2520
http://www.upress.umn.edu

Library of Congress Cataloging-in-Publication Data
Joseph, Miranda.
    Debt to society : accounting for life under capitalism / Miranda Joseph.
    Includes bibliographical references and index.
    ISBN 978-0-8166-8741-1 (hc : alk. paper)
    ISBN 978-0-8166-8744-2 (pb : alk. paper)
    1. Economics—Sociological aspects. 2. Accounting—Social aspects. 3. Finance—Social aspects. 4. Capitalism—Social aspects. I. Title.
    HM548.J67 2014
    330—dc23

                                                                                2014011998

Printed in the United States of America on acid-free paper

The University of Minnesota is an equal-opportunity educator and employer.

20 19 18 17 16 15 14   10 9 8 7 6 5 4 3 2 1

For Sandy

CONTENTS

INTRODUCTION

Modes of Accounting

The credit score, once a little-known metric derived from a complex formula that incorporates outstanding debt and payment histories, has become . . . so widely used that it has also become a bigger factor in dating decisions. . . . "I take my credit score seriously and so my date can take me seriously," she said. A handful of small, online dating Web sites have sprung up to cater specifically to singles looking for a partner with a tiptop credit score. "Good Credit Is Sexy," says one site. (Silver-Greenberg 2012)

This excerpt from a front-page *New York Times* article is but one of many bits of evidence of the penetration of credit and debt into our contemporary popular culture that I might have plucked from the day's media flow. Social theorists have argued that debt is now *the* determining economic and thus social relation, superseding relations of production or consumption as the socially formative economic dynamic. Maurizio Lazzarato's recent book *The Making of the Indebted Man* (2012, 90, 89) draws on Gilles Deleuze, "who summed up the transition from disciplinary governance to contemporary neoliberalism in this way: 'A man is no longer a man confined [as in disciplinary societies] but a man in debt [in a control society],'" to argue that "debt constitutes the most deterritorialized and the most general power relation through which the neoliberal power bloc institutes its class struggle."[1] Certainly, debt plays a particularly prominent role in the contemporary regime of capital accumulation, as debt-related financial instruments from sovereign bonds to securitized credit card debt, student debt, and mortgages are traded on global markets, while stripping assets from individuals in their roles as citizens and consumers. No doubt, debt plays a hegemonizing function: disciplining (or even accumulating) individual and collective subjects of capital by linking their sense of

independence to normative participation in particular social formations as they "freely choose to take on debt" (Heintz and Balakrishnan
2012, 390) under the constraints of that same double-edged freedom
Marx (1977, 271) ascribed to "free labor."

While acknowledging this prominence of debt to contemporary subjectivity and social relations, I take as axiomatic Janet Roitman's (2003,
212) argument that debt is not exterior to social relations, not a "per-
version or deviation," but a fundamental and constitutive social fact.
Debt as a dimension of social relations may then have no history (as,
per Louis Althusser, "ideology has no history" [1971, 159]). However,
any particular indebtedness must be the product of history; moreover,
any particular *fact* of indebtedness must be the product of a process of
knowledge production. So, rather than approach debt as an origin or
cause or crisis to be analyzed, I posit debts, and credits, as components
of complex performative representational practices that I refer to collectively as *accounting*.

In this book, I explore modes of accounting—techniques for constituting and attributing credits and debts—as they are deployed to
create, sustain, or transform social relations. I envision accounting
very broadly and inclusively: sometimes I talk about accounting in
the narrow sense of the production of corporate financial statements,
or financial and nonfinancial calculations and documents produced
for management purposes, such as budgets and performance metrics;
sometimes I mean accounting as the domain of finance-related representations produced and consumed in the context of "personal finance";
sometimes I consider accounting as the calculation of the "debts to society" paid by those deemed "criminal";[2] and sometimes I refer to the
social accounting through statistics that Foucauldians have identified
as the core technology of biopolitical governmentality.[3] Sometimes I
consider nonnumerical accounting, as various kinds of narrative strategies are frequently offered as potentially transformative or disruptive
alternatives to quantitative accounting. Across all of these modes, accounting technologies, I argue, constitute, bind, link, graft, subsume,
and integrate *particular* concrete subjects with the abstract social processes that those subjects manifest;[4] or, to put this in more explicitly
Marxian terms, accounting practices articulate particular subjects in
the dynamic and open *totality* of social relations that are, at the same
time, immanent to those subjects. In making these arguments, I learn
from and have been propelled by the extraordinarily rich literature in

critical accounting studies, the discovery of which has been one of the true pleasures of my work on this project. As I explore diverse instances of accounting practices, then, I advance and elaborate an argument for recognizing and engaging the *dialectics* of abstraction and particularization through which capitalism operates and through which we can gain a critical grasp of that operation.

For the most part, the discursive materials that sustain the argument of this book are artifacts of the current conjuncture, frequently named neoliberalism. *Neoliberalism* refers simultaneously to a particular regime of capital accumulation and a regime of biopolitical governmentality. Life under neoliberalism has been shaped by the intertwined accounting practices through which these regimes of accumulation and governmentality have been implemented. These two domains of accounting are really inseparable. Those attending to neoliberalism as an economic phenomenon point out that the combination of privatization and personal responsibilization with the "financialization of daily life," as Randy Martin (2002) calls it, or the "everyday life of global finance," in Paul Langley's (2008) phrasing, requires us all to manage our own lives through financial accounting practices. Meanwhile, our daily financial lives are shaped by statistical practices, such as credit scoring. Financial accounting at its more sophisticated levels is also interdependent with statistical practices; for example, the valuation of many financial assets and instruments is based on calculated probabilities. (The financial crisis of 2008 is sometimes blamed on a statistical error in that the correlation in the values of mortgage-backed securities was assumed to be lower than it turned out to be.) And Foucauldian scholars of financial accounting articulate its operations as, like statistical accounting, integral to governmentality (see, e.g., Jones and Dugdale 2001, 35; Miller 1994; Miller and O'Leary 1987; Power 1997). These intertwined accounting practices pervade lived neoliberalism across a wide array of institutions and domains: financial accounting in its managerial mode (cost accounting) and the "metrics" (statistical measurements) meant to track the efficacy of practices and programs are the technologies by which most public institutions are managed (and held "accountable"), including, as cultural studies scholars often bemoan, the universities in which we work. The same technologies are used to run health care and criminal justice systems and K–12 educational systems. But it is important not to be narrowly literal about "governmentality"; these life-shaping accounting practices are not deployed only or even primarily by state agencies.

This book's chapters examine various intersections of financial accounting, juridical accounting (assessment of so-called criminals' debts to society), managerial accounting (specifically, "performance measures" in public higher education), and social accounting (the statistical and/or narrative production of populations) through which neoliberalism has been lived. For example, as I discuss in chapter 4, "Accounting for Gender," statistical analyses produced by financial services companies, nonprofit organizations, and academics are circulated through a wide variety of old and new media (television and books as well as websites) that serve as vehicles for the marketing of financial products and services to populations constituted through the statistical narratives. These accounts produce and deploy gendered norms, in the form of statistical and narrative claims about the attitudes and behaviors, competence or incompetence, of women as financial practitioners, household managers, retirement investors, and so on. But crucially, these gendered norms are deployed not only to constitute markets for financial products and services but also, more fundamentally, as a pedagogy of "entrepreneurial" subjectivity: stories about women's financial pathologies mark the boundaries of the normative ideal for all. In fact, these narratives work as marketing tools because, as Kathleen Woodward (1999, 180) points out, we are hailed by statistics—we learn who we are, and the norms to which we should aspire, through statistical stories.[5] But, as I discuss in chapter 3, "Accounting for Time," to a great extent we live these aspirational norms in the mode of failure—we don't measure up, and sometimes we don't even try.

Stark divergences in whether and how differently situated subjects are held accountable for their failures constitute one of the scandals revealed by the recent financial crisis, even as the representations of that scandal conceal more than they reveal. Scholars attending to the neoliberal project of dismantling the welfare state have focused on how the promotion of "personal responsibility" is used to justify the upward redistributions of wealth and infrastructures of support. If *responsibility* is a seductive term, calling us to voluntarily "do the right thing," as the Liberty Mutual Insurance Company's "Responsibility Project" would have it,[6] *accountability* has a different set of connotations. *Accountability* suggests a regime in which you *will* do the right thing (act responsibly) or be punished. Throughout the past few crisis years, the debate over who is to blame and who should be held accountable has obsessed the media.

For instance, on August 1, 2012, the *New York Times* featured a story on the left side of the first business page headlined "Jury Clears Ex-Citigroup Manager of Charges" (Lattman 2012). It reported that an executive had been accused by the U.S. Securities and Exchange Commission (SEC) of misrepresenting a deal to clients—a deal in which the bank put together a derivative financial instrument (a collateralized debt obligation, or CDO) that it sold and simultaneously "bet against"—but had been acquitted. However, the article reported, the jury also offered a statement urging the SEC to continue "investigating the financial industry." The article then offered this interpretation: "The statement appears to echo frustration felt by many Americans that Wall Street executives had not been held responsible for its questionable actions leading up to the financial crisis." Meanwhile, on the right side of the same page, an article reported that the Federal Housing Finance Agency (FHFA), which oversees Fannie Mae and Freddie Mac, had once again rejected the idea of offering debt (principle) forgiveness to mortgage holders (Appelbaum 2012). The crux of the reasoning seemed to come at the end of the article, which reported that the head of the agency, Edward DeMarco, feared that doing so would provide an incentive for mortgage holders to default.

I note this (deliberate?) juxtaposition because it presents precisely the divergence in regimes of accountability of concern to the jurors in the first article, where the financiers who controlled the accounts were not only *not* held accountable, but various policies allowed them to believe that they need not aspire to responsibility. By contrast, excessive concern for "moral hazard" stopped the FHFA from offering any aid to suffering individuals.[7] The jurors' view was expressed more bluntly by the guy next to me on a plane recently who saw me reading Michael Lewis's exposé of life at Salomon Brothers investment bank in the 1980s, *Liar's Poker* (1989). As we talked about the repetition of similar financial dramas over time, he argued that "the Wall Street guys need to be locked up and lose their fortunes, so that their wives would have to live in condos like Bernie Madoff's wife"; only then, he suggested, might those guys be incentivized to stop. They might, but they won't; they know that but for the rare exception of a few individuals, their kind do not actually have to pay their debts. And while we may share the jury's frustration, some caution is warranted before we pile on to demands for accountability that ultimately affirm the juridical regime of accounting "debts to society" that has been so central to the reproduction of racial hierarchy in the United States.[8]

It took some time for accounting to emerge as the through line of this project. This book has been written slowly, in fits and starts, over quite a few years. I began—and my investigation of the phrase *a debt to society* began—as an effort to contribute to antiprison scholarship; I hoped the tools at my disposal, my scholarly training, my approach to thinking about economic processes and social formations in relation to each other, might be useful in responding to the urgent injustice of mass incarceration. And at the same time, as I was finishing *Against the Romance of Community* (Joseph 2002, 98–100), where I first perceived the abstraction/particularity dialectic that will be developed more fully here, I started to realize the centrality of debt to the community–capitalism relation (there discussed briefly with particular reference to microcredit). And, having investigated the performativity of production and consumption, I knew that my next task would be to examine the role of finance capital in social formation. While my contribution here to the prison-abolition effort is ultimately indirect at best, the issue of what form of accounting puts so many people in prison, and what alternative accounts we might offer, remains an animating question for this project.

In the early days of this work, my attention to debt and finance might have been prescient—those issues were not yet headline news. But then in 2007 subprime loans became newsworthy,[9] British bank Northern Rock failed, and Merrill Lynch and Citibank CEOs Stan O'Neal and Chuck Prince lost their jobs due to losses on mortgage-related financial instruments (see Bajaj 2007). And then it was 2008, when the subprime mortgage crisis became a financial crisis and, with the Lehman Brothers bankruptcy, evolved into an economic crisis. Suddenly this project became timely, even urgent. Now the so-called crisis has passed; a "modest economic recovery" (Associated Press 2010) has restored the profitability of banks. Meanwhile, too many people continue to suffer long-term unemployment and underemployment. Much incisive analysis of the financial crisis has been offered by scholars across a number of fields, making this project seem belated. But, as Lauren Berlant argues in "Slow Death" (2007b; discussed more fully in chapter 3) crisis

temporality does not provide the greatest insight into the ongoing, ordinary, endemic processes of exploitation, or into (at least some forms
of) what David Harvey (2003) calls "accumulation by dispossession"
and Costas Lapavitsas (2009) calls "expropriation."

Necessarily, then, working beyond crisis temporality, learning from
and thinking along with others, my hope is to contribute to the collective efforts to generate analyses of the current conjuncture that enable
us to nudge the present in a different direction, toward more broadly
shared well-being and less widely experienced deprivation. I join the
effort among contemporary cultural studies and feminist studies scholars to understand the affective qualities of daily life under neoliberalism and, now, neoliberalism-in-crisis. At the same time, in alliance
with those in critical finance studies, I seek to provide a structural
account of "the crisis" against the individual blame game. In the early
years and even now, media representations of the ever broadening,
deepening, lengthening disruption of the flows of capital tack back and
forth between quantitative abstractions (percentages of homes in foreclosure, billions of dollars lost by financial institutions) and qualitative
narratives (the troubles of particular homeowners or financial institution CEOs) as they ponder how to distribute blame between greedy,
irresponsible banks and greedy, irresponsible borrowers. Muckraking
reports from nonprofit organizations use statistical analyses to identify
patterns of differential and predatory marketing of subprime loans to
people of color and to women. Such reports suggest that there might
be something more going on than individual greed or irresponsible behavior, and yet they do not have the theoretical tools or political intent
to provide a substantial account of that "something more." While such
an account would never have had any impact on the efforts of mainstream policy makers to restore the power and health of the machinery
of capital accumulation, I can only hope that a better analysis might
help those of us who would interfere with that machinery.

During the time of writing, the world has changed. I, too, have
changed. As I began to investigate incarceration, I was increasingly
absorbed by my own institutional inhabitations: the public university,
the mortgaged house. Some of my adventures and meanderings during
these years are described more or less explicitly in various chapters
of this book. Others are not described and are not interesting except that
they make me a participant observer, of a particular class and location,
in the experience of neoliberalism at its height and through its crisis.

My partner and I bought a house, took out a couple of mortgages, and saw the value of the house rise and fall quite dramatically, with our state, Arizona, being an epicenter of the mortgage debacle. Likewise, I saw the state budget collapse and the funding of the state university in which I work slashed, in consequence of which the university restructured in typical ways.

Living through these times, through some of the most "normal" life and work projects—from personal financial management to the increasingly administrative job of an academic[10]—has shaped this book, for better and worse. While I participate in such projects with great privilege—as a tenured faculty member, I have a degree of financial security almost unknown in the current global economy—one of the animating puzzles for this project has always been the participation, or at least aspiration, of so many to such conformity, in the face of good evidence that for most people the effort will not produce well-being. That is, I have been interested in what Berlant (2011) has so incisively named and theorized as "cruel optimism." And if this book has something to offer to the already rich literature on the political economic dynamics of this period, it may well be through a sometimes embarrassing exposure of and reckoning with my own attachment to normative striving as well as that attributed to others. As will become evident but cannot be represented adequately through quotations and citations, this project is indebted to Berlant: hearing and reading and rereading and discussing what is now the essay "Slow Death," as presented in talks and a manuscript shared for discussion in a work-in-progress seminar, shaped my questions and provided language for my inarticulate pondering. But the conversation with Berlant and her work also helped me to make sense of, tolerate, and incorporate into this project the self-interruption in which I myself was engaged.

That self-interruption often entailed participating in university administrative projects. Chapter 5, "Accounting for Interdisciplinarity," corrals two of those life-course tangents, revisiting my participation so as to transform it into an additional opportunity to examine conjunctures of accounting practices and regimes of accountability. I am aware that in certain ways these experiences transformed me and thus have reshaped the book in ways that I can only partially recount. Most notably, this project proposes a more intimate engagement with quantitative knowledge production than do most feminist cultural studies projects. I always intended to engage the question of cultural studies method; my administrative adventures reframed and broadened my concerns about method. I had to confront and engage in a personal and active way the greater ability of certain methods of knowledge production to attract support for their very existence; and at the same time, I had to confront the apparently greater potency of certain methods of knowledge production to govern, as I engaged (in) those methods, in the role of both governed and governor (by which I mean bureaucrat). I say "apparently" because this has also been a period in which science has been most disdained/denied at the highest levels of mainstream politics, with the administration of U.S. president George W. Bush claiming to make its own reality and cutting funding for research and education (see Suskind 2004). The upshot, as I will elaborate momentarily, is that this project refuses at the outset the common dismissals of quantification, resituating some quantitative accounts as what Stuart Hall (2003, 129), after Marx, calls the "complex concrete," the empirical provocation to analysis, while it stakes out an argument for abstraction as a crucial form of knowledge production. By reemphasizing the value of certain methodological insights of Marxist cultural studies that have been relatively neglected, this project aims to articulate techniques for seeing the less visible social processes taking place not so much *behind* the veil of the visible fetish as *immanent* to it.

The uneven distribution of accountability and the centrality of diverse practices of quantitative accounting to the depredations visited by neoliberalism have led many scholars to attribute these violences to the technologies of quantification, calculation, and abstraction themselves. In "Can Numbers Ensure Honesty?" Mary Poovey (2003, 28) describes an emergent "culture of finance" as a "new axis of power," in which "quantification, . . . an inherently abstracting process," produces a "conflation of representation and exchange" that allows financiers to manipulate accounted values at will for their own benefit while putting others at great risk. In addition, Poovey's essay "The Twenty-First Century University and the Market" (2001b, 9, 12) posits "the language of numbers" as the instrument by which "market logic" has devalued and diminished "the humanities." Likewise, as I will discuss at length in chapter 1, in his widely circulated book *Debt: The First 5,000 Years,* David Graeber (2011, 14) argues that quantification allows debt to become "a matter of impersonal arithmetic—and by doing so, to justify things that would otherwise seem outrageous or obscene." Meanwhile, he articulates abstraction as the physically violent removal of things and people from their embeddedness in social relations for purposes of commercial exchange (159). Similarly, Woodward (2009, 209) suggests that abstraction separates or detaches: "A statistic is completely detached from the world, much as today's global financial markets are detached from actual production in a local economy. . . . statistical probabilities seem to implicate us as individuals in scenarios of financial ruin or disaster by disease and weather; that is, abstraction, expressed by the ultimate abstraction, one that is infinite—numbers."

These scholars can draw on and generally expect a supportive reception for their arguments based on a long history of critique of abstraction, and especially as quantification. Some of those arguments have been articulated as political theory. As Marx points out in "On the Jewish Question" (1978, 30), political liberalism envisions an abstract "political emancipation" that depends on and constitutes particular difference and thus comes at the cost of what he calls real "human emancipation."[11] Feminist and critical race studies critiques of political liberalism have theorized the abstracted citizenship of liberalism as marginalizing or excluding some particular differences in order to privilege others, positioning women and people of color as the embodied and marked subjects inadequate to abstract citizenship.[12] (This structure sets up the yearning for universality on the part of subjects entrapped by particularization that Andrea Smith describes; Smith 2010b, citing Denise Ferreira da Silva 2007.) The form of some of these political critiques has been reiterated in feminist critiques of quantitative knowledge production. Feminists have expressed concern about the ways that quantification reduces or erases particularity, difference, and context in the processes of categorization; often depends on categories that reconstitute and reconfirm existing social hierarchies; and produces an illusion of objectivity while breaking the connection between researcher and researched thought to be necessary for better knowledge production.[13]

In *Making a Social Body* (1995, 28–29), Poovey argues that the practices of quantification that produce these outcomes are integral to a "distinctively modern form of abstraction," articulated at a philosophical level in the works of Descartes, Hobbes, and Petty and embodied in and epitomized by the nineteenth-century factory, which would, if it could, produce a "totalized field of power" (25–26). This form of abstraction is ontologically dependent on representation (26), dematerializes and generalizes (27), and creates uniformity and thus equivalence.

This leads to the "notion that value is a function of quantity" (29) and thus is more concerned with aggregates than with individual cases. Such abstraction, then, is presumably contradicted by alternative rationalities (such as those that do value personal experience, or that do not treat all cases/subjects as functional equivalents) and especially alternative, nonnumerical forms of representation: "dramatic tableaux rather than catalogues of aggregates" (51). At the same time—and this is a crucial insight—Poovey recognizes that modern abstractions tend to be "instantiated" in "concrete instances of the phenomenal world and institutionalized as codified practices" (9); however, in keeping with her understanding of abstraction as tending toward totalization, she reads this instantiation as only one-directional, in which the instance is given its meaning and power by the abstraction, in a "process of vivification that . . . Marx and Freud referred to variously as reification, commodification, and fetishization" (9).

Despite this reference to Marx, Poovey's analysis of the emergence of modern forms of knowledge in *Making a Social Body* (as well as in *A History of the Modern Fact*, where she provides the history of an earlier stage in the development of modern abstraction) is better understood to be in dialogue with and a contribution to the Foucauldian literature, for which the critical type of quantification is statistics. The Foucauldian literature figures statistics not as an inadequate representation but rather as *the* preeminent technology of governmentality, enabling the production and management of populations—the exercise of power through the selective and directive encouragement of life captured in the term *biopolitics*—as well as disciplinary strategies directed toward the formation and management of individuals.[14] In *Against Prediction,* Bernard Harcourt (2007) describes in detail the rise and deployment of a particularly pernicious instance of such accounting practices, in which statistical prediction of criminal activity creates institutionalized and systemic practices of racial profiling and racialized incarceration.

No doubt, quantification and abstraction are powerful and dangerous. And for some scholars, refusal, evasion, and flight are the only possible and necessary responses. Less able to envision detachment from the apparatuses of governmentality, my project here is to explore the extent to which their very potencies—the productivity of accounting, accountability, and abstraction in constituting subjects and social formations—are subject to engagement, transformation, and appropriation.[15] What would such an engagement look like?

Cultural studies scholars' attribution of violence to quantification is too often accompanied by dismissal of statistical knowledge. But such dismissal ignores our reliance on the work of colleagues in the social and behavioral sciences to identify disturbing social patterns that we are provoked to investigate and explain using methods and social theories foreign to those who have produced that provocative work. This suggests that identification of otherwise invisible patterns is a useful, even maybe indispensable, tool in the kinds of social criticism practiced by cultural studies scholars. This is the argument that Donna Haraway (1997, 197–202) makes in her discussion of "the statistics of freedom projects." But we must also recognize the limits of such statistical pattern recognition as a descriptive step on the path toward another level of analysis that would allow us to see/grasp/articulate/understand/conceptualize the dynamics generating those observed patterns.

We can draw from Marx and Marxist theory a strategy of critical abstraction through which invisible social processes can be perceived beyond the visible empirical phenomena that are the instantiations of those processes. I am hardly the first to suggest this; in fact, I need to quickly differentiate my position from that of Marxist scholars such as Teresa Ebert, who mirror the critics of abstraction by demonizing what they consider to be a fetishization of the concrete among poststructuralist scholars of culture in favor of analyses that aim to grasp the abstract social totality (see Ebert 2009), offering an equally one-dimensional approach. Woodward's argument for interpellation by statistics suggests that statistical abstractions don't just "seem" to implicate us but are *lived* particularly and concretely, just as it turns out that global finance has an "everyday life" lived by mortgage holders and student debtors, among others. This suggests that what Poovey calls "instantiation" gives life to, as much as it receives life from, abstraction. So, as I will elaborate in chapter 1, "Accounting for Debt," I join Stuart Hall and Alberto Toscano, among others, who build on certain key passages in Marx's works to develop a critical practice adequate to grasping what I have called the dialectic of abstraction and particularization.

Chapter 2, "Accounting for Justice," explores the relation of accounting to justice. Noting the frequent contemporary deployments of numerical accounts by social justice advocates, I turn back to the nineteenth century to investigate the emergence of the intertwined strategies of knowledge production and inscription, of juridical and financial accounting, that undergird the modern regime for the constitution and management of "criminals" and "debtors," categories that are related and differentiated, generating social—and especially racial—hierarchies. I make use of Derrida's critique of liberal "law" (as opposed to "justice") in "Force of Law" (1992) to articulate the "force" of accounting. I then explore some important efforts to critique and promote alternative modes of accounting (such as social accounting and restorative justice) that might be more just or at least more enabling of social justice efforts.

Chapters 3, 4, and 5 engage contemporary conjunctures of accounting, responding to particular provocations in somewhat diverse styles and voices. Chapter 3, "Accounting for Time," which was written slowly over time as the "crisis" unfolded, gives particular attention to the role of accounting in shaping time and thus the temporal structuring of life itself, while dwelling in/on the inherent contradictions of entrepreneurial subjectivity. The chapter thus takes up an approach I elicit from the work of Berlant and of Saba Mahmood, who argues in *Politics of Piety* (2005, 23) for attending to "the variety of ways in which norms are lived and inhabited, aspired to, reached for and consummated," while working through a variety of minicases, including self-representations offered by participants in a small organization in Tucson, Arizona, for formerly incarcerated women called the Women's Re-entry Network; media representations of those said to be subjects of the "culture of poverty"; and media representations of subjects of personal and global finance (in part through readings of the extensive attention given to these issues before and during the financial crisis in the *New York Times*).

As I have noted above, chapter 4, "Accounting for Gender," examines the constitution of gendered norms for personal financial attitudes and behaviors through the production and circulation of knowledge, especially statistical articulation of populations, across the domains of popular culture, marketing research, and legitimate social science. It thus addresses a nexus of the two central features of neoliberalism I have described here: governmentality and financialization. I argue that gendered norms play a key role in articulating neoliberal norms more broadly. Specifically, negative, pathologized portrayals of women as impulsive shopaholics on one hand and paralyzed noninvestors on the other indicate the boundaries of responsible entrepreneurial subjectivity. At the same time, these portrayals, found across a range of discursive sites, proffer images of proper femininity and masculinity, to be achieved through the enactment of different configurations of financial attitudes and behaviors. Noting the diversity and internal contradictions implicit in responsible entrepreneurial subjectivity (really, subjectivities), I conclude the chapter with a consideration of the implications of the recent financial crisis and concomitant shifts in the evaluation of gendered behaviors.

Chapter 5, "Accounting for Interdisciplinarity," reflects on the production of academic knowledge as it is shaped by practices of accounting and discourses of accountability. Noting that "interdisciplinarity," especially in the sciences, has become a priority for many public research universities as they seek to expand "tech transfer" and produce marketable intellectual property, I explore the relationship between interdisciplinarity in science ("the way business is done") and cultural studies' use of interdisciplinarity as a strategy for progressive political intervention ("no business as usual"). Disassembling what sometimes seems a "regime" of accounting and accountability into a miscellany of diverse, contradictory, and ever-changing sets of performance measures, I suggest that there are openings for intervention and the development of alternate accounts.

1 ACCOUNTING FOR DEBT

Toward a Methodology of Critical Abstraction

You are not a loan.

—Strike Debt slogan

Money, credit, and capital are, quite literally, systems of writing. . . .
Understanding finance as a performative practice suggests that processes of knowledge and interpretation do not exist in addition to,
or of secondary importance to, "real" material financial structures
but are precisely *the way in which finance materializes.*

—Marieke de Geode, *Virtue, Fortune, and Faith*

THE EFFORTS of the Occupy Wall Street spin-off Strike Debt to incite collective disidentification with financial debts are inspiring and
often brilliant. Strike Debt is premised on the primacy of debt, rather
than labor or consumption, to the contemporary economy: "As individuals, families, and communities, most of us are drowning in debt
for the basic things we need to live, including housing, education,
and health care."[1] Part of the brilliance of the "You are not a loan"
slogan is that it crystalizes, even as it rejects, that the 99 percent,
those whose American Dream has become nightmare, whose aspirations and expectations have been disappointed, *identify* with their
financial debts.

Highlighting the subjective dimension of the financialization that is
such a prominent aspect of the neoliberal regime of capital accumulation, Strike Debt proclaims:

Debt keeps us isolated, ashamed, and afraid—of becoming homeless, of going
hungry, of being crippled or killed by treatable illness, or of being trapped
in poverty-level jobs. Those facing foreclosure, medical debt, student debt,

or credit card debt feel alone, hounded by debt collectors, and forced into unrewarding work to keep up with payments.[2]

Strike Debt, maybe inadvertently, thus recognizes the internality of debt to social relations and subjectivity—as well as the internality of social relations and subjectivity to debt.

Commodification indicates a process of appropriation and transformation that integrates ever more arenas of life into the social relations of exploitation symptomatized by the commodity form; *financialization* can be understood to refer to the extension and intensification of the social relations entailed by the creation, exchange, and management of financial instruments. I join Dick Bryan, Randy Martin, and Mike Rafferty (2009, 460) in understanding financialization as "a development within rather than a distortion of capitalist production," which nonetheless has specific and "extensive" "ramifications" worthy of investigation and explication. Such ramifications involve not merely increases in the absolute and relative size of financial markets but also increases in the socially formative role of finance. In this context, *debt* should be understood as a "form of appearance," as Marx (1977, 148) might say, of the broader social processes of exploitation and dispossession, an immanent component of social relations rather than an external imposition. I thus depart from the rhetorical strategy of Strike Debt—maybe "you" are a loan after all, or at least a debtor, as you might once have been a consumer, or a worker—to investigate how you are somehow managing, materializing in your own very being, the tensions and contradictions between concrete use value and abstract value that drive capitalist social formation processes.

As I recognize the immanence of debt, I surface the role of accounting in constituting the social relations of credit and debt. The centrality of accounting, the writing of credits and debits, is clear with regard to "high finance." Marx (1990) and Hilferding (1981) referred to financial instruments as "fictitious" capital. Financial instruments are representations and derivations of many and various moments in the accumulation and circulation of capital, titles to claims on interest or dividends (or the obligations to pay), so-called paper wealth that exists only "in an accounting sense" (Hilferding 1981, 111). Nonetheless, referring to these as "fictitious" is unfortunate because it wrongly suggests that they are false or illusory. We can have no doubt of the real role of financial practices—the creation and circulation of financial instruments—in accumulating, circulating, dividing, distributing, and redistributing capital accumulations, as well as structuring the relations among those engaged in such practices. What Strike Debt and the theorists of neoliberal financialization recognize is that the socially formative practices of financial accounting are no longer limited to some esoteric world of "high finance." Later chapters of this book join the collective effort to describe and critique the subjectivity and social relations of this regime of accumulation.

In this chapter, I aim to articulate a theoretical and methodological framework. I begin with an examination of David Graeber's (2011) theorization of debt, which I take to be a kind of "repressive hypothesis" (Foucault 1978) that relies on a demonization and reification of abstraction to cast debt as only destructive of some autochthonous or natural communal energy. Explicating Graeber's position provides an opportunity for me to lay out, in contrast, my understanding of the dialectic of abstraction and particularization—built on Marxian elaborations of moments in Marx's texts—and the strategy of critical abstraction necessary to confront it. In the second section, departing from Janet Roitman's (2003) articulation of the productivity of debt, I offer a representation of credit and debt as socially formative social formations. In other words, like commodities, credit and debt depend on and articulate a complex of abstract determinations. Following Roitman, I begin to articulate the performative role of accounting in that articulation.

Theorizing Debt for Social Change: What Is the Problem?

Credit and debt have been written into what I have elsewhere identified as the Romantic discourse of community, a discourse pervasive in the social science literature as well as in the popular imagination that situates community as the "other" of modernity and especially of capitalism, which is generally understood to destroy community. This discourse, I have argued, reveals even as it denies the supplementary role of community for capitalism. The development and expansion of credit is explicitly seen to have participated in or at least to be symptomatic of the destruction of community, and community is often posited as a bulwark against the evils of indebtedness.

The inscription of credit into the Romantic discourse of community turns on a story of a decline in interpersonal trust. In one of many instances of such inscription, Avram Taylor (2002, 2) connects the history of credit with the discourse of community in his assessment of "the effect of credit on working class communities" and his attempt "to relate this to the debate about the decline of the working class community" in the post–World War II period in Britain. Taylor argues that forms of credit characteristic of prewar working-class communities, such as neighborly mutuality, corner-store credit, and street lenders, which evidenced an "interpenetration of instrumental and affectual rationalities" (35), declined in the postwar period, replaced either by more impersonal forms of credit demonstrating, he says, a decline in trust or by forms of credit that instrumentalize affectual bonds. Taylor is helpfully explicit in naming the sociological tradition that elaborates the Romantic narrative of community: he states that his theoretical perspective is based on "Weber's ideas about the rationalisation of social life, Ferdinand Tönnies' notion of Gemeinschaft and Gessellschaft, as well as the more recent work of Anthony Giddens on the nature of modernity" (10).

The same story of coincident expansion and depersonalization of credit is narrated in a March 2007 *New York Times* article by Lynnley Browning:

> The old way of processing mortgages involved a loan officer or broker collecting reams of income statements and ordering credit histories, typically over several weeks. But by retrieving real-time credit reports online, then using algorithms to gauge the risks of default, Mr. Jones's software allowed subprime lenders like First Franklin to grow at warp speed. . . . "It takes the subjectivity out of the good ol' boy system in which Martha knows Joe, who approves the loan—then you end up with a bad decision," Mr. Jones said.

But the article expresses some ambivalence, suggesting that the depersonalization enabling the ultimately disastrous subprime bubble had a silver lining of more rational and thus fair lending practices. One might hope. Unfortunately, according to the complaint filed by the city of Baltimore against Wells Fargo in the wake of the subprime crash, this was not the case:

> Wells Fargo also created a unit called the "Affinity Marketing Group" in its Silver Spring, Maryland office to target African Americans, including members of African-American churches. Paschal Decl. ¶ 12. All the employees of the Affinity Marketing Group were African American. *Id.* Subprime loan officers in the group who targeted African Americans were selected on the basis of their race and Wells Fargo's desire to use African-American employees to target African-American customers. *Id.*
>
> 55. Another way in which Wells Fargo targeted African Americans was by tailoring its subprime marketing materials on the basis of race. *Id.* ¶ 11. It devised software to print out subprime promotional materials in dif-

ferent languages, one of which was called "African American" by Wells Fargo. *Id.* . . .

56. Wells Fargo's subprime loan officers held derogatory stereotypes of African Americans, which contributed to their targeting of African Americans in and around Baltimore for subprime loans. Jacobson Decl. ¶ 28; Paschal Decl. ¶ 8, 16. Subprime loan officers described African-American and other minority customers by saying "those people have bad credit" and "those people don't pay their bills," and by calling minority customers "mud people" and "niggers." Paschal Decl. ¶¶ 8, 16. They referred to loans in minority communities as "ghetto loans." *Id.*[3]

This predatory targeting of subprime loans suggests that the "personal" and "communal" provided a critical supplement here, too. Racism is often at the core of efforts to constitute "community," defining the boundaries of inclusion and exclusion. In this case, while attributing negative personal characteristics—especially lack of creditworthiness—to borrowers, the bank deployed racialized communality by hiring African American loan officers in order to solicit (misplaced) trust from African American borrowers (see also Powell 2010, who reports a similar dynamic in Memphis). Thus the "sophisticated underwriting technology and data that allow [Wells Fargo] to predict with precision the likelihood of delinquency, default or foreclosure" (*Baltimore v. Wells Fargo*, 3), and that would seem to depersonalize the process, in fact became a technology for articulating particular and local subjects of dispossession with/into the global financial system.

The most prominent contemporary inscription of debt into a discourse of community has been performed by David Graeber in his 2011 book *Debt: The First 5,000 Years*, which has received a great deal of attention in academic, activist, and popular media venues (see Hann 2012; Kear 2011; Luban 2012; Meaney 2011). He tells a story not so much of the decline of community as of its violent destruction; moreover, he extends the story into a historical past far older than even the most generous historical periodization of emergent modernity. Graeber has been credited as instigator and theorist of the Occupy movement, and his book clearly aims to support Occupy by encouraging detachment from the sense of moral obligation too many people feel to pay financial debts to financial institutions that feel no reciprocal obligation. Given the leading role debt now appears to play among the strategies of capital accumulation (deployed to strip assets from variously targeted populations) and that our sense of moral obligation can only be accounted as an instance of what Lauren Berlant (2011) calls "cruel optimism," or an attachment that will be self-undermining, Graeber's effort to debunk the "myths" (of barter and primordial debt) that subtend our sense of moral duty with regard to financial debts is valuable and commendable. Like Marx (but not in explicit conversation with Marx), Graeber argues against the projection of exchange (Adam Smith's trucking and bartering) into a mythical past that secures its place in human nature and thus naturalizes and legitimates contemporary relations that have been produced through a history of violence. And like Nietzsche (whose work Graeber does directly engage), Graeber points out that conceptualizations of the social bond as essentially a relation of permanent indebtedness—in which we are always already in debt to the existing social order and/or its representatives—can serve to legitimate established power dynamics and social hierarchies, an important point that I take up in the next chapter.

However, his analysis of—and, I fear, his and others' efforts to generate collective opposition to—our attachments to our debts is limited by the reaffirmation of yet another "myth." In this myth, again and again, across the globe in different times and at different speeds, communal relations based on interpersonal trust are displaced by depersonalized calculation (Joe and/or his pay stubs by the anonymous credit score) and the particular is disrupted or destroyed by being *abstracted*. Thus, despite my admiration for Graeber's accomplishments and precisely in response to the unusually broad impact of his work, I undertake an in-depth exploration of his argument to demonstrate the ways that this myth, like the ones he debunks, has some unfortunate implications, concealing rather than revealing what I will describe as dialectical processes of abstraction and particularization, potentially undermining efforts to mobilize/galvanize a movement of the 99 percent.

The first half of his book, Graeber states, is intended to answer "the central question . . . What does it mean when we reduce moral obligations to debts? What changes when the one turns into the other?" (13).[4] Or, as he puts it later, "How is it that moral obligations between people come to be thought of as debts, and as a result, end up justifying behavior that would otherwise seem utterly immoral?" (158). This question incorporates his answer in that it presumes/establishes a dichotomy between interpersonal obligation and "impersonal" accountable debt. And in his use of the word *reduce* he indicates from the beginning that he understands quantification and depersonalization—the movement away from face-to-face relations—to be a loss, a reduction.

Graeber claims that there are three principles of economic interaction or "systems of moral accounting" (114):

- Communism, which he defines as a relation of distribution rather than ownership. "'From each according to his abilities, to each according to his needs'" (94) is for Graeber the "foundation of all societies" (96). Communism is the domain of the unmeasured: "The surest way to know that one is in the presence of communistic relations is that not only are no accounts taken, but it would be considered offensive" (99).
- Hierarchy, which regulates distribution by custom and habit (109–13).
- Exchange, which distributes goods through reciprocal trade of equivalent values by people who are, therefore, likewise equivalent, and who can end their relationship by settling their debts (102–8). "What marks commercial exchange is that it's 'impersonal': who it is that is selling . . . or buying . . . should in principle be entirely irrelevant. We are simply comparing the value of two objects" (103).

Although Graeber spends much of the chapter in which he lays out this schema demonstrating the intertwinedness of these three modes, and thus that humans cannot be reduced to *Homo economicus,* over the following chapters he reduces this synchronic complexity to a linear diachronic trajectory in which violence brings exchange to dominance over the other two dynamics and "human economies" are destroyed/ perverted by commercial economies.

Human economies are those in which "social currencies" serve primarily "to create, maintain, or sever relations between people rather than to purchase things"; in human economies "each person is unique and of incomparable value, because each is a unique nexus of relations with others" (158). By contrast, in commercial economies, in which money is used for profit, "qualities are reduced to quantities, allowing calculations of gain and loss" (159). When commercial economies come into contact with human economies, Graeber argues, those unique human relations are destroyed.

Initially, it seems that quantification is the crucial problem. It is the technology of depersonalization and thus provides immunity for, or blindness to, immoral or harmful behavior:

> A debt, unlike any other form of obligation, can be precisely *quantified.* This allows debt to become simple, cold, and *impersonal.* . . . it doesn't really matter who the creditor is; neither . . . of the two parties ha[s] to think much

about what the other party needs, wants, is capable of doing. . . . One does not need to calculate the human effects; one need only calculate principal, balances, penalties, and rates of interest. (13; emphasis added)

Sounding a bit like an early Marx figuring money as the root of all evil, Graeber continues, "The crucial factor . . . is money's capacity to turn morality into a matter of impersonal arithmetic—and by doing so, to justify things that would otherwise seem outrageous or obscene" (14).

The emotional appeal of this argument in our current historical moment is clear, as mortgage holders faced with foreclosure bang their heads against impenetrable loan servicing companies. And Graeber's scenario resonates with one of the (many) persistent explanatory tropes for the recent subprime crisis turned financial crisis turned economic crisis: the depersonalization of mortgage lending (noted above). According to this story, in some imagined "once upon a time," often evoked by references to Frank Capra's classic 1946 film *It's a Wonderful Life,* loans were made and held by the neighborhood savings and loan, whose officers made those loans to bank customers they knew personally. Indeed, Floyd Norris begins a December 2007 *New York Times* column on possible government solutions to managing the subprime mortgage crisis with quoted dialogue from Capra's film. This is meant to illuminate a contemporary set of rules proposed by the Federal Reserve "to keep bankers from doing mean and stupid things." In the film, the odious banker Mr. Potter challenges George Bailey's father, a kind and compassionate agent at a small-town building and loan society, demanding mortgage payments from customers at any cost:

> "Have you put any real pressure on these people of yours to pay those mortgages?"
> "Times are bad, Mr. Potter. A lot of these people are out of work."
> "Then foreclose!"
> "I can't do that. These families have children."
> "They're not my children."

Norris asserts the impossibility of Potter, Pa Bailey, or even George Bailey imagining how our contemporary, twenty-first-century mortgage market functions. He notes that the Fed acknowledges, "When borrowers cannot afford to meet their payment obligations, they and their communities suffer significant injury." And he concludes, "Pa Bailey understood that, which is one reason he was unwilling to foreclose during the Depression. He knew his borrowers and they knew him. This generation's lenders did not know their borrowers, but figured that did not matter."

In the run-up to the current debacle, brokers used computer programs to determine loan eligibility and generate mortgages that they aimed to sell off to financial firms that turned them into globally tradable securities. Presumably this new depersonalized and globalized mortgage market harmed bankers' ability and even willingness to make appropriate assessments of creditworthiness: they could feel no sense of responsibility toward borrowers they did not know, or for the quality of loans they were not going to keep on their books. Of course, this explanation runs headlong into the vast evidence of predatory lending by race and gender, which suggests that the characteristics, capacities, and desires of the borrowers were crucial, though not in the way they are imagined to have operated in the "once upon a time" fairy tale.

Despite its emotional appeal and resonance with some of the articulations of alienation to be found in the early Marx, Graeber's articulation of the problem as depersonalization by way of quantification, or abstraction more broadly, like the popular narrative, reaches its limit precisely at this point. His story cannot account for the predatory attention to the particulars of borrowers *enabled* by the apparently depersonalized technologies of mortgage lending. The inscription of debt into a story of the destruction of community by quantification and abstraction fails to account for the generative role of abstraction in social formation. This role *is* articulated in the critique of abstraction that can be found in, and has been developed from, a handful of key passages in the works of the mature Marx.

For Graeber, the emergence of capitalism is but one among many moments in which warring states create markets that turn "human relations into mathematics" (14). Like Marx, Graeber historicizes, but he offers a different history. Marx is concerned with the diverse violences (including, certainly, those undertaken by warring and colonizing states) that produce the specific preconditions for capitalism: on one hand, accumulation of wealth by a minority that can be used as capital and, on the other, dispossession of the majority, who become "free" labor. By contrast, for Graeber state violence plays a decisive role, and what it does is bring exchange to dominance over the other economic dynamics.[5] While for Marx and Marxists such as David Harvey, violent accumulations of wealth, "so-called primitive accumulation"

(Marx 1977) or "accumulation by dispossession" (Harvey 2003, 144), are supplements to exploitation, for Graeber it is the intimate relation of violence and exchange that is at issue.[6]

In discussing the processes by which state-driven commercial economies destroy human economies, Graeber uses the term *abstraction*: "There is every reason to believe that slavery, with its unique ability to rip human beings from their contexts, to turn them into abstractions, played a key role in the rise of markets everywhere" (165). For Graeber, one is turned into an abstraction by a process of physically violent removal from embeddedness in social relations:

> To make a human being an object of exchange, one woman equivalent to another for example, requires first of all ripping her from her context; that is, tearing her away from that web of relations that makes her the unique conflux of relations that she is, and thus, into a generic value capable of being added and subtracted and used as a means to measure debt. This requires a certain violence. To make her equivalent to a bar of camwood takes even more violence, and it takes an enormous amount of sustained and systematic violence to rip her so completely from her context that she becomes a slave. (159)

Where Marx, in the opening pages of *Capital,* articulates the commodity as simultaneously a use value and a value, concrete and abstract, particular and equivalent, Graeber suggests here that these modes are mutually exclusive, that particularity must be destroyed to constitute abstract value. While Graeber is quite right to recognize the material reality of abstraction, in rendering it a noun (or sometimes an adjective) rather than a verb, he positions abstraction (or the abstract thing) as the result of a process, not the process itself, as evidence only of the destruction of social relations, not the construction of such relations.

What is at stake here? "Social relations" are too often relations of oppression, relations that we might want to understand so as to transform. Recognizing abstraction as process rather than product is crucial in this endeavor. So, for instance, Ruth Wilson Gilmore (2002, 16) argues:

> Racism is *a practice of abstraction,* a death-dealing displacement of difference into hierarchies that organize relations within and between the planet's sovereign political territories. . . . *the process of abstraction* that signifies racism produces effects at the most intimately "sovereign" scale, insofar as particular kinds of bodies, one by one, are materially (if not always visibly) configured by racism into a hierarchy. (emphasis added)

In fact, more broadly she argues, "The violence of abstraction produces all kinds of fetishes: states, races, normative views of how people fit into and make places in the world" (16). Despite this potential for violence, she nonetheless identifies "abstractions" as necessary to her own critical analysis:

> My purpose is to use research techniques to piece together a complex (and not necessarily logical) series of abstractions in order at once to analyze and produce a multiscalar geographical object of analysis. . . . For researchers, purpose and method determine whether one reifies race and state—chasing down fetishes—or, rather, discovers dynamic processes that renovate race and state. (16)

Using abstractions to reveal processes of abstraction can also reveal, she argues, "the ways that relatively powerless social actors—e.g., prisoners' mothers and families—renovate and make critical already existing activities, categories, and concepts to produce freedom . . . processes of abstracting and reconstructing geographies of liberation" (17).

Gilmore's complex deployment of the term *abstraction* is indebted to Marx, for whom abstraction is both a social process that really happens as a component of the capitalist mode of production, implied in the production and exchange of commodities, and the necessary mental exercise for the critic who would perceive that social process. Granted, Marx actually says a rather dizzying array of different things about abstraction, using the term to refer to different practices and processes. In efforts to sort out his position, many scholars have turned to two key parts of his texts: the "1857 Introduction" to the *Grundrisse* and the opening chapters of *Capital*. In the *Grundrisse*, Marx offers an explicit discussion of methodology, comparing the "abstractions" deployed by the political economists to his own techniques and conceptual tools. As I have already noted, in the opening chapters of *Capital*, Marx uses the term *abstraction* in describing the difference between (exchange) value and use value. In "The Open Secret of Real Abstraction," Alberto Toscano (2008) provides a very helpful review of some of the key Marxist appropriations and interpretations of these passages in works by Roberto Finelli, Louis Althusser, Jacques Rancière, Alfred Sohn-Rethel, Slavoj Žižek, and others, on which I draw here. But I first learned to read the "1857 Introduction" through Stuart Hall's interpretation of it and continue to rely on his explication as well.

In the "1857 Introduction," Marx offers a critique of abstraction as reductive generalization, as deployed by the political economists, that resonates with feminist critiques of abstraction such as Mary Poovey's (discussed in the introduction). Marx describes a form of abstraction that creates categories by finding commonality through a process of stripping away; this practice "reduces, by abstraction, specific historical relations to their lowest common, trans-historical essence" (Hall 2003, 116). This kind of abstraction is of limited value, as Marx (1973, 85) explains, with reference to "production":

> Whenever we speak of production, then, what is meant is always production at a definite stage of social development. . . . However, all epochs of production have certain common traits, common characteristics. *Production in general* is an abstraction, but a rational abstraction in so far as it really brings out and fixes the common element and thus saves us repetition. Still, this *general* category, this common element sifted out by comparison, is itself segmented many times over and splits into different determinations. Some determinations belong to all epochs, others only to a few. . . . the elements which are not general and common, must be separated out from the determinations valid for production as such, so that in their unity . . . their essential difference is not *forgotten.*

The crucial flaw in "those modern economists who demonstrate the eternity and harmoniousness of the existing social relations lies in this *forgetting*" (85). As Hall (2003, 120) summarizes, "What is 'common' to production, then, as produced by the process of mentally abstracting its 'common' attributes, cannot provide a method which enables us to grasp, concretely, any single, 'real historical stage of production.'" Moreover, abstraction as a stripping away to some essential core can land you in a Hegelian realm, in which "thought" operates independently (119).

However, Marx offers alternative and more useful conceptualizations of abstraction. As Toscano (2008, 274) says:

> The first point to note is that Marx promotes . . . a theoretical break with an empiricist or neopositivist usage of the terms "abstract" and "concrete." . . . Marx reformulates the distinction such that the sensible and the empirical appear as a final *achievement* rather than a presuppositionless starting point.[7]

As Hall (2003, 115) puts it, and as the quote above indicates, "The most concrete, common-sense, simple, constituent starting-points for a theory of Political Economy, turn out, on inspection, to be the sum of many, prior, determinations." In relation to this "complex" "concrete," which is a product of history and of many determinations, related in a particular configuration, abstraction cannot be "fictitious hypostases of a positive, underlying generic essence" (Toscano 2008, 274–75, citing Finelli 1987). Nor can abstraction be separation or alienation, a distancing from reality that leaves the human essence behind (Toscano 2008, 277, citing Rancière 1989, 78–79)—as it seems to be in Graeber[8]—a position that, Jacques Rancière (1989, 98) argues, leads to an "ideology of the concrete," what one might even call a fetishization of the concrete. Instead, for Marx and Marxists, as indicated in Toscano's title, "The Open Secret of Real Abstraction," abstract thought is the product of and strategy for grasping abstraction as a historical, real, social force.

The reality of abstraction for Marx is both historical and structural, located both in the market and in production. In *Capital* (1977, 127), the focus is on the structure and on exchange: "The exchange relation of commodities is characterized precisely by its *abstraction* from their use-values," which further entails the abstraction and homogenization of various specific labors (128). While, in order to perceive this real abstraction, the critic must momentarily "disregard the use-value of commodities" (128–29), the abstraction entailed by the exchange relation is not a mental process undertaken deliberately by the exchangers but rather "a social process" that, as Marx says, "goes on behind the backs of the producers" (135). It is "already present in the social effectivity," according to Žižek (1989, 17, interpreting Sohn-Rethel 1978), that producers confront as the reality of the proportions in which particular commodities can be exchanged, proportions determined by the interaction of "a wide range of circumstances; . . . the level of development of science and its technological application, the social organization of the process of production . . . the conditions found in the natural environment" (Marx 1977, 130). Each of these determinants is itself the product of history.

In fact, both the real social processes of abstraction and the abstract categories through which we initially (if only partially), ideologically, grasp that reality are the products of history, as Marx (1973, 104) emphasizes in the "1857 Introduction" with regard to labor:

> As a general rule, the most general abstractions arise only in the midst of the richest possible concrete development where one thing appears as common to many, to all. . . . Indifference towards specific labours corresponds to a form of society in which individuals can with ease transfer from one labour to another and where the specific kind is a matter of chance for them hence indifference.

Moreover, "the example of labour shows strikingly how even the most abstract categories, despite their validity—precisely because of their abstractness—for all epochs, are nevertheless, in the specific character of the abstraction, themselves likewise a product of historic relations" (105). While some scholars have noted the modularity and interchangeability of labor to which Marx referred, a then-emerging corollary of industrial production, they argue it has since been supplemented by new, real abstractions associated with so-called cognitive capitalism: the "general intellect" for Virno (2004, 63–66), or "the proliferation and production of new procedures, of codes of production, of transmissible 'hows' rather than measurable 'whats'" (Toscano 2008, 284, with reference to Cillario 1996).

The crucial point remains that concrete particularities are the products and bearers of abstract social processes and relations, socially effective, generative, "real" abstractions. This has important epistemological implications:

> The concrete is concrete because it is the concentration of many determinations, hence unity of the diverse. It appears in the process of thinking, therefore, as a process of concentration, as a result, not a point of departure. . . . the abstract determinations lead towards a reproduction of the concrete by way of thought. (Marx 1973, 101)

Or, as Hall (2003, 129) puts it, the epistemological challenge of Marx's theorization of abstraction is

> to "think" this real, concrete historical complexity, [to] reconstruct in the mind the determinations which constitute it . . . [such that] what is multiply determined, diversely unified, in history, already "a result," appears, in thought, in theory, not as "where we take off from" but as *that which must be produced.*

Recognizing the concrete as the point of arrival, some Marxists (famously, Georg Lukács 1971) have urged analysis of any/every phenomenon in relation to the "totality" of determinations. While I do not want to take on the whole totality debate here, I acknowledge that some enactments of totality thinking tend toward "totalization," in the sense of a one-dimensional determinism that prioritizes certain social dynamics over others, thus, for instance, trivializing sexuality as "not only 'merely cultural' but . . . always already localized and particularized" (Floyd 2009, 5, quoting Butler 1993). This kind of totalization—that prioritizes ahead of time some determinations over others—risks a kind of hubristic imagination of a closed system, positively grasped, fully accounted for, and, moreover, fundamentally missing the point; as Floyd argues, "The effort to think totality is itself [or ought to be] a critique of ontological and epistemological particularization," the "severing of connections" promoted by capitalism itself (6). Marx suggests that we can understand abstract determinations as the generators of the particular distinct historical formations; likewise we can and should deploy abstractions in thought, not in order to ignore, suspend, or destroy differences, but rather, as Gilmore (2002, 16) does, to de-fetishize, to discover "dynamic processes that renovate" such formations.[9] So, against trivializations of "particular" formations of social difference on one hand and demonizations of abstraction, as in Graeber, on the other, our challenge is to sustain an appreciation of their dialectical and supplementary relation.

Addressing this relation, Avery Gordon offers "haunting" as a name for the "mediation" between the abstract system and the concrete particular structure and subject. Haunting answers the dangers of totalization by marking simultaneously the limits of our knowledge and the open dynamism of overdetermining social forces, for, according to Gordon (1997, 19),

> in haunting, organized forces and system structures that appear removed from us make their impact felt in everyday life in a way that confounds our analytic separations and confounds the social separations themselves. . . . Could it be that analyzing hauntings might lead to a more complex understanding of the generative structures and moving parts of historically embedded social formations in a way that avoids the twin pitfalls of subjectivism and positivism?

The mediations to which I attend in this book are not hauntings but accountings, seemingly much more accessible processes. And precisely for that reason, it is crucial to join Gordon's effort to honor a "Marxian concept of haunting" (20) that attends to the lived immanence of what is absent, invisible, abstract, and potent.

As a matter of social theory, then, it becomes clear that by articulating "abstractions" *only* as the reified consequence of violence, Graeber misses the dialectical and generative dimensions of the processes in which abstraction participates. And conversely, such a rendering idealizes the uniqueness of the interpersonal relations he posits as prior to such abstraction, ignoring the social processes generating those relations. This "repressive hypothesis" regarding abstraction has important political implications. A review of two alternative interpretations of Graeber's key case studies is revealing.

Graeber notices that the exchange of women depends on a hierarchy in which women are lower than men (the objects exchanged rather than the subjects of the exchange). Graeber's (2011, 137) anthropological example here is the Lele, "an African people who had, at the time Mary Douglas studied them in the 1950s, managed to turn the principle of blood debts into the organizing principle of their entire society." For Graeber, however, as the scaling up from exchange of women to exchange of women for soap to systematic enslavement suggests, the real problem is the transition from human economies to commercial ones. And, in fact, he moves right along to the Atlantic slave trade as his primary example: slaves are "people stolen from the community that made them what they are. As strangers to their new communities, slaves no longer had mothers, fathers, kin of any sort" (146). But it seems to me that his readings of both the exchange of women and enslavement are revealing of the limits of his theoretical framework.

Gayle Rubin argues that "the exchange of women" is a highly problematic concept both theoretically, insofar as Claude Lévi-Strauss locates it as a prerequisite of culture, and empirically. She argues that the Lele people are actually quite unusual in *explicitly* exchanging women; and while such exchange might be plausibly interpreted as occurring in some cultures where it is not explicit, in others, according to Rubin (1975, 176), "the efficacy of the concept becomes altogether questionable." She suggests that the concept of "exchange of women" is useful only insofar as it indicates a "sex/gender" system, in which women "do not have full rights to themselves" (176–77). As Rubin theorizes it, a sex/gender system generates social relations and the subjects of those relations. The exchange of women enables men to enact and sustain relations, "the flow of debts and promises" (182), among themselves and their kinship groups. But this exchange also depends on prior constructions of gendered divisions of labor and norms of heterosexuality that constitute gendered divisions of people, to whom different characteristics are attributed and of whom those different characteristics are required (178–80). While women may be treated as objects of exchange, this does not mean that they actually lose all qualities or, for that matter, all subjectivity. Rather, Rubin assumes that there is a subjectivity; it may manifest as submission, as a "sexuality [that] responded to the desire of others," or as resistance, "female attempts to evade the sexual control of their kinsmen" (182). For Rubin, the question is how, by what interaction of psychic and social regulation, that subjectivity is constituted.

Precisely because of its socially constitutive function, Graeber wants to understand the exchange of women as illustrative of so-called human economies. But this requires underreading the systemic production of the category or class or subject position of "women" as social currency; while particular women may be exchanged in particular transactions due to their unique interpersonal relations, their exchangeability is constituted by and constitutive of their subjection as *women*. Women are not ripped from their context but rather are exchanged in context. Meanwhile, Graeber wants to mark as catastrophically different the exchange of women from the moment it involves violence or money (and again he argues, "The equation [of human life with money] was established at the point of a spear" [144]). In this moment, despite his recognition that wives created through enslavement "quickly develop new ties" (145), human economies are perverted and become dehumanizing economies, in which, as far as Graeber can see, particular relations no longer play a meaningful role.

Graeber's description of the violence of turning people into commodities through enslavement both resonates with and differs importantly from Saidiya Hartman's examination of that process in *Lose Your Mother* (2007). Hartman too emphasizes the estrangement of enslavement, the violent separation of those enslaved from their kin. And she claims as her own perspective, as a living legacy of slavery, a constitutive lack of and yearning for belonging that is not to be satisfied by her return to Africa to explore the history of enslavement. But where Graeber insists that the violence occurred through "the very mechanisms of the human economy" (155), perverted as they were by the slave trade, Hartman does not romanticize prior communal relations in Africa; she argues that Africans enslaved other Africans who were already perceived as others and outsiders (4). Like Graeber, Hartman marks the destructive role of money; but in her account, although Africans accumulated money—cowrie shells, demeaningly called "Negro money" (207)—primarily for prestige rather than as capital, that did not stop the accumulative effort from driving extraordinary depredation. Further, the destruction of that currency by Europeans, far from rehumanizing social relations, actually served to consolidate European domination. Meanwhile, Hartman argues that for Europeans, the color line was constituted through the slave trade, establishing a "hierarchy of human life" that "determined which persons were expendable, and selected the bodies that could be transformed into commodities" (6). Her emphasis, it seems to me, is on the production of social relations as much as on their destruction. Relations of hierarchy, of disrespect, of disregard within and between racialized social formations are constituted in the process and wake of extracting people from their prior relations. And then also, but only through extraordinary effort, a community among the fugitive (225) and the enslaved—as Hartman discusses in *Scenes of Subjection* (1997, 59–61)—may also be constituted.

As Hartman (2007, 24–25) describes them, these social relations entail a particular slave subjectivity, a subjectivity of limited agency, "legally recognized as human only to the degree that he is criminally culpable" and socially recognized as joyful and seductive in order to "deny, displace, and minimize the violence" of "white enjoyment" of "wanton uses of slave property." And then, she argues, in the wake of formal emancipation, freed slaves were resubjected as morally and economically "indebted" subjects. While under slavery economic abstraction (the treatment of racialized persons as commodities) constituted the particularity of slave subjectivity, after emancipation the political abstraction of liberal citizenship—liberal freedom—constituted racialized economic subjects, always already indebted for their very freedom as well as for their economic survival, through an intertwined regime of labor contracts and criminal codes (125–27). (I discuss the role of accounting in the resubjection of freed slaves in chapter 2.)

My point here is not to set up a debate over "the facts" between Rubin and Graeber or Hartman and Graeber, but rather to notice that their different theoretical orientations generate different apprehensions of the problem. Rubin and Hartman reveal constitutive relationships between abstraction and particularization. Graeber dichotomizes particularity and abstraction, demonizing only abstraction, as if it could be disentangled from processes of particularization, and offers particularization as a cure.

Graeber's approach directs our attention to the evil 1 percent and helps us to disidentify with the masters of the universe. Whereas Brent White (2009) has gained some popular infamy for encouraging individuals to throw off their moral bonds to their debts and join the rationality of the financial institutions by "walking away" from mortgages that it would be financially irrational to repay, Graeber sees the real cure in a repersonalization of credit relations. Rather than individual rational financial evaluation, Graeber's approach calls for a collective debt strike and thus a more fundamental rejection of financial rationalities.

But Graeber cannot give an account of the process that produces not only the radically unequal distributions of wealth and power between the 99 percent and the 1 percent but also the differences *within* the 99 percent on which the abstract circulation and calculation of capital, for the benefit of the 1 percent, also depend. Rubin's and Hartman's approaches (which I would suggest align in important ways with a Marxist analysis) do enable an understanding of the generation of the particular differences on which the abstractions depend. As Angela Davis noted in her speech for the Occupy protesters in New York: "There are major responsibilities linked" to the decision "to come together as the 99 Percent. . . . How can we be together, in a unity, that is not simplistic, and oppressive? How can we be together in a unity that is complex, and emancipatory?"[10] While the socially destructive power of capitalism's processes of abstraction certainly needs to be addressed, we cannot answer Davis's question unless we recognize the socially constructive particularizing power of capitalism as well.

Credit, Trust, and the Extension of Social Relations

Janet Roitman's essay "Unsanctioned Wealth; or the Productivity of Debt in Northern Cameroon" (2003, 211–12) suggests an alternative to the "repressive hypothesis" with regard to debt:

> I would like to consider the ways in which debt is plenitude and not simply lack. Perhaps economic debt is not just the constraint of society, the rubber stamp of a certain social status: being liable, a liability. . . . debt can be a mode of either affirming or denying sociability. . . . What is the difference between debt that disturbs and what one might call socially sanctioned debt? How is it that some forms of wealth are socially sanctioned in spite of their origins in debt relations while others are denounced . . . ? Ultimately, these questions are oriented toward the matter of the productive nature of debt and debt relations.

Writing about Cameroon in the late twentieth century, Roitman recognizes the instrumental role of debt in "the construction of an 'extraverted' political economy" (212), deployed to open a postcolonial national economy in service to the interests of global capital. At the same time, however, she also draws on Nathalie Sarthou-Lajus's work to conceptualize debt not only as an external imposition but as *"already there"* (212). Roitman understands *debt* in a way that recalls Althusser's (1971, 161) articulation of *ideology,* modeled on but also "not unrelated to" the unconscious, "endowed with a structure and functioning such as to make it a non-historical reality, i.e. an *omnihistorical* reality ... in the sense in which the *Communist Manifesto* defines history as the history of class struggles." Debt, Roitman suggests, is a structure that constitutes the subject as dependent and inevitably located in asymmetrical relations (213). As a form empty of content, debt in this theorization is crucially different from the primordial debt myths deployed in the constitution of hegemony that Nietzsche and Graeber critique. However, for Roitman, specific debts, like ideologies, are of course historically determined: "The mediation between the ontological status of debt and the sociology of debt is, then, a matter of history, or the production of truths about the history of debt and indebtedness" (213). This theorization of debt usefully directs our attention to the determinate relations constituting any achieved state of indebtedness as the noninevitable outcome of dynamic processes, in which debts and credits are articulated through practices of knowledge production. Moreover, in this view, debt is not a product of other events but the name for a dimension of social formation processes, of the active structuring of social relations through deferral across time and space of the completion or closure of an exchange (213).

When viewed as the positive extension of relationality, an unclosed, uncompleted economic exchange is often called *credit* rather than debt. The relationship between credit and debt can be understood in a number of different ways. Like production and consumption, as Marx articulates their relation in the "1857 Introduction" (1973, 91–94), credit and debt can be understood as immediately *identical*: credit received is simultaneously a debt owed. They can also be understood as *mediating* of each other: credit is fully realized only when the loan is made and the borrower accepts the debt; the need for borrowed funds gives credit its reason for being; the existence of loanable capital creates the need it satisfies. And they can be understood as constitutive of each other. But one might object, as Marx does to the Hegelian sort of identity and unity that might be imagined for production and consumption, that it is important to recognize the ways credit and debt are *separated* across social space and time in any particular instance (93–94). As production is separated from consumption by distribution, the producer's relation to the product becomes an "external one" (94), so credit is separated from debt by the social distance and difference between creditor and debtor, the time between loan and repayment, which creates the potential for contradiction and crisis—the loan might not be repaid. With the complexities of this relation in mind, I start this part of my argument with credit because, while it inevitably entails debt, it does have the positive, socially productive connotations that I aim to evoke. In fact, credit is often thought to depend on—or even to be—*trust,* a prized social substance, said to grease the wheels of the economy while providing stability to social institutions (such as governments and banks).[11]

Precisely because of the association of credit with trust, histories of credit, of the nearly incredible increases in the sheer quantity of credit of all kinds during the modern period, become stories of the development of social formations as much as stories of the destruction of prior formations. Some versions of this story fit in quite well with the narrative of communal decline in that they describe a replacement of "interpersonal trust" with "system trust" (Luhmann 1979). Presuming that trust must be established on some basis beyond the transaction itself, histories of credit describe a shift in the location of that external basis from personal relationships to the state, corporations, and monetary systems. For instance, in *A Republic of Debtors* (2002), a narrative of the emergence of bankruptcy law in the nineteenth-century United States, Bruce Mann attributes to economic expansion a rapid depersonalization of credit through the invention of bills of exchange and other credit instruments that allowed owners of debt to be far removed from the original transactions and the original social relationships in which those transactions were embedded. In a sense, this depersonalization fostered a destruction of social bonds as creditors turned to the courts and prisons to deal with debtors. In Mann's story, however, these social bonds are restored in a more depersonalized form through bankruptcy legislation, which allows debtors (of a certain class) to maintain, at least to some extent, their social position. Likewise, in assessing the conditions that enable the development of "good" credit systems (through a comparative history of European nations), free market enthusiasts Scott B. MacDonald and Albert L. Gastman (2001, 3) argue that the crucial factor is the development of third-party guarantors for impersonal credit relationships—that is, the ability of merchants to trust not each other but the rule of law and states as enforcers of contracts.

In his history of credit in early modern England, Craig Muldrew revises this opposition between interpersonal and system trust. Muldrew accepts Niklas Luhmann's contrast between preindustrial interpersonal trust and modern system trust, between what Muldrew describes as "the early modern web of tangled interpersonal obligation" and "a utilitarian world in which a massive body of economic knowledge is used to operate systems which seek to reduce economic agency into predictable patterns of behavior" (1998, 6). However, he argues *against* Luhmann's functionalist presupposition that trust sustains credit relations, that it is a means for creating such structures, proposing instead that trust is the substance of social process itself, that it *is* credit (and vice versa). As Rowena Olegario (2006, 6) argues with regard to the nineteenth-century United States, "'trust' did not refer primarily to the personal ties that gave members of small and tightly knit groups the confidence to trade with one another. Instead . . . trust denoted the willingness of creditors to risk their capital."[12]

Muldrew, noting the complexity of interpersonal trust in early modern English trade, suggests that interpersonal trust—precisely in the form of credit, which represents, indistinguishably, both reputation and economic ability—is both possible and necessary even in relatively complex societies (7). In Muldrew's account, as the dramatic expansion of the early modern English economy extended social relations beyond their prior scope and thus required new management strategies, creditor–debtor relations were the medium, the language, the means of communication through which social relations were negotiated and performed (5). That is, while recognizing vast changes in social and economic relations, Muldrew's arguments point to the significance of interpersonal relations in modern, apparently depersonalized systems. These arguments suggest that we might see the "system trust" Luhmann describes not only as abstract trust in a system but also as a commitment to an "imagined community" (Anderson 1983).

MacDonald and Gastman (2001, 128) emphasize the centrality of the imagined community of the nation: the "process of nationalism," which, as "the cause and the result of wars and imperial expansion, multiplied national debt and produced crises of public credit . . . as well as the creation of a working public and private credit system ca-

pable of allowing the state to function and private enterprise to flourish." Likewise (though obviously from a very different perspective), in
his discussion of "so-called Primitive Accumulation," Marx (1977, 919)
argues:

> The only part of the so-called national wealth that actually enters into the
> collective possession of a modern nation is—the national debt. . . . And
> with the rise of national debt-making, lack of faith in the national debt
> takes the place of the sin against the Holy Ghost, for which there is no
> forgiveness. . . . The public debt becomes one of the most powerful levers of
> primitive accumulation.

The central role of nationalism suggests that interpersonal relations
are not replaced by an impersonal state acting merely as an administrative enforcer of contracts.

Rather than understanding the growth of credit as actually disinte-
grative of social bonds, Poovey argues that we might understand the
narrative of lost trust (of communal decline) as integral to the development of credit. To make this point, Poovey (1998, 41) quotes John Mellis,
a sixteenth-century promoter of double-entry bookkeeping, who

> conjures a fictitious "time past" when a merchant's honesty could be signi-
> fied by using a single phrase ["By the faith of a good faithfull merchant"]
> both to establish historical precedent for the prestige he now claims and to
> designate the present as a fallen or debased age, whose "decay" is signaled
> by the distrust now generally directed against merchants.

Poovey thus presents the narrative of lost trust and declining communality as a performance aimed at establishing creditworthiness, that is,
repute as an opportune site through which abstract capital might flow.
Meanwhile, Poovey also suggests that the narrative of lost trust elides
other transformative and constitutive social processes: it is not merely
coincidental that Mellis is a promoter of double-entry bookkeeping,
which, as I will discuss below, Poovey describes as another crucial
technique for performing creditworthiness (41). Despite, or rather precisely through, new modes of accounting—of knowing and constituting subjects—persons and their relations continue to play a crucial role
in the circulation of credit.

In emphasizing the elaboration of relations of trust and credit, I
do not mean to suggest some sort of effusion of sweetness and light.
As Marx (1977, 875) makes clear in connecting nationalist faith in the
national debt to "so-called primitive accumulation," the "historical

process of divorcing the producer from the means of production . . . written in the annals of mankind in letters of blood and fire," the constitution of credit relations that are also social relations incorporates diverse subjects as unequal subjects of capitalism, of exploitation and domination. And it can produce wrenching and painful transformations to existing social relations as particular subjects embody abstract economic processes that are in a sense beyond them.

In her ethnographic study of Midwestern farm loss in the 1980s and 1990s, Kathryn Dudley (2000) argues that access to credit had everything to do with the reputation and family name of the recipient, with assessments of the farmer's character and work ethic. By contrast, farm loss had everything to do with shifts in international markets and international relations leading to a crash in the value of the farmland and crop prices. Dudley highlights that the loss of a farm was nonetheless accounted as a matter of personal responsibility by the farmer's friends and neighbors, who distanced themselves from the farm loser and bought up the farm loser's means of production (land, equipment, and so on) in the foreclosure auction. Similarly, in his discussion of credit in early America, Mann (2002, 16) shows the central role of communal relations in constituting creditworthiness, while emphasizing the constitutive and transformative role of credit in those relations:

> Not surprisingly, sureties [additional signatories to loans] almost invariably were friends or relatives of the debtors whose debts they warranted—suretyship rested on blood, affection, and honor, not profit. Family ties notwithstanding, by securing the express written promises that constituted commercial transactions, sureties were creatures of a commercial economy, not a traditional one.

When debtors failed, they put their families and friends at risk, often pulling them into insolvency. As Mann says, "Every suretyship was thus a potential creditor–debtor relationship, both between the original creditor and the surety, and between the surety and the original debtor" (16). Here, interpersonal relations constitute creditworthiness even as those interpersonal relations are reconstituted by debt.

As I suggested above, the contemporary subprime mortgage debacle provides another example. Popular narratives blame the "depersonalization" of credit for the recent crisis. And it does seem that the financial structure of the subprime mortgage market—in which high fees and interest rates, as well as prepayment penalties, were expected to ensure profitability across thousands of loans, especially when securitized, even if a relatively large percentage failed—was meant to enable a *disregard* for the person and creditworthiness of the individual borrower. But the displacement of redlining by predatory lending across the full array of consumer finance indicates a financial structure that is not impersonal, does not disregard the persons involved, but rather actually depends on a *disrespectful regard* for particular borrowers. As Vikas Bajaj and Ford Fessenden note in a pair of 2007 *New York Times* articles that first appeared in print under the joint headline "The Subprime Landscape, from Detroit to Ithaca,"[13] specific groups of people were targeted, based primarily on race but also on gender, age, and neighborhood, for these "high-cost" loans; even holding income stable, the concentration of subprime loans was reportedly dramatically higher in Black and Latino neighborhoods. In the collapse of the market, it was precisely those specific people who were first and most severely subjected to accumulation by dispossession, stripped of their homes and home equity (Dymski 2009). Of course, subprime mortgage finance is not an isolated case. In fact, all the diverse strategies for what Gayatri Chakravorty Spivak (1999, 237) has called "credit-baiting," at scales ranging from microcredit development programs to "payday" loans to International Monetary Fund lending to "developing" nations, might be said to depend on or produce debtor subjects whose racial, sexual, national, and class identities and communal membership are crucial to the transaction. Disrespectful regard, I propose, needs to be understood as a social relation.

The Performativity of Financial Accounting

Recognizing disrespect as a social relation suggests that particular subjects and communities do not stand outside credit relations and do not provide protection from them. Rather, predatory lending in a globalized, computerized, securitized market evidences the articulation of abstraction and particularity. We might then want to turn our critical attention to the technologies of articulation, to distinguishing particular regimes of accounting as they constitute credits and debits, creditor and debtor subjects, the spatial dimensions of financial markets and social relations, and the temporalities through which our financialized lives are played out. Understanding accounting in the broadest sense, exploring various particular regimes, is the project of the various chapters of this book. But the field of critical accounting history has undertaken the project in a very direct and concrete way.

There is a fundamental debate in accounting history between those who see the development of accounting techniques as merely utilitarian, with techniques developed as needed by business, and those associated with critical accounting history who read the development of accounting as constitutive and particularly as playing a role in discipline (if they are Foucauldians) or exploitation (if they are Marxists).[14] Some have argued that the invention of double-entry bookkeeping in the early modern period was constitutive of the emergence of capitalism itself given its role in rendering "into objective, quantified terms the concept of capital as claims against listed resources" (Previts and Merino 1998, 5). Across this divide, developments in accounting practice are seen to have shifted over time such that under mercantilism, the purpose of accounting was to keep track of transactions; managerial or cost accounting (arguably serving the functions of discipline and exploitation) emerged only with industrialization; and accounting for the purpose of public accountability became significant only for corporations aiming to attract and pool capital from multiple sources and did not truly come into its own until the development of capital markets such as the New York Stock Exchange in the nineteenth century.

Describing the functions of double-entry bookkeeping in the sixteenth century in England, Poovey (1998, 59) suggests that discipline and public accountability are inherent in the form of double entry itself (see also Thompson 1994; Aho 1985, 2005; Hoskin and Macve 1988, 1994, 2000). She argues that the newly invented double-entry bookkeeping did not serve the function of actually rendering any sort of realistic account of one's assets. Rather, it was a rhetorical strategy for demonstrating precision, accuracy, and balance. As "one of the earliest systems to privilege both things in themselves (the objects and money the merchant traded) and a formal system of writing numbers that transformed representations of these things into usable facts" (29), double-entry bookkeeping constituted a precursor of what Poovey calls "the modern fact"—a particular kind of particular that can stand as evidence for induced abstraction.

Reading Mellis's textbook, Poovey notes that early double-entry accounting systems included at least three books that gradually rendered financial transactions more abstract: the first was a "memorial" in which the "master or his agent" used both narratives and numbers to "chronicle each day's business transactions as they occurred"; the second was a "journal" into which an accountant would transcribe the transactions, using fewer words and more numbers in an indexable arrangement (42–43). Finally, the double-entry ledger itself categorized and generalized transactions, created a balance of credits and debits through the introduction of fictitious personas (particularizations of abstract capital) such as "Money" or "Stock," to or from whom debts might be owed, and elided the potential temporal gaps between money owed and money actually in hand (59). Double-entry bookkeeping thus required the subordination (and translation into numbers) of particulars (which seemed to be privileged because they appeared to, but did not quite, refer to specific transactions in the world) to a formal system in which the particulars became meaningful (64).

As a rhetorical strategy, the formal precision created an impression of accuracy and thus of transparent representation of empirical particulars (64). According to Poovey, "The balances produced by this system of writing proclaimed the creditworthiness of the individual merchant; more generally, the system's formal coherence displayed the credibility of merchants as a group" (xvii). And further, as a public and rule-bound system of writing, double-entry bookkeeping not only linked particular economic transactions to an abstract system but also linked particular subjects to abstract subjectivity. On this point, it is worth quoting Poovey more fully:

> Double-entry bookkeeping's writing positions weakened status differences by making every writer who was willing to write to rule equivalent . . . interchangeable. Most analysts who have noticed this effect have emphasized its disciplinary quality. . . . more significant from a historical perspective . . . is that the generalized subject positions created by double-entry's preference for writing to rule anticipate the universal human subject. (65)

Here, she locates early double-entry bookkeeping as playing a groundbreaking role in the development of the procedures of abstraction and particularization that define not only modern science (as she points out) but also capitalism and liberal governmentality. As I will argue in the next chapter, accounting turns out to be a central technology for constituting and articulating particular subjects as differentially creditworthy bearers not only of abstract capital, of financial credits and debts, but also of juridical credits and debts.

There is much to be learned from Poovey's reading of double-entry bookkeeping in early modern England, and she is no doubt right that a social, as well as epistemological, transformation is "anticipated" in double-entry bookkeeping. But as the accounting historians indicate, financial accounting did not take on until later the widespread and pervasive role in social formation processes that it now seems to have. In keeping with Marx's call to attend to the particular configurations of determinations that constitute a given historical conjuncture, after a brief contemporary interlude I turn in the next chapter to the nineteenth-century United States to observe the intertwined transformations of criminal justice and debt management coincident with the growing centrality of accounting to social formation.

2 ACCOUNTING FOR JUSTICE

Beyond Liberal Calculations of Debt and Crime

> In a sense we have come to our nation's capital to cash a check. When the architects of our republic wrote the magnificent words of the Constitution and the Declaration of Independence, they were signing a promissory note to which every American was to fall heir. This note was a promise that all men, yes, black men as well as white men, would be guaranteed the unalienable rights of life, liberty, and the pursuit of happiness.
>
> It is obvious today that America has defaulted on this promissory note insofar as her citizens of color are concerned. Instead of honoring this sacred obligation, America has given the Negro people a bad check, a check which has come back marked "insufficient funds." But we refuse to believe that the bank of justice is bankrupt. We refuse to believe that there are insufficient funds in the great vaults of opportunity of this nation. So we have come to cash this check—a check that will give us upon demand the riches of freedom and the security of justice.
>
> —Martin Luther King Jr., "I Have a Dream" address

WHAT IS THE RELATION of accounting to justice? Derrida's essay "Force of Law" (1992) explores the relation between law and justice. Derrida argues that law is the site of force, "always an authorized force, a force that justifies itself or is justified in applying itself" (5). "Justice" exceeds the law, depending on a "decision" that cannot be fully guided or guaranteed by application of the law. Law is inhabited by force not only because it is organized to serve "the economic and political interests of the dominant forces of society," Derrida argues, but also because "the founding and justifying moment that institutes law implies a performative force" (13), an inherent, ungrounded, constitutive force, that is in evidence again in each implementation of the law. I take accounting to be, like law, a set of rules and procedures that can and should be subject to critique not only as an instrument of established dominant powers but also as a performative force, a socially formative force. And, as in the case of law, in relation to accounting the question of justice is not fully answered by conformity to rules and procedures.

The relation of accounting to justice is a question not only for philosophers but also for those engaged in activist work for social change, practical work of all kinds on behalf of those who have suffered injustice. Martin Luther King Jr.'s most famous speech features an accounting; imagining the social contract through a financial metaphor, his accounting suggests that financial fraud has been perpetrated—a bad check has been passed. Justice is a matter not just of calculating and paying the unpaid debt but simultaneously of crime—though a crime that King seems willing to forgive should the debt be paid. King is not alone in understanding the social contract through a banking metaphor; Cesare Beccaria, one of the key figures in articulating modern liberal criminal justice, describes crime as an overdrawing of one's account in the social contract bank. But, crucially, King reverses the creditor–debtor relation; his accounting posits the society as criminally indebted, where for Beccaria the metaphor articulates the debt of an individual criminal to society.

The deployment of counting and accounting to mark injustices is a nearly inevitable rhetorical strategy for those who seek justice. The opening paragraph of an earlier version of this chapter included the following: "Approximately two million people are currently incarcerated in the United States (a tenfold increase in the last thirty years), and those incarcerated include a disproportionate number of people of color, the poor, the uneducated."[1] These claims are true (actually, the total number is larger now than when I first wrote those words), but my rhetorical strategy of deploying those numbers to indicate a crisis worthy of attention is a formulaic and potentially dangerous use of "the master's tools."[2]

In her 1997 essay "Race and Criminalization: Black Americans in the Punishment Industry," Angela Y. Davis (1998, 63) offers a critique of the use of statistics in debates over crime. She suggests that proponents of more incarceration "employ statistics in the same fetishistic and misleading way as Malthus did" in arguing for solving poverty by killing off the poor. She quotes a Heritage Foundation document that presents a complex calculation: "'If the 55 percent of the estimated 800,000 current state and federal prisoners who are violent offenders were subject to serving 85 percent of their sentence, and assuming [each] . . . would have committed 10 violent crimes a year . . . , then . . .'" In this kind of accounting, Davis points out, "the real human beings— a vastly disproportionate number of whom are black and Latino/a men and women—designated by these numbers in a seemingly race-neutral way are deemed fetishistically exchangeable with the crimes they have already committed or will allegedly commit in the future. The real impact of imprisonment on their lives never need be examined." Lauren Berlant (2007b, 761), noting the frequency with which "social justice activists engage in the actuarial imaginary of biopolitics" in their efforts to generate a sense of crisis, also points to the fetishizing function of such numerical presentations; she contends that emotionally moving statistical representations of suffering populations, addressed to the privileged, may ultimately serve merely to "measure the structural intractability of a problem the world can live with" (762).

Interruption

In December 2006 and January 2007, in collaboration with the University of Arizona's Student Union Gallery, the Women's Studies Department presented *Interrupted Life: Incarcerated Mothers in the United States,* curated by Rickie Solinger through her organization WAKEUP/Arts.[3] This traveling exhibit, composed of eight installations, would seem intended to answer Davis's concern about the erasure of real lives by statistics. The brochure suggests that the exhibit "provides a powerful occasion for paying attention to the fact and experiences of incarceration in the US."[4]

The installation *Stretched Thin: Irishtine and Her Mother,* by Stephen Shames, explores the relationship between one incarcerated woman and her daughter. It includes a poster-size photograph of them displayed between and behind two clothing racks filled with hanging T-shirts. In front of the shirts is a music stand, which supports a binder containing photographs of the daughter with other girls goofing around and with her mother, interspersed with photographs of their letters to each other as well as the girl's journal entries. Letter fragments and some of the same images are printed on the fronts and backs of the T-shirts. Both the shirts and the binder emphasize the

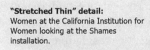

"Stretched Thin" detail:
Women at the California Institution for
Women looking at the Shames
installation.

Photographs and caption from the *Interrupted Life* brochure, provided by
Rickie Solinger with the *Interrupted Life* exhibit. Created by Stephen Shames
for WAKEUP/Arts.

fragmentary and irregular nature of the relationship between mother
and daughter. In the letters the mother answers pleas for more letters—
and the daughter's complaints that the mother is actually less available when out of prison than when inside—with great protestations
of love ("I love you and yes I know that I have not been there for you,
however I never stop loving you or worrying about you") and warn-
ings ("I just want you to be very careful. . . . see me, I jumped into the
fast life . . . got caught up in fast money, stealing and doing drugs").
Both write about other family members—the people now functioning
as mother and family to the daughter as well as the daughter's father,
who is not an active part of the family.

As the title *Stretched Thin* suggests, what we see here, in addition to
the continuity of the connection between mother and daughter, and with
other family members, are the damage, fragmentation, disordering,
and reordering of those relations that seem to result from the mother's
failures, her drug addiction and incarceration. Despite its warm attention to individual lives, this piece might be understood to reaffirm the
persistent image and etiology of the "pathology" of "the Negro family,"

as Daniel Patrick Moynihan called it in his 1965 statistics-filled report, which makes the source of the problem inherent to the troubled woman herself. This structure has been called victim blaming, but it can also be read as a form of fetishism, in that the empirically visible object (here "the incarcerated mother") obscures constitutive social processes. As Ann Cvetkovich (1992) points out in her essay on Marx's use of sensationalism in *Capital,* the visible presentation of the body in pain can interfere with the analysis of the invisible social processes to which the pained body is meant to draw attention. Here, I'm suggesting that such an effect is redoubled because, like the fetishized commodity, the value of which is taken to inhere in its substance, the pathology manifested by the incarceration of the mother and disruption of her family is taken to inhere in those subjects themselves.

Another installation, *THE RULES,* by Sasha Harris-Cronin, represents the rules that shape, limit, and constrain the relations between inmates and visitors. Each of the panels addresses a different set of rules: the application forms and other paperwork that potential visitors, particularly those bringing children with them, must fill out; the searches to which visitors' persons and things may be subjected, and the items they are and are not permitted to bring with them; the dress code to which they must conform; and the limitations on physical contact between visitors and inmates. This work conveys the total relentlessness of the rules, laid out, as they are, as a continuous stream, in all caps, with no space between the lines; the type fades out, blurs, in the middle of each panel, suggesting both the endlessness and the incomprehensibility of the rules. Like *Stretched Thin,* this piece suggests that prison interferes with relationships between inmates and their children—but the visual presentation attributes the interference to the cold officiousness of the system. The very orderliness of the prison system is presented as disrupting the order of human relations (of kinship and community).

Centerpiece is quite complex and a bit overwhelming. Hundreds of four-by-six-inch cards, each decorated or written on by an incarcerated woman, are mounted together in a grid of twenty-four per panel, without separating space or framing. The organizers of this piece, working through various groups that work directly with incarcerated women, sent blank cards into prisons: "We asked women to respond—with visual art or otherwise—to the prompt 'From where I sit, this is what being a mother means to me . . .'" (Solinger 2007, 66). This installation

Centerpiece and *Sonic Wallpaper* in *Interrupted Life* exhibit. (P1270985) license copyright; all rights reserved by daviscenterart. Courtesy of the University of Vermont, Dudley H. Davis Center. http://www.flickr.com/photos/30917988@ N08/4113132147/in/photostream.

too seems to respond to Davis's critique; it offers an implicit invitation to look more closely, to do our time looking at particular cards, to disaggregate the mass of cards, of incarcerated women, and to see the humanity, creativity, emotion, individuality of the particular woman represented by each card. In keeping with the prompt, this is a humanity often marked by or achieved through the woman's role as a mother in relation to her children.

Looking again, other unthematized relations also emerge. Many cards communicate through standard symbols: broken hearts, clocks, images (or, rather, abstracted indexes) of water, sun, birds, flowers. Others offer a single, similarly symbolic word: Love, Freedom, Home, Faith, Shame. Yet others use materials collaged from pop culture (mostly magazines). In depending on these abstract indexical symbols and media artifacts to constitute their individuality, the creators don't so much reveal the meager resources available for their self-expression as situate themselves in a social context that extends beyond their relation to their children.

Taking up a different rhetorical strategy, three comic books produced by an organization called the Real Cost of Prisons Project,[5] originally published separately in 2005 and now collected as *The Real Cost of Prison Comix* (Ahrens 2008), present numerical aggregates and statistical patterns. *Prisoners of a Hard Life: Women and Their Children* begins with a page that juxtaposes statistics about women in prison with images of faces, thus asking us to remember the people referred to by these numbers. This deployment of numbers is no surprise. Davis herself cannot resist citing the numbers:

> While I do not want to locate a response to these arguments on the same level of mathematical abstraction and fetishism I have been problematizing, it is helpful, I think, to consider how many . . . over 5.1 million. . . . According to the Sentencing Project, . . . black people were 7.8 times more likely to be imprisoned than whites. . . . 32.2 percent of young black men and 12.3 percent of young Latino men. . . . A major strength of the 1995 report, as compared to its predecessor, is its acknowledgment that the racialized impact of the criminal justice system is also gendered. (64)

She suggests that these numbers impose on us a "responsibility of understanding," specifically of understanding the "racist logic" (and the "encounter of gender and race") that determines this empirically documented, statistically represented result (64). But, of course, as she argues, the numbers do not speak for themselves; they might very well be deployed to evidence the inherent criminality of Black people.

Representations of large total numbers or dramatic increases of prisoners would seem to be intended to shock or to produce recognition of the seriousness of the issue, though this requires a predisposition on the part of the audience to think incarceration is bad; high rates of recidivism would seem to suggest that prison as a method for dealing with social problems is not working, but this presumes that the auditor is interested in solving social problems and not, for instance, making a profit from prison-related industries or producing social inequality; and the use of comparative rates of incarceration by race can be used as Davis uses them, to point to something—but what?—going on beyond the numerical fetish and beyond the fetish of broken laws. Davis does not counter numbers with individual lives but challenges them with something far more abstract, her analysis of the "logic of racism."

Another comic book from the Real Cost of Prisons project, *Prison Town: Paying the Price,* tells the story of a prison being placed in a rural town that has suffered job loss through farm decline and de-industrialization. The narrative moves back and forth between a story about a boy and his parents who live in "Anytown, USA" and "numerical facts." It tries to make the raw numbers meaningful through comparisons: more prisons than Walmarts, more prisoners than farmers. Both in its narrative of rural job loss and its mention of Walmarts, the comic directs our attention to the forces of economic globalization and transformation. Narrative sections of the comic book portray decision makers and decision-making processes, emphasizing the lack of accountability associated with decisions about whether and where to build new prisons, depicting these prison-siting processes as deliberately evading democratic participation and overriding the desires of local residents, as power-laden processes revealing another kind of force that is beyond the borders of, but nonetheless crucial to, the law. Neither narrative nor number uses the familiar rhetorical strategies of provoking emotion through supplementary presentations of the suffering humanity of singular individuals in their human relations and shocking statistical facts. Rather, as in Davis's deployment of statistics, here both narrative and number point us beyond the empirical outcome, whether for individuals or for populations, toward an analysis of social processes.

Accounting for Crime and Debt

> The prison sentence, which is always computed in terms of time, is related to abstract quantification, evoking the rise of science and what is often referred to as the Age of Reason . . . precisely the historical period when the value of labor began to be calculated in terms of time and therefore compensated in another quantifiable way, by money.
>
> —Angela Y. Davis, *Are Prisons Obsolete?*

It is a commonplace to say that "criminals" pay their "debt to society" by spending time in prison. But this commonplace naturalizes a mode of accounting that deserves to be interrogated: How is crime understood as a debt? Why is the debt to society (rather than to, say, a particular victim), and what is meant by *society*? How is responsibility for the debt assigned to a particular "criminal"? How has time become the general equivalent for crime? We might take the use of the term *debt* in "a debt to society" to be metaphorical. But the link between debt and prison is by no means simply rhetorical—or, rather, the rhetorical

Details from second and third (unnumbered) pages of *Prison Town: Paying the Price* (2008), by artist Kevin Pyle and writers Kevin Pyle and Craig Gilmore, in the comic book series produced by the Real Cost of Prisons Project. Reproduced by permission from Lois Ahrens, Real Cost of Prisons project director.

link is not so simple. I do not mean to point, as the *Prison Town* comic book does, to the bonds that pay for prison building or to the financial debts accumulated by prisoners, though both of those are meaningful components of the apparatus of contemporary mass incarceration in the United States. Rather, I investigate the intertwined emergent strategies of knowledge production and inscription, of juridical and financial accounting, that undergird the modern regime for the constitution and management of criminals and debtors, categories that are related and differentiated, generating social hierarchies. I explore efforts to critique and promote alternative modes of accounting (such as social accounting and restorative justice) that might be more just or at least more enabling of social justice efforts.

Starting in the 1790s in the United States, and participating in the broader transformation of penality described by Foucault in *Discipline and Punish* (1977), criminal justice reform movements instigated the replacement of corporal punishment with incarceration: these movements invented and built penitentiaries where those convicted of crimes were to be imprisoned for "determinate sentences" (of predetermined lengths of time) and made to labor and pray on a highly regulated schedule, with the expectation that doing this time would uplift and reform the criminal.[6] Of course, over its now more than two-hundred-year history, the use of incarceration as the predominant penalty for crime has been articulated in a variety of ways. Determinate sentencing was, from the 1870s, supplemented by indeterminate sentencing (in which length of time of incarceration is adjustable based on numerous factors, including assessments of the prisoner while incarcerated): "Full-blown indeterminate sentencing existed in every American jurisdiction from the 1930s to the mid-1970s" (Tonry 1999, 3). Then, from the mid-1970s onward, as a 1995 Bureau of Justice Statistics report notes,

> legislatures around the Nation have sought to reduce discretion in both the sentencing process and the determination of when the conditions of a sentence have been satisfied. Determinate sentencing, use of mandatory minimums, and guidelines-based sentencing are illustrations of approaches that limit discretion and increase the predictability of penalties. (Beck and Greenfeld 1995, 1)

Driven by a set of political economic dynamics detailed in Ruth Wilson Gilmore's *Golden Gulag* (2007), the past forty years of "tough on crime" ideology and mass-incarceration policy making have diminished both desire and apparatus for rehabilitation; incarceration has come to

MAXIMUM RELEASE DATE

Sample 1

Inmate was received on January 1, 2011 with a total term of 6 years and was granted 200 days presentence credit (100 actual days per PC 2900.5 plus 100 days conduct credit per PC 4019). There is 6 days of postsentence credit plus 6 days of vested credits.

Case Number(s): ZZ000000	Section B - Recalculation of EPRD (change in credit earning status, credit loss/credit restoration, etc.)
Section A – Original EPRD Calculation	
This is the initial EPRD calculation that is done upon reception. Unless there is a change in work group (credit earning status) and/or credit losses occur, the EPRD remains throughout the term.	**STEP 1:** Accumulation of CDCR Incarceration Credit for days previously earned and projected future credit. Record fractional amounts of credit (2 decimal pts.) apply whole amounts only;
Credit Code 1	**B1. Maximum Date (Line A6)** = _____
A1. Start Date **01/01/2011**	B2. Minus CDCR Incarc. Credit Earned - _____ (See Reverse)
A2. Plus Time Imposed + <u>6 YRS 0 MO</u> = <u>01/01/2017</u>	B3. Plus Net Credit Loss (See E1.) + _____ Leave Line B3 Blank if Credit Code 2
A3. Minus PRE & Post Sentence Credit - <u>200 PRE 6 PST</u> = <u>06/09/2016</u>	B4. Equals Current Release Date (CRD)* = _____ Calculation ends here if: - Credit Code 2, 5
A4. Minus Vested Credit Credit Code 1, Divide by 1 or 2 Credit Code 2 or 3 Divide by 2 - <u> 6 </u> Credit Codes 4 or 6 Divide By 5.66 Credit Code 5 – Zero (Round Down Fractions) = <u>06/03/2016</u>	- Credit applied is to the CRD/Max. Date Carry date down to Line B13
A5. +Dead Time/-Merit credit = <u>0 DT - 0 MC</u>	B5. Minus Date Credit Applied Through - _____
A6. Equals Maximum Date = <u>06/03/2016</u> Note: Credit Code 5 (zero credit) calculation stops here.	B6. Equals Days remaining to serve as of = _____ date credit applied.
If change in work group, credit loss, Reeves, MCC, etc. stop here and proceed to Section B	B7. Divide Line B6 as follows to project CDCR Incarceration Credit Credit Code 1: WG - A1/U/A2/B/D1 divide by 2; WG - F divide by 3 then multiply by 2 Credit Code 3: Divide by 5 Credit Code 4 or 6: Divide by 6.66
A7. – Day Before Start Date (Line A1) - _____	CC-WG ▶▶
A8. Equals Days to Serve = _____	Equals Projected CDCR Credit = _____
A9. Minus Dead Time - _____	B8. Total CDCR Incarceration Credit - Accumulate Fractional Credit Line B2 _____ (include fractions) Line B7 _____ (include fractions) = _____ +
A10. = Days where credit may be applied = _____	
A11. = CDCR Incarceration Credit by dividing Line A10 by: Credit Code 1 – Divide by 2 (round down); Credit Code 2 – Divide by 3 (round up, also see section G) Credit Code 3 – Divide by 5 (round down) = _____ Credit Code 4 or 6 – Divide by 6.66 (round down)	**STEP 2: Recalculate EPRD**
	B9. Maximum Date (Line B1/A6) = _____
A12. Maximum Date (Line A6) _____	B10. Minus Total CDCR Incar. Credit - _____ (Line B8, round down) B11. Plus Net Credit Lost (See E2.) + _____
A13. – CDCR Incarc. Credit (Line A11) - _____	B12. Minus Milestone Credit (Sect. F1) - _____
A14. Equals Original EPRD = _____	**B13. Equals Adjusted EPRD*** = _____ *The CRD is an intermediate date and may exceed the maximum date; however, the Adjusted EPRD cannot exceed the maximum release date

Sample calculation worksheet in *CDCR Calculation Methodology Handbook* (California Department of Corrections and Rehabilitation 2011, 4), which states, "CDCR's calculation worksheets were created to provide step-by-step instructions and uniformity to calculate the Earliest Possible Release Date (EPRD) for inmates sentenced to serve a determinate (DSL) term in state prison." This worksheet reproduces a portion of form "CDCR 1897-U (1/10) Access Version" (5) and appears on page 12 of the handbook.

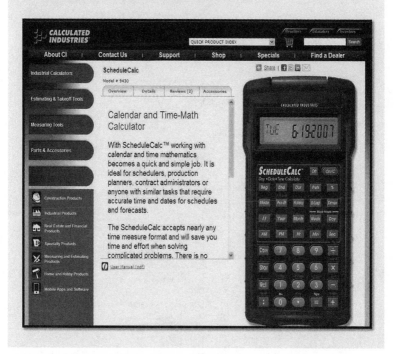

Advertisement in *CDCR Calculation Methodology Handbook* (California
Department of Corrections and Rehabilitation 2011, 55).

be understood primarily as punishment and incapacitation. Most recently, in the first decades of the twenty-first century, economic pressure on U.S. states, in combination with social movement resistance to
the mandatory-minimums approach, has provoked some reconsidera-
tion of sentencing policies.

The complexity of the political and economic calculations driving

CrimeTime California Worksheet Sample Screen

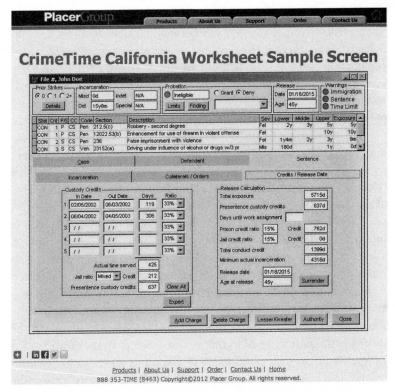

Screen shot from online advertisement for Placer Group, http://www.placergroup
.com/ctCalScreen_Worksheet.aspx (accessed March 2013).

sentencing policy is outdone only by the complexities of calculating
the time to be spent in prison in any particular case. The California
Department of Corrections and Rehabilitation provides a handbook
with model forms and instructions and worksheets for figuring, adding, and subtracting "time imposed," "Pre and Post sentence credit,"
"Vested credit," "Dead time," and "meritorious credit" that bear a
remarkable resemblance to tax forms; various online services have
been developed to assist corrections departments, lawyers, and their
clients in figuring out the stakes of the plea negotiations that determine
the outcomes of most criminal cases, as well as prisoners working to
minimize their time. These complex technical calculations of time for
crime are the culmination, both logically and historically, of processes
joining accounting and criminal justice as intertwined procedures of
social formation.

Sometimes understood to be a response to a decline in communal social control (driven by the very same economic expansions that are said to have driven the shift from interpersonal to system trust in the financial domain; see, e.g., Colvin 1997; see also Garland 1990 for an overview of theories of punishment), the Enlightenment regime of criminal justice was, per Foucault (1977, 80), intended to be more centralized and pervasive, more efficient. But as in the case of the development of credit discussed in chapter 1, here too we can see the emergence of a new communality in the supposed replacement of interpersonal with system trust. While this new communality may appear (as Marx argues in "On the Jewish Question," 1978) in the alienating and mystifying form of the liberal state, disavowing the interested and particular relations of civil society, it nonetheless depends on those social and economic interdependencies. This new communality works not merely through abstraction but also through processes of abstraction and particularization that constitute and bind the particular subject to the abstract.

For Foucault, the transformation of penality that resulted in the self-evident naturalness of incarceration as punishment for crime actually sutured two initially distinct emergences (232–33). On one hand, he describes the shift in penal techniques as a shift from the prioritization of sovereignty to the prioritization of discipline, a new governmentality that laid hold of the soul rather than the body (or rather, given the hard labor and physical brutality incorporated into the penitentiary, a new governmentality that laid hold of the soul in addition to the body). Discipline—which distributes and coordinates the activities of dociled bodies in precisely measured and divided times and spaces, monitoring the subjects of those activities through surveillance and examination—was first developed in other sites, such as the military and schools. It was only later jerry-rigged, in the form of incarceration, to the other, juridico-economic, determinant of the shift, the development of Enlightenment juridical philosophy. That juridical philosophy, more interested in the abstract juridical subject than in the body or the soul, initially proposed a different approach to punishment, a very specific and differentiated matching of crime and punishment; but incarceration fit its needs in that the deprivation of liberty is an equal penalty for all regardless of class and has the potential for quantification by time and thus, Foucault notes, takes a "wages-form" that enables it to appear as a reparation (debt payment) while allowing quantitative equivalences between time and crime (232).

Foucault is, of course, far more interested in incarceration as a site of discipline, where the criminal is constituted as an individual text to be read, measured, transformed, in the space opened up by incarceration for the disciplines of criminology, psychology, and anthropology—those disciplines of "moral accounting"—which thrive in and constitute the technologies of surveillance and examination that incarceration entails. With regard to the juridico-economic, Foucault reiterates more than he explains the naturalness of prison time as quantifiable repayment of debt. His work traces the early development of the technologies for reading not merely the crime but the criminal—his "passions, instincts, anomalies, infirmities, maladjustments, effects of environment and heredity" (1977, 17). Leps (1990) builds on Foucault's work with an account of the rise of positivist criminology, suggesting that over the course of the nineteenth century, increasingly powerful epistemological tools were developed for writing and reading particularities. As a site for the elaboration of social Darwinism and eugenics, positivist criminology enabled not only the examination—quite literally the measurement—of the physical and moral features of the individual criminal but also the reading of these particulars as evidence of abstractions or generalities, as classed, raced, gendered traits, as the products of unsanitary neighborhoods or hereditarily inferior families. And I will argue that, like double-entry bookkeeping, Enlightenment juridical accounting is organized to articulate particularized individuals to abstract rules; in other words, less jerry-rigging was necessary than Foucault suggests.

The transformation of criminal justice was intertwined with a transformation in the management of debtor–creditor relations: the previously normative practice of imprisoning debtors was, like the treatment of criminals, the object of "reform" (sometimes explicitly addressed by the same organizations seeking to reform criminal punishment) (Coleman 1974, 255–56; see also Mann 2002; Daniels 1995). Reforms included providing the option of debt servitude, providing imprisoned debtors with enough freedom to work, shifting the costs of jail to creditors, physically separating debtors from those deemed "criminals," and passing insolvency laws that released impoverished debtors who owed small debts, although access to these various particular forms of relief differed by age, sex, marital status, and class (Coleman 1974, 252, 253, 257).

Meanwhile, debtors' prison was not just reformed—it was displaced.

Other mechanisms emerged for managing financial relationships. Increased use of written documents, such as promissory notes that could be enforced or discounted as they were exchanged, gave creditors alternatives in dealing with overdue debts. (Cohen [1982, 4] offers a rich story of the growth of numeracy in order to help explain why "in the 1820s and 1830s there suddenly appeared many types of quantitative materials and documents that previously had been quite rare," and why "not only government agencies but private associations and individuals were eagerly counting, measuring and churning out data.") Various and ultimately successful attempts to establish bankruptcy laws enabled the resolution of creditor–debtor relations through legal procedures that identify and distribute the assets of the debtor to creditors and then relieve the debtor of further responsibility for those debts: federal bankruptcy laws were passed (and shortly repealed) in 1800, 1841, and 1867, and then passed more durably in 1898.[7]

In addition, an elaborate nongovernmental apparatus of credit reporting was developed that sought to manage debtor–creditor relations in advance by providing creditors with information about potential borrowers (Olegario 2006; Lauer 2008). Rather than shifting from reliance on interpersonal to system trust, early credit reporting, as described by Rowena Olegario and Josh Lauer, simply sought "to extract and reproduce the individual's local reputation for a national audience" (Lauer 2008, 309). According to Olegario, building on a prior practice of businessmen making use of letters of reference when seeking to conduct business with strangers, early credit reporting firms, such as the New York–based Mercantile Agency (which evolved into the Dun of what was eventually Dun & Bradstreet, one of the "Big Three" Wall Street credit-rating agencies), gathered and sold information about "'THE HOME STANDING of the merchant'" (2006, 51) provided by "'correspondents'" (49) such as attorneys (and sheriffs, merchants, postmasters, and bank cashiers) located in towns throughout the United States. Such a correspondent could draw on "'long and personal acquaintance and observation . . . having his eye upon every trader of importance in his county, and noting down, as it occurs, every circumstance affecting [the merchant's] credit'" (51). Unlike contemporary consumer credit reporting, which primarily assesses the consumer's payment history, nineteenth-century U.S. credit reporting determined creditworthiness through narratives describing "reputation," especially regarding "character, capacity, and capital." Olegario states that "in addition to capital [guesstimates of "worth"] and 'capacity' (business ability), the criteria for determining creditworthiness included the so-called character traits of honesty, punctuality, thrift, sobriety, energy, and focus. Experience, marital status, and age were also deemed important" (82).[8]

In the 1850s, the credit reporting firms began to organize the information they gathered with coding systems and ultimately produced ratings, using systems of letters and numbers to briefly convey the conclusions drawn from the narrative data (Olegario 2006, 65–67; Lauer 2008, 317–19). The shift from "narrative to number" also included increasing use of financial data to supplement the personal reports on reputation (Lauer 2008, 315, 317). Lauer argues that "the textualization of credit risk became increasingly abstract and, in contrast to earlier modes of credit assessment, disembodied and impersonal" (319). On the other hand, if the credit reporting system abstracted, it also particularized, producing individual behaviors; Lauer points out that "the information documented in the mercantile agency's 'thousand folios' represented a system of disciplinary surveillance that sought to regulate business behavior under its omnipresent gaze" (321). And "despite the veneer of objectivity provided by the credit-rating system— particularly as affected by the separation of capital from personality— ambiguities abounded" in the actual application of the rating system to particular cases (319). On this point Lauer quotes a contemporary critic of the system "who lambasted the logic of the capital estimates ('the millionaire and the $20,000,000 millionaire are "all one" to the agency') and the meaningless terms employed to designate creditworthiness (what is the difference, he asked, between 'very good' and 'high'?)" (320).[9]

Meanwhile, the nineteenth century was quite a dynamic period in the development of accounting in the United States. While Schultz and Hollister (2004, 144) point to the persistence of book debt, "personified" ledger accounts, and single-entry accounting to "keep track of payables and receivables," and Previts and Merino (1998, 45) note that double-entry bookkeeping was already widespread by the time of the American Revolution, significant innovations occurred in the deployment of accounting for management purposes. According to T. Colwyn Jones in *Accounting and the Enterprise* (1995, 25–26):

> These involved the creation of regular, periodic returns forcing "the natural rhythm of work into a straitjacket of comparable sections of time." Here,

accounting both reflected the new imposition of time discipline (Thompson, 1967) and may be supposed to have provided one of the means of enforcing it—through the periodic measurement of performance.

Taking an explicitly Foucauldian approach, critical accounting scholars Keith Hoskin and Richard Macve (1994, 86) argue that building on techniques for quantifying human qualities developed in educational contexts (their primary case is West Point Military Academy, as transformed in 1817 by the introduction of a new regime), by the mid-nineteenth century businesses (first, and not coincidentally, the Springfield Armory) began to deploy "writing, examination and grading" practices to "*integrate* the surveillance and control of time, activity and cost, [which] made the modern concerns with productivity, performativity and profitability articulable." But discipline is only part of the story here. Thomas Tyson (1990), while also recognizing new deployments of accounting in the service of labor control, efficiency, and productivity, is not persuaded by Hoskin and Macve's causal narrative. He gives more emphasis to a decline in collaboration among employers and the provocations offered by "a period of strikes, union activity, and a reduction in daily working hours" by workers whose work had been accounted and paid on a piece-rate basis (52). That is, Tyson correlates accounting developments with contested processes of social and economic formation.[10]

The elaborations of these new financial and juridical regimes are, of course, not merely analogous but also rather deeply intertwined processes. As Foucault (1977, 87) points out, the new techniques of punishment were intertwined with a new "economy of illegalities," "restructured with the development of capitalism," such that the property crimes of the poor were subject to normal courts and punishments while the commercial crimes of the bourgeoisie were subject to "special legal institutions," "accommodations, reduced fines, etc.," such as, we might add, bankruptcy law. Precisely for this reason, I would suggest that something more/other than discipline is at stake. These procedures for inscribing debt and creditworthiness advanced processes that Foucault might have called biopolitical but seem better characterized, somewhat less technically, as social formation, especially but not exclusively racial formation. That is, in the United States, this new economy of illegalities enabled the differential attribution of criminal versus financial debt to serve as a central strategy of racial formation.

The Rules

For the nineteenth-century U.S. reformers and for Foucault, Cesare Beccaria's 1764 treatise *On Crimes and Punishments* was a symbol for the "enlightenment" of criminal justice; and it continues to be such a symbol for contemporary legal scholars (see, for instance, Sherman 2003 and Harcourt 2008, although debate over the meaning of the text is evidenced in Beirne 1994). Beccaria clearly articulates the procedure for subjecting particular individuals to abstract justice. He argues that society is established by social contract, which he (laying the ground for Martin Luther King Jr.) conceptualizes through a banking metaphor: the contract is established through "deposits" of liberty (1963, 11–12; see also Zeman, 178–79). He says:

> The sum of all these portions of liberty sacrificed by each for his own good constitutes the sovereignty of a nation, and their legitimate depositary and administrator is the sovereign. But merely to have established this deposit was not enough; it had to be defended against private usurpations by individuals each of whom always tries not only to withdraw his own share but also to usurp for himself that of others. (12)

Beccaria argues for "the rule of law," the establishment of general laws, applicable equally to all, by the legislature (14). He asserts that the role of judges is "to complete a perfect syllogism in which the major premise must be the general law; the minor, the action that conforms or does not conform to the law; and the conclusion, acquittal or punishment" (14–15), thus proposing precisely that particulars (particular crimes) are to be abstracted in order to be subject to the abstract law. As Foucault suggests, the new juridical regime that Beccaria's treatise proposes (and that has become the dominant liberal approach) was a transformation in juridical accounting that begins to answer some questions about the phrase "a debt to society."

Previously, the criminal was accountable to the sovereign; now, under the ideology of the social contract, the criminal was to be accountable to the society. Previously, there was no proportion between crime and punishment, or rather there was a deliberate disproportion, aimed at displaying the superior power of the sovereign; now, with deterrence taken as the primary aim, there was to be a careful balance between the two (though maybe not the perfect zero balance of debits and credits of the double-entry balance sheet), based on the idea that subjects are rational calculators and/or that the close relation between the crime and the punishment and the inevitability of punishment will make an "impression" on men's minds. Previously, the accounting of crimes and punishments took social status and hierarchical relationships (as much of those doing the judging as of those being judged; 78–81) into account; now, these would, supposedly, be excluded from consideration. And previously, under the rules of the old "penal arithmetic," as Foucault calls it, each piece of evidence produced a piece of guilt (36), and partial proof equaled partial guilt; now, evidence and guilt were to be accounted differently, according to what Foucault calls the rule of common truth, modeled on mathematics and common sense (96–97). A person was to be innocent until proven guilty, and all evidence had to be assessed together.

What to make of this new regime of juridical accounting? In proposing a juridical system based on the rule of law, Beccaria is proposing a new mode of legitimating the law, by its very regularity, its systematicity. That is, as merchants were made credible by writing accounts to the rule of double-entry bookkeeping, the legal regime is to be made credible by its rule-boundedness. (This mode of legitimation was evident in the response of the U.S. Congress to the Enron scandal, which was to undertake to "restore investor confidence in capital markets" by passing the Sarbanes–Oxley Act, which strengthened the rules for corporate auditing and accounting controls—in effect, the rules for following rules.)[11] The legitimacy thus gained specifically elides what Derrida calls the "force of law"—the force that cannot be justified or accounted for within the law and yet animates it—and the space of decision inherent to but uncontained by the application of a rule to a case.

In relation to Beccaria's scheme, the judge's syllogism, this force might be seen to operate in the determination of the major premise (the general law). That is, with Nietzsche we might reject Beccaria's sentimental attribution of ongoing social indebtedness to a "contract" and instead attend to what Derrida (1992, 6) calls the "originary violence that must have established this authority," that was necessary to "the welding of a hitherto unchecked and shapeless populace into a firm form" (Nietzsche 1989, 86). In imagining the social bond through a banking metaphor, Beccaria installs accounting as the technology through which social standing, social creditworthiness, is to be ascertained. Moreover, Beccaria's understanding of crime as a violation of the social contract implies that the "debt to society" that criminals are said to pay by spending time in prison is not incurred in the moment of a crime; rather, a crime is said to have occurred when it is determined that there has been a failure, or active refusal, to maintain an ongoing debt, to fulfill obligations. Nietzsche famously makes this structure of permanent indebtedness explicit: "The community . . . stands to its members in [the] relation . . . of the creditor to his debtors. . . . The aim now is to preclude pessimistically, once and for all, the prospect of a final discharge . . . until at last the irredeemable debt gives rise to conception of irredeemable penance" (70, 71, 91). A criminal conviction might then be understood as a foreclosure of social credit, which helps to explain (but does not excuse) the fact that most felony convictions become life sentences through a morass of "collateral consequences," barring felons from everything from voting to receiving social services such as food stamps and public housing to qualifying for barber's licenses; and it also helps in making sense of the structure of incarceration as a kind of exile, separating people from their social networks.[12]

We might also look for the role of force in the determination of the minor premise of the syllogism (the particular case) and, of course, in the articulation of major and minor. With regard to the minor premise of the syllogism—What happened in the particular case? What crime has been committed?—Beccaria proposes an array of rules of evidence that interestingly seem not unlike the procedures for establishing creditworthiness through bookkeeping: he suggests the assembly of a variety of independent proofs or pieces of evidence that are adequate to persuade what has come to be called "the reasonable man" (20–21). In other words, like early double-entry bookkeeping as Poovey describes it (see chapter 1) and financial accounting more generally as a technology of demonstrating creditworthiness, rather than providing an absolute accounting of assets or, in this case, facts, the accounting of evidence must perform a rhetorical function of persuasion.

Moreover, with regard to certain crimes and juridical procedures, accounting is not merely *like* evidence; it *is* the evidence. Beccaria devotes a chapter of his book to debt, arguing that through "rigorous examination" "innocent bankrupts" should be distinguished from "fraudulent" ones. Those found to be innocent should not be punished but rather simply made to pay, or to work until they can pay. Meanwhile, echoing his own call for publication of laws, Beccaria urges that financial frauds be prevented by laws that require "public and open registration of all contracts, and liberty for all citizens to consult the well-ordered documents, a public bank formed out of intelligently apportioned revenues . . . designed to provide timely financial assistance" (78). For Beccaria, then, with regard to debt, the issue of criminality explicitly turns not on whether or not one is a debtor but rather on how one represents that debt.

Here, as in the "reform" of criminal justice, Beccaria's approach was realized in nineteenth-century U.S. practice. In fact, according to Mann (2002, 226), early bankruptcy law explicitly exposed debtors to "rigorous examination" in place of imprisonment:

> To receive that discharge, the debtor had to submit to a minimum of three examinations under oath within forty-two days . . . and there make full disclosure of his property and accounts, including the details of any recent transfers. Creditors could attend the examinations, produce witnesses and documents, and question the debtor. . . . The debtor could be freed from jail if imprisoned for debt and was shielded from arrest during the examination period.

According to Wootton and Moore (2000), unlike British courts, where common law disallowed "shop books" from being entered as legal evidence, from the colonial period onward American courts allowed accounting records to serve as legal evidence of debts. This was rationalized by "necessity" and by the "circumstantial guarantee of trustworthiness." That is, the records were allowed to be used as evidence in order to facilitate credit—creditors could use their own records to prove debts were owed to them, making them feel more free to give credit. But also, as stated by Judge Learned Hand in 1927—affirming, according to Wootton and Moore, one hundred fifty years of precedent—the "circumstantial guarantee of trustworthiness" is precisely the formal systemization that Poovey points to:

> Records . . . are in practice accepted as accurate upon the faith of the routine itself, and of the self-consistency of their contents. Unless they can be used in court without the task of calling those who at all stages had a part in the transactions recorded, nobody need ever pay a debt, if only his creditor does a large enough business. (*Massachusetts Bonding v. Norwich Pharmacal* 1927, 937)

The attribution of credibility to account books and their supposed ability to stand in as reliable substitutes for the actual people who participated in transactions reiterates the displacement of the body of the debtor by various forms of written security for loans in a way that might seem depersonalizing but in fact is more analogous to the displacement of the body by the *soul* of the criminal, as Foucault puts it (1977, 16ff.).

As Mann points out, the examination required within the law was not the only sort of examination involved; financial accounting was supplemented by a social accounting. Most early bankruptcy procedures were limited to those engaged in "commerce" and to those who owed more than a certain substantial minimum debt. This suggests, and Mann argues, that the restoration of social bonds and social standing for debtors made possible by bankruptcy law was motivated by the incarceration of debtors who were also creditors—wealthy businessmen, not those who were indebted because they were poor. That a certain force, a social formation process, was at work in the establishment of bankruptcy law, the major premise of the syllogism, is also evidenced by the arguments made by debtors against their imprisonment.

Debtors tried to establish their social creditworthiness by distinguishing themselves from slaves, criminals, and women. According to Mann (2002, 141), they mobilized "images of the absolute power of the creditor and of heartless creditors tearing families apart, images that require the reader only to substitute 'master' for 'creditor' to be transported into the world of plantation slavery," and, citing the Rights of Man on their rightful independence, objected to the dependency of indebtedness as feminizing; further, they claimed they were inappropriately treated as (or worse than) criminals. Mann quotes from an article in *Forlorn Hope,* the prison newsletter published by William Keteltas (1800), objecting to the fact that incarcerated criminals were provided with food and clothing while incarcerated debtors were not:

> Why should the state nourish and protect the violators of its institutions (who are in that respect debtors to the public) [by providing them food and clothing in penitentiaries, unlike debtors, who had to provide for themselves while incarcerated] and yet give up the necessitous man for a failure in a private contract? As the law now operates . . . it is a greater crime to run into debt, however fair the prospect of paying, than to rob a man on the highway, commit a rape or burn a house. (105)

It appears that the distinction between criminal (fraudulent) debtors and innocent debtors turns not only on the representation of the debt through a financial accounting that can be subjected to "rigorous examination," as Beccaria suggests, but on a social accounting as well.

Meanwhile, just when bankruptcy law was finally and fully established for creditors (Mann's tale of the emergence of bankruptcy law concludes in the 1870s), a new regime of financial accounting and public contracts was applied to debtors of another sort with the aim of restoring their social position, but this time as slave labor. As Fleischman, Oldroyd, and Tyson (2011) point out, the emancipation of slaves in the wake of the Civil War in the United States presented those who sought to control and deploy that labor force for profit with some challenges, depriving them as it did of the extensive array of techniques of physical coercion legitimated by ownership. In response, Saidiya Hartman (1997, 125–63) argues, during Reconstruction a broad and multifaceted effort was undertaken to constitute those who had been "emancipated" as indebted subjects, obliged to docile hard work; this effort involved pedagogical projects such as the freedmen's handbooks that Hartman reads as well as a number of legal and financial practices. Southern white employers, as well as the government agencies seeking to manage the transition from slave to wage economy, began to make greater and different uses of management accounting and contract enforcement to discipline labor.

During slavery,

> best practice in the USA was typified by Thomas Affleck's (1851) account and record-keeping book, which helped reassure slave-owners that they were engaging in a perfectly rational business activity by providing them with a uniform and apparently scientific scheme of plantation accounting. . . . the emphasis in the Affleck book was on tracking revenues with a lack of interest in cost management and worker productivity. Indeed, upon examining scores of surviving Affleck books . . . the clear impression created . . . is that quantifying labour output was not deemed worth the effort. (Fleischman et al. 2011, 757)

After the Civil War (and unlike in the British West Indies, where the post-slavery transition did involve an immediate and extensive implementation of government-required management accounting on plantations), Fleishman et al. argue, the disintegration of the plantation system determined that a different set of technologies would dominate: "Labour control at the micro level depended primarily on evidencing the performance of contracts" that "compensated workers in permutations of crop-shares, wages, rent-free house or land and provisions. . . . share-based contracts or monthly wages were common approaches used to entice the freedmen to remain on the fields until crops were harvested. Share contracts specified work rules, effort levels, and the fines or physical punishments that could be imposed" (760, 762). In relation to these contracts, the state did not even appear to be an abstract or neutral third party, merely implementing an impersonal system. During Reconstruction, the Freedmen's Bureau was often called upon to arbitrate contract disputes in which the evidence presented consisted of elaborate bookkeeping records that seem to have been primarily detailed notations of deductions of various amounts from the payment due to the worker, not only for materials and cash advances but also for time: "Time lost to sickness was to be deducted from the worker's wage or share, while time lost to idleness or absence without leave was to be penalised at three times the normal rate. Again these exactions had to be supported by accounting data to be effective in law" (764; see also 762–64). Accounting was thus a means of reenslavement insofar as it turned most Black farmers into debt peons (Clarke 1998, 180–81).

In addition, state enforcement and laws that directly articulated with these contractual arrangements took advantage of the phrasing of the Thirteenth Amendment, which abolished slavery and involuntary servitude "except as punishment for crime" (Clarke 1998, 110). The infamous "Black Codes" and the slightly less explicitly racial successor laws criminalized vagrancy and unemployment, thus reinscribing the obligation to labor under conditions of domination in addition to the (merely) exploitative relations of free labor (Clarke 1998, 68–69, 178; see also Fleischman et al. 2011, 767–69). Once found to be criminals for failing to fulfill these obligations, former slaves could be and were forced to labor (Colvin 1997). Direct leasing of convicts was one technique for putting convicts to work; another was criminal surety laws, which enabled whites to pay fines for convicted African Americans, who then were obliged to work off their (involuntarily acquired) debts to those whites (Clarke 1998, 112). If, in the case of creditors, the "rigorous examination" associated with bankruptcy law enables the circulation of capital by staving off social, if not financial, foreclosure (by determining that they are innocent bankrupts), in this case the circulation of capital is enabled precisely by foreclosure, of both the newly gained citizenship and the property rights of African Americans, who are, through the supplementation of financial accounting by social (racial) accounting, constituted as "fraudulent" bankrupts.

Restoring Justice

The relation of accounting to injustice is often all too clear, with accounting deployed as a tool of discipline, exploitation, expropriation, and domination in both financial and juridical realms. As Mariana Valverde (1999, 658, quoting Derrida 1992, 17) points out, the Enlightenment regime of justice can be and has been critiqued for its participation in procedures of abstraction and commensuration associated with accounting:

> Law is, for Derrida as for Marx, hopelessly caught up in the violent logic of abstract equivalence through which all human experience, including time itself, is reduced to an abstract quantity in the process of exchange. . . . In this sense, law is the opposite of justice, since Derrida, following Emmanuel Levinas, argues that justice "must always concern singularity."

However, as Valverde notes, "Derrida does not counterpose law to justice in a binary fashion" (659). For Derrida (1992, 16), justice depends on a space of decision that is intertwined with law—"For a decision to be just and responsible it must . . . conserve the law and also destroy it or suspend it enough to have to reinvent it in each case" (23)—and yet exceeds law:

> Every time that we placidly apply a good rule to a particular case, to a correctly subsumed example, according to a determinant judgment, we can be sure that law may find itself accounted for, but certainly not justice. . . . Law is the element of calculation, and it is just that there be law, but justice is incalculable, it requires us to calculate with the incalculable. . . . the decision between just and unjust is never insured by a rule. (16)

Derrida emphasizes the necessity of calculation as a constraint against the appropriation of the "incalculable" by those who might excuse genocidal violence as divine justice:[13]

> That justice exceeds law and calculation . . . cannot and should not serve as an alibi for staying out of juridico-political battles, within an institution or a state. . . . justice is always very close to the bad, even to the worst for it can always be reappropriated by the most perverse calculation. . . . And so incalculable justice *requires* us to calculate. . . . Not only *must* we calculate, . . . but we *must* take it as far as possible. . . . This requirement does not properly belong either to justice or law . . . exceeding each one in the direction of the other. Politicization . . . is interminable. (28)

The excess of justice over law imposes a "responsibility" to examine the boundaries of the law, "recalling the history, the origin and subsequent direction, thus the limits, of concepts of justice, the law and right, of values, norms, prescriptions that have been imposed and sedimented there" (19), and pursue the ongoing effort to make the law fulfill "the classical emancipatory ideal" (28). As Martin Luther King Jr. (1963) proclaims, "We [must] refuse to believe that the bank of justice is bankrupt. . . . So we have come to cash this check—a check that will give us upon demand the riches of freedom and the security of justice."

My own argument thus far has suggested that injustice occurs not only through abstraction but in the inscription of particularities as well. Rather than emphasize the opposition of abstract law to singular justice, I have tried to show that it is valuable to attend to the procedures of abstraction and particularization by which particularities are articulated in, through, with generalized laws. If we understand that the circulation of capital and the elaboration of the liberal state operate through racializing technologies of accounting that simultaneously deploy abstraction and particularization, then we recognize that each is not likely to pose much of a barrier to the other. Meanwhile, it is useful to recognize that accounting through processes of particularization and abstraction is a representational strategy, a performative act that constitutes creditworthiness by writing and reading. The centrality of accounting suggests that epistemological interventions are possible, that alternative writings and readings might produce alternative particularizations and abstractions, might bind subjects differently or not at all. Hartman (1997, 131–32), for instance, notes that the constitution of indebted subjectivity among former slaves did not go uncontested: "As many former slaves asserted, they had not incurred any debt they had not repaid a thousandfold. In the counterdiscourses of freedom, remedy was sought for the injuries of slavery not through the reconstruction of the Negro . . . but through reparations." She argues that the "fiction of debt was premised upon a selective and benign representation of slavery" (132); justice demands an alternative account, one that relocates responsibility (debt) from the individual former slave to the "circumstances . . . the culmination of three centuries of servitude" (133) in which former slaves collectively struggled.

So, what would accounting for justice look like? Since its emergence in the 1970s, the restorative justice movement has gained substantial popularity. It is but one of many initiatives that explicitly invoke community as a key to reforming criminal justice; others include community policing, community service sentencing, and community justice

(Garland 2001; Pranis 1998; Lacey and Zedner 1995). In a 1996 promotional video titled *Restoring Justice,* produced by the National Council of Churches of Christ in the USA, Howard Zehr explains: "Instead of saying the state is the victim, restorative justice understands that communities and people are the victims, that real people are hurt." The restorative justice movement includes an array of programs (many initiated by faith-based nongovernmental organizations, or NGOs) implemented by local, state, national, and tribal jurisdictions in New Zealand, Australia, Britain, Canada, and the United States. The programs incorporate elements such as victim–offender mediation, family group conferencing, circle sentencing, and community reparative boards (Bazemore and Umbreit 2001). Restorative justice advocates imply that the victim and the offender, their family members and friends, and a miscellany of others (social workers, teachers, police, the restorative justice facilitator) who might be present at restorative justice procedures are members of a "community." In most of these procedures, the offender and victim are required to tell their stories in the presence of these others, and it is through this storytelling that indebtedness is articulated: restorative justice advocates express the hope that in hearing the story of the victim, the offender will feel shame and remorse, offer an apology, and receive forgiveness from the victim, who will then experience "closure."[14] So in place of assessing a debt to society, restorative justice envisions a much more concrete form of debt paying that brings criminals and victims into direct interaction and accountability. The regime of accounting they offer would seem to reject the abstraction required for articulating particular cases with general rules entailed in the Enlightenment juridical regime.[15]

While restorative justice is sometimes offered as an "alternative to incarceration" (Smith 2010a, 39), contesting incarceration is not central to restorative justice rhetoric. Some of the sentences that emerge from restorative justice processes include time in prison; John Braithwaite (2002, 31–32), author and editor of many books promoting restorative justice, proposes a "regulatory pyramid" that maintains incapacitating punishments as a final resort. However, restorative justice does claim to be a strategy for dramatically reducing the use of incarceration in that restorative justice processes more often result in financial restitution to the victim, community service orders, required participation in treatment programs, and, crucially, apologies. Its potential to reduce the use of incarceration as well as its appropriation by numerous governments at various scales suggests that restorative justice warrants both generous and critical evaluation.[16]

As Derrida might have them do, advocates of restorative justice attend to the history of modern criminal justice and to what they view as its violent foundation. Whereas Foucault focuses on the emergence of the penitentiary, and the shift in accountability from the sovereign to society, as the most meaningful flashpoint in the history of punishment, advocates of restorative justice see the key moment as the establishment of the "king's peace," the "capture" of criminal justice from local communities by the state (Delgado 2000, 755; Braithwaite 2002, 5; Zehr 1990, 115). And while liberal juridical philosophy posits prior approaches to criminal justice as brutal and arbitrary, advocates of restorative justice idealize past modes, focusing on the centrality of shaming, fines, victim compensation, and social reintegration in a vast array of premodern and indigenous societies, rather than on the centrality of corporal punishment and execution.[17]

The storytelling that is at the center of restorative justice processes, a mode of accounting that claims to be very different from the assembling of evidence required by liberal justice, would seem to create an opportunity for the singularity and uniqueness of the situation to emerge. And in aiming to restore community, advocates of restorative justice might in fact be understood to be seeking to open or reopen social relations, lines of credit as it were, where criminal justice is a process of foreclosure. However, the emphasis on producing "closure" for victims suggests that the credit relations aimed at here are still the permanent indebtedness, penance, and submission to norms of which Nietzsche writes.

Some critics of and participants in restorative justice recognize that the intended closure might not actually be achieved, given that immediate communities (for example, families) as well as the larger "community" within which the offender and victim come together are riven by power differences (Alder 2000). Barbara Hudson (1998), for instance, argues that what will persist through and beyond the restorative justice ritual is not an open-ended ethical relation but rather a structural relation of domination. To address this problem, George Pavlich (2001) recommends the active recognition of alterity within restorative justice processes and a constant examination of the social processes that determine the identity of the community and its members. While this Derridean recommendation might seem like a reiteration of the call to attend to singularity and difference as against generalization, one might understand it to require just the reverse, that is, precisely the abstraction and calculation that restorative justice rejects.

Richard Delgado (2000, 769) has argued that "such particularized mediation atomizes disputes, so that patterns, such as police abuse or the overcharging of black men, do not stand out readily." Calling for the kinds of statistical evidence that Davis uses to incite our responsibility to understand the racist logic determining criminal justice practices, Delgado's critique returns us to the question of the relation of accounting to justice. That is, rather than reject accounting, might we identify practices of accounting that would enable justice?

Critical accounting scholars have generated a number of proposals and practices that aim to rework accounting to serve social justice projects. In a remarkable move, Gallhofer and Haslam (2003, 22–65) seek to appropriate for emancipatory purposes Beccaria's Enlightenment linkage of accounting with justice. They conceptualize accounting as a tool for publicity in the public interest through a reading of the works of Jeremy Bentham—yes, that Jeremy Bentham—whose proposed juridical and penal reforms, including the Panopticon, made infamous by Foucault, were directly influenced by Beccaria and who apparently wrote a great deal of previously ignored material on accounting. Gallhofer and Haslam understand accounting as a communicative social practice that has the potential, when used to hold the powerful accountable rather than in an exercise of control by the powerful, for "enlighten[ing] with the effect of social betterment" (7). They present a number of examples from both the nineteenth and the late twentieth centuries demonstrating the use of accounting by social reformers to offer alternate and more negative views of activities of corporations and governments. They point out that these practices, sometimes called "social accounting," necessarily transform some key components of accounting practice: social accounting or "accounting publicity" is addressed not internally among corporate managers for purposes of cost saving or other business decision making, or externally to actual or potential shareholders (owners) by managers seeking to demonstrate their success and creditworthiness; rather, such accounting is addressed to a broader public engaged in democratic processes or to the workers who might thereby come to recognize themselves as an exploited class (Gallhofer and Haslam 2003, 113). Moreover, the form and content of the accounts are reshaped to reveal, for instance, exploitation and to do so in a nontechnical language appropriate to the intended audiences (121).

For Tony Tinker, a transformative accounting practice would not simply place the conventional tools in new hands, as "publicity at the service of different masters" (Gallhofer and Haslam 2003, 115). Tinker (1985, xx) posits that "members of a society are interconnected through their economic and social interdependencies. . . . Accounting information is not merely a manifestation of this myriad interdependence: it is a social scheme for adjudicating these relationships." And he asks, "How should we decide on the rules?" Tinker offers what he calls a Marxist vision of emancipatory accounting that aims to engage the socially constitutive role of accounting. Noting that conventional accounting relies, nearly unconsciously, on a "marginalist" theory of value (107), Tinker argues that conventional accounting actively defines socially meaningful entities as individuals (or individual corporations as legal persons) and delimits their domains and relations to objectively observable market activity. For Tinker, then, one important innovation related to so-called social accounting is its effort to account for "externalities," such as environmental damage, that are not market-priced costs to the individual corporate entity. However, as restorative justice has largely been captured by the state it is meant to critique, social accounting has been almost entirely captured by corporations seeking to defer critique and regulation by demonstrating their green credentials through self-reported social and environmental accounts (Tinker 1985; Gallhofer and Haslam 2003; Spence 2009).

Here we might also recall that Berlant and Davis criticize the deployment of numerical accounts for fetishizing the objects represented, leaving the audience of the numerical presentation in emotional thrall to the "fact," "the crisis," when what is needed is actionable analysis. In an effort that begins to answer this concern, Christine Cooper, Phil Taylor, Newman Smith, and Lesley Catchpowle (2005) propose a strategy of critical social auditing or accountability that takes a Marxist understanding of social process seriously. Like Tinker, they reject conventional or "positivist accounting," which accepts that "the facts of a situation are pretty much as they appear when we first observe them" and "the compartments in which we find such facts [are] the inevitable and unalterable properties of the things themselves, not the products of historical developments" (Rees 1998, quoted in Cooper et al. 2005, 956). Instead, they propose that "accounting practice, regulation, information and so on cannot be understood on its own but only as part of a totality," a totality characterized by "deep contradictions (and conflicts)" that are generative of systemic "change" (957).

Cooper et al. undertook a survey of college students aimed at understanding the consequences of the increasing gap between financial aid and the cost of attending college. They asked students if and how much they worked, how much they got paid, and in what types of jobs they worked; they also asked about the impact of students' work on their time spent on classwork as well as on their levels of stress, depression, and so on. The authors interpreted the results as demonstrating a contradiction in which students were turned into particularly exploitable (low-wage, contingent) workers suited to a transformed economy of part-time service industry jobs, even as this work undermined the students' ability to engage and succeed in the academic endeavor supported by this employment. While not an earth-shattering revelation, this account certainly tells a story different from one of student achievement viewed in isolation from the "totality" of the changing regime of financial support for that education and the changing employment market. (I can easily imagine a "kids these days" conclusion about the declining commitment and ability of the students.) The authors provide a useful example of a social accounting designed not simply to present facts of suffering or failure but also to reveal constitutive determinants.

Like the *Prison Town* comic book, an accounting that points beyond itself—using number and narrative to ask the right questions rather than serving up one right answer—Cooper et al.'s contribution can be read as a gesture in the direction of a de-fetishizing accounting. Across this chapter, as I have sketched the work of accounting in the constitution of injustices, I also mean to have collected several such gestures toward justice, proposals for and examples of a variety of alternative accounting practices that trace dialectics of abstraction and particularization, and hold some potential to help us transform the social hierarchies of credit and debt in which we are inscribed.

3 ACCOUNTING FOR TIME

The Entrepreneurial Subject in Crisis

Begin

In her important essay "Slow Death," Lauren Berlant (2007b, 754) wants to help us conceptualize "contemporary historical experience . . . where life building and the attrition of human life are indistinguishable; and where it is hard to distinguish modes of incoherence, distractedness, and habituation from deliberate and deliberative activity, as they are all involved in the reproduction of predictable life." She develops the concept of "practical sovereignty" to describe constrained agency as it is mediated by "zoning, labor, consumption and governmentality" but also "unconscious and explicit desires *not* to be an inflated ego deploying and manifesting power" (757). By deflating sovereign subjectivity in this way, she argues, we can evade two errors: one overreads any "manifest lack of self-cultivating attention" as "'really' irresponsibility, shallowness, resistance, refusal or incapacity"; the other overreads "habit . . . such that addictions, reaction formation, conventional gesture clusters, or just being different can be read as heroic placeholders for resistance, . . . affirmation . . . or transformative desire" (757).

I have found Berlant's conceptualization of subjectivity enabling as I have observed and tried to understand the efforts and failures of all sorts of people, including myself, to inhabit responsible, entrepreneurial subjectivity. Nikolas Rose (1999, 142) has articulated entrepreneurial subjectivity as a strategy of neoliberal governmentality, one that conceives of the human actor not merely as the nineteenth-century economic subject of interest but also as empowered, self-governing, and thus "*active* in making choices in order to further their own interests and those of their family . . . in their quest for self-realization." For the "responsibilized" (139) entrepreneurial subject, "it is a part of the continuous business of living to make adequate provision for the preservation, reproduction and reconstruction of one's own human capital" (142), as Colin Gordon puts it.[1] This subject, "active in making choices," would seem to be precisely the "sovereign" subject that Berlant, not to mention Sigmund Freud, Michel Foucault, Judith Butler, and Wendy Brown, as well as Rose and Gordon, suggest is a fiction or fantasy. As Wendy Brown (2001, 11, 10) argues, it is difficult to "sustain the conviction that we devise and pursue our own ends when we are so patently the effects of" what she calls "intricate yet disseminated forms of social power." And yet it is important to recognize that one of the constraints shaping agency is this norm of agentiveness, of sovereignty. As Berlant (2007b, 755) argues, the fiction is a consequential one: "It has provided an alibi for normative governmentality and justified moralizing against inconvenient human activity."

The ideal entrepreneurial subject of neoliberalism lives only one side of a contradiction: she borrows and invests to build a future for herself and her family. Meanwhile, she somehow avoids the dialectic that transforms credit received into a debt and binds the present to the past. I take Berlant to be arguing that we must be alert for just these kinds of contradictions. In the context of the recent economic crisis— the credit crisis—such contradictions have become more visible. And the possibility of drawing a line between responsible, future-oriented behavior and irresponsible, immature, shortsighted risk taking has all but vanished. That is to say, the norm of entrepreneurial subjectivity is likely to be inhabited in the mode of failure.

Of course, to say that the contradictions are more visible is to reveal my own perspective; they are more visible to me in the way that poor African Americans in New Orleans became visible to "us" in the context of television coverage of Hurricane Katrina. And Berlant specifically argues against the deployment of crisis rhetoric (her case is the so-called obesity epidemic), which not only misrepresents the duration and scale of an endemic, "structural or predictable" situation as an epidemic event—making a "population wearing out in the space of ordinariness" "radiant with attention, compassion, analysis and sometimes reparation" (761)—but also, while appearing to call for heroic action, in fact becomes "a way of talking about what forms of catastrophe a world is comfortable with or even interested in perpetuating" (761).[2] So in what follows I attend not only to the most immediate moment of economic crisis but also to the contradictions of a broader neoliberal present, even while it is my hope that alongside the passing televisual crisis there is a crisis of a more Marxist variety in which that endemic, structural situation has reached its self-induced breaking point.

In alliance with Berlant, I attend to the contradictions by exploring the specificity and diversity of the norms of contemporary subjectivity and something of the diversity of the ways those norms are inhabited. In undertaking this project I am also trying to learn from Saba Mahmood's work. In *Politics of Piety* (2005), Mahmood suggests that much is lost if one assesses any particular set of practices in terms of a binary opposition of resistance versus subordination (or even subversion versus reinscription of norms) and if one associates agency with only resistance or subversion. Mahmood points out that such an approach depends on a liberal presumption of inherent desire for autonomy and freedom. Her own agenda is to make it possible to perceive the agentiveness among women in the Islamic piety movement in Egypt; but she also notes: "Many societies, including Western ones, have flourished with aspirations other than [freedom and liberty]. Nor, for that matter, does the narrative of individual and collective liberty exhaust the desires with which people live in liberal societies" (14). So even in "the West," things get more interesting if one attends to those other desires and attachments and, as Mahmood says, to "the variety of ways in which norms are lived and inhabited, aspired to, reached for, and consummated" (23).

There was a time (has it passed?) when I thought the goal of this piece of writing would be to address the following question: What does the dialectical negation of entrepreneurial subjectivity look like, the negation on which it depends, that it itself produces but that embodies a contradiction or even entails a crisis—an opportunity for change? And, provoked by Lee Edelman's 2004 book *No Future: Queer Theory and the Death Drive*, I added: Does it look like the death drive? This question, troubled if not completely displaced by the project I have just articulated through Berlant and Mahmood, emerged this way: I had noticed that liberal theorists, promoters, and policy makers had spent a great deal of energy in hand-wringing and theorizing over the fact that many people are, ostensibly, *not* good enough capitalist subjects, working, saving, and consuming as they should. Likewise, I had also noticed that Marx's prediction that capitalism would produce its own "gravediggers" has always, even in Marx's own work, been hedged by theories aimed at understanding why we *do not* foment revolution. This similarity between Marxist and capitalist concerns over inadequate subjectivity—subjectivity not coherently, completely animated or organized by the pursuit of its interest, be that capital accumulation or revolution—might be understood to be the corollary of a similarity between capitalist and Marxist affirmations of productivism that *has* been noticed by a number of theorists.

In his 1975 text *The Mirror of Production,* Jean Baudrillard argues that Marx, like the political economists he critiques, articulates production as the only possible "imaginary" (in the Lacanian sense) through which subjects can recognize themselves. Baudrillard suggests that radical social transformation depends on a critique of this productivist imaginary. He offers "primitive" symbolic exchange, understood to involve wasteful expenditure, as an alternative to productivism. Arguing that under consumer capitalism production is no longer the real site of social control, Baudrillard holds up the social movements of the time, and most especially youth movements, as contesting the new site of social control: "the code," the "symbolic." Baudrillard's text is both brilliant in its critical anticipation of the neoliberal elaboration of responsible entrepreneurial subjectivity and a cautionary tale in its romanticization of, on one hand, "primitive societies" and, on the other, the social protests of and around 1968.

More recently, in her 2002 book *The Protestant Ethic and the Spirit of Capitalism,* Rey Chow has likewise recognized the pervasiveness of production as the mirror through which the subject—including or especially the subject of social transformation—is constituted. She argues:

> Any consideration of ethnic subjection would need to include not only the manner in which ethnics have been subjected to and continue to "resist" their dehumanizing objectification but also the psychological mechanism of "calling" . . . "work ethic"— . . . a dynamic built into the rationalist process of commodification itself. (33)

Chow suggests that ethnic protest seeks the very same wealth and grace promised by the Protestant ethic (as conceived by Max Weber 2000). Chow draws not only on Weber but also on Slavoj Žižek's Lacanian reworking of Louis Althusser's concept of interpellation. She notes that for Žižek,

> the point of interest . . . is not whether there exists a resistive subject who may or may not answer the call; rather, it is that, only by answering such

a call, only by more or less allowing one's self to be articulated in advance by this other, symbolic realm, can one avoid and postpone the terror of a radically open field of significatory possibilities. (110)

Chow does not propose a direct embrace of that "ontological terror" but rather, in a Butlerian move, proposes disrupting the symbolic through excessive and parodic reproductions of stereotypical ethnic images.

Meanwhile, in an argument that resonates with Baudrillard's, Edelman offers an incisive critique of the contemporary imaginary of *reproduction*. Against the cult of the child and the future, Edelman (2004, 7) does propose an embrace of the death drive, the drive toward that terrifying unfixity of meaning, which implies letting go of "the fantasy, precisely, of form as such, of an order, an organization, that assures the stability of our identities as subjects." Where Baudrillard romanticized the youth movements of the 1960s, Edelman, writing at the beginning of the twenty-first century, turns to *queerness*. By *queer* he does not mean any actually existing LGBT people, and specifically not LGBT rights–seeking movements, which he sees as embedded in the productive/reproductive imaginary. Rather, *queer* "is called forth to figure" "the death drive . . . both alien and internal to the logic of the Symbolic, . . . the inarticulable surplus that dismantles the subject from within . . . the negativity opposed to every form of social viability" (9). Edelman would even have us "refus[e] as well any backdoor hope for dialectical access to meaning" (6).

José Esteban Muñoz (2007, 363) criticizes Edelman's "queer," as well as his absolute rejection of futurity, as dependent on a disavowal of racial difference. Because of Edelman's failure to recognize that "all children are not the privileged white babies to whom contemporary society caters," Muñoz argues that Edelman "reproduce[s] a crypto-universal white gay subject that is weirdly atemporal—which is to say a subject whose time is a restricted and restricting hollowed-out present free of the need for the challenge of imagining a futurity that exists beyond the self or the here and now" (364). I concur with this assessment and will suggest that this temporality is class-specific, dependent on control over technologies of temporality, such as accounting rules, and the imposition of alternate temporal regimes on less privileged others.

Edelman deploys many characters from literature and film to sketch this queerness that "figures the availability of an unthinkable jouissance" that "reduc[es] . . . fantasy's promise of continuity to the meaningless circulation and repetitions of the drive" (39). Among them are

Charles Dickens's Scrooge and George Eliot's Silas Marner, both of whom prefer, are oriented toward, not other people of any gender or sex but rather the money that they take apparent pleasure in hoarding, counting, fondling. Interestingly, Edelman does not in this context discuss Bartleby, Herman Melville's scrivener who "would prefer not to," and who serves better those theorists who would keep open that dialectical back door.

In Melville's short story "Bartleby, the Scrivener: A Story of Wall Street," Bartleby is an employee of a Wall Street lawyer who, as narrator of the story, describes himself as increasingly stymied by the refusals of his scrivener to work and, more generally, to do what he is told. Bartleby thus provides a highly serviceable figure in the efforts of numerous theorists, including Žižek, Giorgio Agamben, Michael Hardt and Antonio Negri, and Gilles Deleuze, to locate a mode of intervention within the neoliberal discourse of entrepreneurial subjectivity, a discourse that has been so pervasive it has seemed almost impossible to read (or perform) a politically meaningful refusal of productivism or reproductivism.[3] In fact, as I will discuss further in the next chapter, inactivity has been pathologized as depression, to be treated with medication (Ehrenberg 2010; Cvetkovich 2012). Like Baudrillard and Chow, Žižek (2006, 382) recognizes that efforts to resist (precisely because they are *efforts*) wind up participating in that which they seek to oppose, and thus proposes Bartleby as a model for

> how we pass from the politics of "resistance" or "protestation," which parasitizes upon what it negates, to a politics which opens up a new space outside the hegemonic position and negation. . . . not only the obvious "There are great chances of a new career here! Join us!"—"I would prefer not to"; but also "Discover the depths of your true self, find inner peace!"—"I would prefer not to"; or . . . "What about all the racial and sexual injustice that we witness all around us? Isn't it time to do more?"—"I would prefer not to."

More modestly, Hardt and Negri (2000, 204) take Bartleby as evocative of a refusal that, while a performance of passivity, can be a first step toward collective action: "The refusal of work and authority, or really the refusal of voluntary servitude, is the beginning of liberatory politics . . . but it is only a beginning. . . . as part of that refusal, we need also to construct a new mode of life and above all a new community." Seeking to interpellate Occupy Wall Street (OWS) as "*the active subject of a refusal capable of building a community* starting out from its estrangement from the interests of capitalistic society" (Berardi 2009, 23; emphasis added), Occupy Wall Street protesters read "Bartleby" out loud in Zuccotti Park, and commentators have linked the lack of positive demands offered by OWS to Bartleby's enigmatic refusal—and the impact of Bartleby's language on the lawyer, who begins to "prefer" as well—to the impact of the phrase "the 99 percent."[4]

The efforts to expand the impact of OWS by using Bartleby to attribute meaning to the protests is actually a very savvy form of solidarity, of collaboration with OWS. Nonetheless, I would suggest that the celebration of Bartleby risks the sort of "overreading" that Berlant warns against—attributing too much sovereignty and intentionality, or just too much meaning, to what might be failures rather than refusals of (re)productivism. In "Cruel Optimism," a companion piece to "Slow Death," Berlant (2007a, 36) turns our attention elsewhere: "Cruel optimism is . . . a concept pointing toward a mode of lived imminence, one that grows from a perception about the reasons *people are not Bartleby*, do *not* prefer to interfere with varieties of immiseration, but choose to ride the wave of the system of attachment that they are used to" (emphasis added). Understanding our attachments to the status quo strikes me as absolutely critical to strategizing social movement for social change. So, for now, I look where Berlant points.

Learning from Berlant and Mahmood, I have tried not to turn the conflicted and self-contradictory subjects I encounter into heroes; instead I try to attend to the neither/nor subject, neither fully subordinate nor meaningfully resistant and, more important, neither entirely good capitalist subject nor revolutionary subject. That is the subject who tries, hits roadblocks, gets tired, stops trying so hard, picks up the object nearest to hand rather than making the effort to do the right thing, but then tries again. By exploring the lived contradictions, I am in hopeful search for a less than intentional crisis in the discursive apparatus sustaining capitalist accumulation in its current mode.

Begin Again

I read the *New York Times*—too much. I waste some of my most potentially productive time each day obsessively reading the *Times*. I can, sort of, legitimate this time spent with the *Times* as research, since the *Times* has persisted as the authoritative voice of neoliberalism before, during, and after the neocon George W. Bush years. So, for instance, in the years preceding the start of economic/financial crisis, the paper featured relentless reiterations and revisions of "culture of poverty" arguments. A front-page news article of March 20, 2006, by Erik Eckholm, headlined "Plight Deepens for Black Men, Studies Warn," states "experts . . . show that the huge pool of poorly educated black men are becoming ever more disconnected from the mainstream society. . . . finishing high school is the exception, legal work is scarcer than ever and prison is almost routine." What is the explanation? As Eckholm reads the studies, "terrible schools, absent parents, racism, the decline in blue collar jobs and a subculture that glorifies swagger over work . . . all these intertwined issues must be addressed." Fair enough. But then, "Joseph T. Jones, director of the fatherhood and work skills center here, puts the breakdown of families at the core. 'Many of these men grew up fatherless.'"

In a column the following August, Bob Herbert (2006)—whose beat among *Times* regular opinion columnists was U.S. poverty and minorities—identifies "a depressing cultural illness, frequently fatal, that has spread unchecked through much of black America." He concludes, "It is up to blacks themselves to embrace the current opportunities for academic achievement and professional advancement, to build the strong families that allow youngsters to flourish, and to create a cultural environment that turns its back on crime, ignorance, and self-abasement." And then, on the anniversary of Hurricane Katrina, Juan Williams (2006)—who became a political contributor on Fox News after twenty-three years at the *Washington Post* and service as an NPR correspondent—pipes up with a "prescription" for curing poverty: "Finish high school, at least. Wait until your 20s before marrying, and wait until you're married before having children. Once you're in the workforce, stay in: take any job, because building on the experience will prepare you for a better job. Any American who follows that prescription will be at almost no risk of falling into extreme poverty. *Statistics show it.*"

Statistics. What exactly do statistics show? As I will discuss more fully in the next chapter, the construction and deployment of "statistics" can and should be engaged at a number of levels. In her 1994 article "Babies and Banks: The 'Reproductive Underclass' and the Raced, Gendered Masking of Debt," written in the context of the early 1990s recession, Brett Williams argues that social scientific portrayals of the "underclass" as pathological serve as a deliberate red herring. She points out that they draw attention away from changes in the banking system, such as the U.S. Supreme Court's 1978 *Marquette* decision that allowed banks to follow the usury laws of the states in which they chose to locate for credit cards distributed nationally. That decision enabled tremendous increases in interest rates, which in turn transformed the credit card industry, making it profitable to lend money to people with so-called bad credit, to begin "'penetrating the debt capacity' of varied groups of Americans," who could then use credit to "mask" their stagnant incomes (351). Meanwhile, Brett Williams points out that the negative portrayals of the so-called underclass emphasize, as Juan Williams does, the idea that the poor get their *life course* wrong, most notably by having babies at the wrong time. And she draws on the work of Arline Geronimus, who has spent more than thirty years building statistical data and arguments to contest the normative accounts, showing that the life-course norms that pay off in health and wealth for white people do not actually pay off so well for poor people of color (349).[5]

In calling these *New York Times* texts reiterations and revisions of a culture of poverty discourse, I invoke Daniel Patrick Moynihan's famously pathologizing 1965 report *The Negro Family: The Case for National Action* and thus seem to suggest that this discourse bemoaning a lack of proper capitalist subjectivity and, in particular, lack of work ethic and ability to defer gratification—and locating the problem in culture—is of fairly recent origin, more or less coincident with neoliberalism. And certainly, it has been aggressively deployed as policy in this period:[6] In the United States one might point to the Personal Responsibility and Work Opportunity Reconciliation Act of 1996, which Bill Clinton claimed would "end welfare as we know it," and which linked intervention in kinship and gender relations (by requiring women to identify the biological fathers of their children to qualify for benefits, limiting the number of children eligible for benefits, and funding various programs promoting marriage) to the coercive promotion of "responsibility" through work.[7] But discourses diagnosing the lack of (and apparently aimed at producing) proper capitalist subjectivity in the poor, especially through intervention in the domestic sphere and gender and kinship relations, are as old as and utterly integral to capitalism itself. In *Making a Social Body,* Mary Poovey (1995) describes the circulation of such a discourse in mid-nineteenth-century Britain; and Saidiya Hartman, in *Scenes of Subjection* (1997), describes the operations of such a discourse vis-à-vis recently freed slaves in the post–Civil War United States.[8]

The resonance of the current discourse with similar discourses of past eras raises a question: What is the relationship between the responsible subjectivity being solicited here and the "entrepreneurial subjectivity" described by Rose, Gordon, and others who, building on Foucault's work on governmentality, have tried to identify a distinct subject of neoliberalism?[9] I would suggest that it should be seen as one of many versions, and that "entrepreneurial subjectivity" varies across the social and economic hierarchy. Elizabeth Freeman (2010, 3) argues that "time binds," "that naked flesh is bound into socially meaningful embodiment through temporal regulation. . . . Schedules, calendars, time zones," and, as I will emphasize, accounting practices "convert historically specific regimes of asymmetrical power into seemingly ordinary bodily tempos and routines." Moreover, Freeman argues,

> the state and other institutions, including representational apparatuses, link properly temporalized bodies to narratives of movement and change . . . teleological schemes of events or strategies for living such as marriage, accumulation of health and wealth for the future, reproduction, childrearing, and death. (4)

As she points out—building on the work of Julia Kristeva (1981) and Dana Luciano (2007)—temporal norms have been differentially gendered: cyclical, as opposed to sequential, norms are associated with Woman-as-symbol, as well as historically specific women's domestic roles (5). Likewise, multiple norms of responsible temporal/financial life management are differentially deployed in conjunction with racial, gender, and class formation projects.

A certain amount of deliberate confusion between different versions of entrepreneurial subjectivity is one of the sites and sources of contradiction and crisis in the current conjuncture. The subject of the culture of poverty discourse, who is meant to work toward deferred gratifications, is a subject of labor and consumption. But the entrepreneurial subject has sometimes been distinguished as the subject of personal finance and risk management from the laboring saver (or the laboring spender/shopper). Randy Martin (2002, 3–5), for instance, states: "Savings rested upon a mass psychology of deferred gratification. . . . In the new psychology, money is not to be left untouched, but constantly fondled, mined daily like a well-stocked refrigerator." Martin notes that the "financial subject" isn't meant to be or can't be universal since a computer and Internet connection are minimum requirements for participation in daily financial self-management; but he also suggests that "financialization" has had an impact on "what are taken as typical habits of life" (7). That is, although not everyone can participate, everyone lives in the shadow of financialized norms and expectations for what a life should be (see also Langley 2010).

To get a better feel for these norms and expectations, I went back to the *Times* to see what personal financial advice it was offering to its own readers at the same time that it was performing for them the scolding of the poor, who I suspect rarely read the paper themselves. The *Times* offers a *lot* of personal finance advice, including "primers" on topics related to identity theft, credit cards, insurance, retirement planning, and estate planning, as well as ongoing advice columns such as Your Money by Ron Lieber, which is apparently aimed at what one article calls "the mass affluent,"[10] as opposed to Wealth Matters by Paul Sullivan, described on the *Times* website as "a column looking at strategies that the wealthy use to manage not only their money but their overall well-being."[11] A search of the *Times* online archive using the term "personal finances" suggests that in recent years the paper has run about 250 articles per year intended to help readers sort through the vast array of financial products and services: individual retirement accounts (do you want an IRA or a Roth IRA?), mutual funds of various specific kinds (index funds, collar funds, target-date funds), annuities, reverse mortgages, and, of course, further financial advice from advisers and books.

Going back to 2005 and 2006, I was surprised at the centrality of what appeared to be old-fashioned budgeting and saving. The need to do these things is cast as a response to a changed world, the "revised social contract" (Martin 2002, 10), in which one cannot count on social security, pensions, or inheritance but must instead take responsibility for oneself.[12] So, an April 2006 article titled "Looking Out for Yourself: Some Tips," by Eric Dash, begins:

The reminders are everywhere.

You turn on the television and there's a commercial depicting a middle-age couple talking with a financial adviser about what they need to do to retire comfortably.

A money expert on her blog discusses the hows and whys of building a nest egg, starting right now. People you barely know ask, "Are you in your company's 401(k) plan?"

No one asked that question 50 years ago. Until recently, most Americans counted on their company for the bulk of their retirement nest egg. Now that responsibility is largely in employees' own hands.

Writing before the writing was on the wall that the good times would end, columnist M. P. Dunleavey must have seemed a bit of a wet rag, with articles criticizing "the inflation of our expectations" (2006), in which she encourages budgeting or writing a "spending plan," an activity that she implies will performatively produce savings (see also Dunleavey 2005). And columnist/humorist Ben Stein (2005) offers financial advice to college freshmen that places hard work at the center.

But this focus on working and saving is a bit misleading (maybe most importantly for the *Times* readers themselves). In January 2006, Paul B. Brown's review of three new investment how-to books begins this way:

> Pity, please, the people who write personal finance books.
>
> More than 150 years ago, Charles Dickens wrote in "David Copperfield": "Annual income twenty pounds, annual expenditure nineteen six, result happiness. Annual income twenty pounds, annual expenditure twenty pounds ought and six, result misery."
>
> Little has changed since.

The thing is, spending less than your income does not appear to be the type of advice offered in the books Brown reviews, which are focused not on budgeting one's spending in a particular year but rather, at least in Brown's representation, on investing for retirement. These books and the *Times* itself are thus speaking to a different audience and in a different voice than, say, *The Suze Orman Show,* which is usually organized around a format titled "Can I Afford It?" in which Suze "approves" or "denies" a request by a caller to buy something (a house, a vacation, a fancy purse) after evaluating the caller's income, debts, and savings. The implication is that you should save and invest those savings, since if you cannot demonstrate that you are doing so, you get "denied"—but the immediate focus is spending, or not. Meanwhile, for the *Times* reader, saving and investing have merged since 401(k)s (defined contribution plans) replaced defined benefit pensions, a shift that, as Martin (2002, 12) says, "asks people from all walks of life to accept risks into their homes that were hitherto the province of professionals." While at least some readers of the *Times* can handle this "risk," in many cases, Martin argues, "without significant capital, people are being asked to think like capitalists" (12).

Life: Time: Responsibility

A key site of such increased risk, in addition to retirement savings invested in a volatile stock market, is of course the housing market, or, maybe more precisely, the mortgage market. In an academic article on the foreclosure crisis in the United States, Susan Saegert, Desiree Fields, and Kimberly Libman (2009, 298) argue that familiar discourses of the Protestant ethic and American Dream have served as a Trojan horse for financialization:

> The policies and financial practices that made homeownership accessible to previously excluded households treated homes like speculative commodities and new homeowners as investors who were increasing their risk postures to aggressively manage growth of overall wealth. [Meanwhile] the [popular/political??] rhetoric of the expansion of homeownership turned on the much older notion of homeownership as the American Dream, the ultimate achievement of autonomy, a better life for the next generation and full citizenship.

Accessibility has been a very deliberate project, but accessibility on what terms? The material consequences of this project of "inclusion" have been, it turns out, devastating.

As Saegert et al. point out, given the personal virtues associated with homeownership, "the damage done by foreclosure is not restricted to material loss. The threat of mortgage foreclosure calls into question homeowners' selfhood and their relationship to society and government" (298). Optimistically, Saegert et al. draw on evidence from focus groups to suggest that the contradictions in which homeowners were caught led some to question "the common sense of neoliberal homeownership and the systems that it upholds" (309). I certainly hope so, but I am, in this chapter, more concerned with understanding—without condemning as dupes—those who did not.

The confusion and manipulation of multiple versions of entrepreneurial subjectivity plays out, to a significant extent, through temporal contradictions apparent in the dynamics of the "neoliberal homeownership" crisis. Saegert et al. might be oversimplifying matters by contrasting homeownership as American Dream with homeownership as financial speculation. Certainly, homeownership has been promoted through the rhetoric of the American Dream; however, as George W. Bush's Department of Housing and Urban Development put it in a brochure titled *Blueprint for the American Dream,* this is a long-term dream not only of building "a better life" for oneself and one's children but also of "accumulating wealth which may be used for retirement or left in an estate."[13] That is, homeownership as a form of liberal citizenship is not separable from homeownership as financial investment. Nevertheless, the temporal framework for that investment *is* the site of contradiction.

Drawing on interviews with homeowners conducted in 1999–2000 in the United Kingdom, where, as in the United States, homeownership has been aggressively promoted over the past couple of decades, Susan J. Smith (2008, 527) argues that homeowners like to imagine themselves as "the figure who wisely distinguishes 'safe' housing investment from riskier styles of money management; the person who is too responsible to gamble." Here the "safe" investors would seem to be distinguishing themselves from the irresponsible rich in a way that echoes my imagined *New York Times* readers' self-satisfied sense of distinction from those who, or so they read, have failed to follow life-course norms involving working one's way up a ladder of education and employment, all the while deferring gratification. However, Smith points out that it is not only the case that the housing market can be more volatile than the stock market, as we have all learned over the past few years; it is also the case that, in conjunction with "financial innovations" that have made it "easier now than it has ever been to withdraw equity" (529), the "ethopolitics" of homeownership have shifted:[14]

> Owned housing is no longer simply a way of trading high outlays in working life for low housing costs in old age [and thus to engage in long-term planning and saving]. It is, rather, an active resource—a housing-market solution for the wide range of welfare needs and consumption desires that households experience [in the present]. Choosing to buy may signal the responsible housing consumer; investing money in, and wresting resource from, owned homes is the mark of an active citizen. (529)

Martin (2002, 108) argues that "financialization implies an extreme form of presentism." And while the value placed on deferred gratification would suggest that presentism correlates with irresponsibility, Smith is suggesting that under neoliberalism, where the ideal entrepreneurial subject is the *active* subject, the presentism of home equity borrowers has been cast not (only) as *irresponsible* but rather (also) as a form of responsibility by sheer dint of activity.[15]

But when and for whom is radical presentism responsible or irresponsible? This gets confusing—and that is precisely the point. Martin points out that for those invested in houses that are also homes, "the present tendency toward leveraging ownership against future increases in valuation" through home equity loans means that "what was once a source of security is now a source of risk" and "generates increased vulnerability to bankruptcy" (31). That is, maybe spending your future housing wealth now is irresponsible: "vulnerability to bankruptcy" sounds like a bad thing; and, certainly, bankruptcy remains shameful for some people and is, no doubt, an indication that someone's life has become very difficult. But it is also important to remember that, as I argued in chapter 2 (and as was reaffirmed by the passage of the Bankruptcy Abuse Prevention and Consumer Protection Act of 2005),[16] *bankruptcy* is a *privilege,* an opportunity for a "fresh start" that is doled out with increasing parsimony in the United States, at least with regard to struggling individuals and families rather than businesses (it has never been available to the poor). And none of the legislation passed in response to the financial crisis (including the comprehensive Dodd-Frank Wall Street Reform and Consumer Protection Act) featured a so-called cram-down provision to allow mortgage debt on a primary residence to be modified or discharged in bankruptcy; meanwhile, the major airlines and auto companies have almost all used bankruptcy procedures to shed financial obligations to their workers (especially long-term obligations for pensions and retiree health insurance).

Karen Ho directly addresses the question of who has access to the privilege of living in the present and who must drag their past around in *Liquidated: An Ethnography of Wall Street* (2009). She describes investment banker norms as including both "temporal identification with the market"—a market in which, according to the efficient market hypothesis, the future is supposedly always already "priced in" and thus absolutely collapsed into the present—and short-termism, evidenced by "relentless deal-making frenzy" and driven by commission or bonus pay linked to sales/deals or short cycles of financial reporting (such as "quarterly bottom lines") (242, 252).[17] In the context of the financial crisis, the apparent role of short-termism (and the gargantuan bonuses received by investment bankers for deal making that, as it turns out, a few moments later destroyed their own firms and damaged the larger economy) has led to populist demands that executive/banker pay be withheld for some amount of time to create longer- rather than shorter-term perspective. Having to live in the present with past decisions is imposed as a punishment. From the financiers' perspective, this longer-term responsibility may seem financially irrational—in conflict with a long run that announces itself now, in market prices—since it makes them less liquid, less able to respond to the new present.[18]

As Ho describes them, bankers understand themselves to have enough personal liquidity to deal with the downside risk of their efforts to "milk the present" (295), moving on to the next present moment when this one goes south; but they do recognize that for others the present becomes a past that shapes the future. She quotes a banker as explaining that, by contrast with his own situation, most people's lives are not adequately "liquid":

> "If you have a skill set, you can't just trade that skill set in for another skill set. It's lumpy. In the same way that a house has less liquidity than cash does. And a skill set has even less liquidity than a house does. A person's family, home and life have even less liquidity. . . . we see that some people, because they have no liquidity in their lives . . . they suffer." (244)

Without liquidity, people might actually need to plan in order to survive. Ho draws on Richard Sennett's argument that, as Wall Street norms have shaped corporate behavior and "stable bureaucratic structures of the corporation have . . . been . . . replaced by a new institutional structure that values disloyalty, irresponsibility, and immediacy" (246), "workers are denied 'the gift of organized time' to engage in the long-term and stable planning of one's work and life, to survive social upheavals and establish some kind of command over one's life narrative" (246, quoting Sennett 2006, 36). But if presentism can be judged as disloyalty and irresponsibility when imposed on those without the "liquidity" to survive it, it is important to remember that the organized, planned life is also a technology of exploitation and domination.

In an academic article that has received a huge amount of attention in the popular media, law professor Brent White (2009) describes differentiated relations to responsibility not in terms of "liquidity" but in terms of double standards, where social norms of "responsibility" keep an individual paying an "underwater" mortgage when a corporation (or investment banker) making a rational financial decision would simply "walk away." The shocked and appalled responses of the news media punditry to White's work have certainly made it clear that the norm of responsibility is alive and well in popular discourse;[19] and, in keeping with that norm, the current crisis has produced broad recognition of the "irresponsibility" of the bankers. Ho (2009, 284) is very much in line with popular discourse in noting with some dismay, "Investment bankers are not compelled to take any responsibility for scandals or bad deals." I understand the impulse to produce/impose a common standard one way or another, to make bankers more responsible or mortgage holders less so. But this approach misses the fact that these different standards are not independent of each other; rather, the liquidity of the financier, the ability of the banker to live in the present, depends on the individual mortgage holder's accepting this long-term responsibility, treating his or her house as an American Dream home, not merely a financial investment. As Paul Langley argues in *The Everyday Life of Global Finance* (2010, vii), "In meeting their obligations, American mortgagors are, for example, often unwittingly ensuring that the wheels of the mortgage-backed securities market continue to turn."

Sennett (2006, 23), despite recognizing that "narratives . . . of how things should happen . . . the stages of a career, steps of increased wealth . . . how to buy a house" are a "bureaucratic imposition" of "military, social capitalism," nonetheless seems to value one particular temporal schema over another as the better way to have a life:

> A self oriented to the short term, focused on potential ability, willing to abandon past experience is—to put a kindly face on the matter—an unusual sort of human being. Most people . . . need a sustaining life narrative, they take pride in being good at something specific, and they value the experiences they've lived through. (5)

The imposition of what has been called "flexibility" on workers by corporations that restructure in time with the stock market is surely painful for those suffering layoffs or other threats to their survival. But keeping in mind the punishing deployment of particular life-course norms for young poor women of color as well as the recent raft of critiques of chrononormativity emerging from queer studies,[20] we should pause at Sennett's suggestion that those who can endlessly start fresh, live in the present, unconstrained by past or future, are "unusual," maybe a little queer.

In Lucy Prebble's 2009 play *Enron,* Jeffrey Skilling, Enron's CEO, is made to say that his entire identity and sense of self depend on the Enron stock price. As it happens, in the play, Skilling explains his identification with the stock price to his daughter:

SKILLING: I have to check the stock price.
DAUGHTER: Why?
SKILLING: Because that's how Daddy knows how much he's worth.
DAUGHTER: Why?
SKILLING: Well, the market knows how many people believe in Daddy. (69)

Unlike the children in Edelman's examples, Dickens's Tiny Tim and Eliot's Eppie, who work bits of magic on Scrooge and Marner, and who reorient the financiers toward humans and futures, Skilling's child is unable to rescue or redeem her father. It may be that the fictionalized Skilling is the truly queer figure in Edelman's sense, a postmodern version of Edelman's nineteenth-century misers, rejecting future-oriented reproductivism (and, in fact, any "real" economy of production) in favor of a permanent present of meaningless repetition and circulation.[21]

To recall the Enron situation, however, is to remember that investment bankers and corporate executives are not merely reactive to the market in an immediate or short-term temporal framework; they also attempt to shape that market by creating, negotiating, struggling over structures of time as constituted by accounting practices. Critical accounting scholars have claimed a key role for accounting in instantiating a capitalist regime of abstract, quantifiable time, in which time is objectified as "interchangeable, measurable units," contrasted with the "concrete" or experiential time (Floyd 2009, 52, with reference to Postone 1993; see also Thompson 1967) thought to precede and persist beyond the domain of capital (see Ezzamel and Robson 1995, 160). Revisiting the transformation of temporality associated with the Industrial Revolution, most famously described by E. P. Thompson, Paolo Quattrone (2005, 196) argues that "the achievement of a notion of time which is shared and objective requires the deployment of a series of techniques, technologies and beliefs," among which "accounting may play an important albeit neglected role." Quattrone continues:

> Could we measure and talk of efficiency without the asset turnover ratio? Probably not. If today no one would contest that "time is money" and that "time is gold" (as stated by Benjamin Franklin), it is likely because this ratio (and the double-entry bookkeeping behind it) has made the flowing of time visible, measurable and worthy. (203)

While attributing to accounting a role in this fundamental transformation of the temporal imaginary and, concomitantly, a practical role in implementing temporal synchronization, Quattrone also recognizes that accounting proliferates diverse temporal regimes tied to various reporting deadlines and rhythms (200); and, quoting Anthony Hopwood, he points to accounting, especially budgeting and planning, as a site of struggle over performance measurement (202).

As Mahmood Ezzamel and Keith Robson (1995, 149) note, accounting practices shape social relations—they "regulate and monitor economic transactions across time and space" (or, as Tony Tinker [1985, 81] would put it, they "arbitrate" or "adjudicate")—through what appear to be "mundane 'technical'" decisions regarding

> the ordering of recorded transactions, the periodicizing of accounting calculations (depreciation, interest charges, determination of periodic profit and loss, discounting of future financial options to the present, etc.) and the monitoring of economic performance (time and motion-based performance targets, frequency and timeliness of reporting, bases of cross sectional and time-series comparisons, etc.). (149–50)

Among the issues always up for grabs in accounting is how to value assets; this turns out to be a question of *when* to value those assets. As one introductory-level accounting textbook explains, for instance:

> The *going concern convention* holds that . . . the market (sale) value of non-current assets is often low in relation to the values at which they appear in the balance sheet, and an expectation of having to sell off the assets [for instance, if the business were going to close] would mean that anticipated losses on sale should be fully recorded. However, where there is no expectation of a need to sell off the assets, the value . . . can continue to be shown at their recorded values (that is, based on historic cost). . . . [Meanwhile,] the *prudence convention* requires that the expected loss from the future sales [of goods intended to be sold] should be recognized immediately rather than when the goods are eventually sold. Profits, on the other hand, are not recognized until they are realized (that is, when the goods are actually sold). (McLaney and Atrill 2005, 49–50; emphasis added).

Manipulation of the timing of valuation was critical to the Enron case.

Apparently in violation of accounting's "prudence convention," which requires that expected losses should be booked now but profits should not be booked until they are realized, for Enron, the ball got rolling when it got permission from the SEC to use "mark-to-market" accounting and thus was permitted to book future revenues in the present. Prebble's play opens with the party Enron supposedly had to celebrate that SEC decision. Prebble has Skilling explain mark-to-market this way:

> If you have an idea, if you sign a deal, say that we're going to provide
> someone with a supply of champagne for the next few years at a set price,
> every month whatever—Then that definite future income can be valued,
> at market prices today, and written down as earnings the moment the deal
> is signed. We don't have to wait for the grapes to be grown and squashed
> and . . . however the hell you make champagne. The market will recognize
> your idea and your profit in that moment. And the company will pay you
> for it. If you come up with something brilliant—You know, life is so short.
> If you have a moment of genius, that will be rewarded now. (9)

Of course, in the recent economic crisis, mark-to-market has not been
so appealing: bankers have fought to change accounting rules that require that they book various assets at their current, negligible market
value and thus acknowledge billions of dollars in losses on mortgage
securities. (I imagine Skilling might say, "If you come up with something stupid—You know, life is so short. If you have a moment of idiocy,
you should not be punished for it, now or later.") And to a significant
extent they appear to have won that fight, although the battle rages on
(see Scannell 2009).[22]

I note this skirmish over the rules not as an instance of meaningful
political economic struggle, but rather as an indication of the control
of the financiers over the means of production of liquidity, of credit.
The larger point is not simply that one particular temporal schema—of
abstract homogeneous commensurable time—provides a victory for
capitalism, but that capital accumulation and the reinscription of social hierarchies proceed through an orchestrated (if at times cacopho-
nous) deployment of diverse temporal norms. Embodying what might
be understood as a radicalization of the abstraction of time attributed
to capitalism (empty, equivalent, temporal units are freed completely
from particular order or location), bankers and the Jeff Skillings of the
world deploy the credit that allows free—liquid—movement through
time and space, enabling them to live in whatever present they might
prefer. They are shielded by a red herring in the form of the apparently particular, but in fact statistically created, present-oriented, irresponsible, childbearing young woman of color. Meanwhile, "responsible" workers and savers (consumers and borrowers) bear the debt,
the obligations and responsibilities, taking credit for their submission
to exploitation and expropriation. Intricately intertwined, neither responsibility nor irresponsibility provides leverage against the social
processes that generate this scenario: insisting on responsibility turns

out to be *ressentiment,* a self-defeating expression of moral superiority by the losers; and irresponsibility certainly cannot be read as any sort of resistance to a norm of responsibility, but rather must be understood as a normal privilege of the powerful and the creditworthy, those in command of the technologies of accounting and thus the attribution of credit and debt. Rather than join in the effort to extend and enforce the norm of responsibility, I will persist in the effort to pick at its cracks and fissures.

Keep Going (Starting Over, Again)

This chapter is the product of interruption, fortunately not the violent interruption of a prison term, but self-interruptions, tangents off the direct path toward professional advancement. I have twice interrupted my work on this scholarly project, allowing myself instead to be absorbed in the daily labor of university administration, including serving as chair of my university's Strategic Planning and Budget Advisory Committee. In that role I coauthored—and later participated in a number of presentations promoting—something called the Instructional Responsibility and Accountability Process, which was aimed at extracting more teaching from the faculty. Is it really possible that I was alone among my faculty leadership colleagues to hear in this title an echo of the Personal Responsibility and Work Opportunity Reconciliation Act of 1996, or the Illegal Immigration Reform and Immigrant Responsibility Act, also of 1996, which dramatically enhanced the criminalization of undocumented immigrants? If participating in a management crackdown on the faculty through the rhetoric of responsibility and accountability gave anyone else the creeps, they did not say so—on the contrary, they appeared sincerely convinced that some colleagues were not pulling their weight. And while department heads (the audience for the presentations) resisted demands to hold their faculty members "accountable," certain that this would be a time-consuming bureaucratic nightmare, they responded in much more positive way to calls for responsibility, envisioning constructive conversations with their colleagues about how to serve more students. The magic of "responsibility."

A few years ago, I spent some time hanging around a small project called the Women's Re-entry Network (informally known as WREN). This was not "research" per se; I got no institutional review board approval, and, for that reason, I quote here only things participants said at public events. I chose the group largely because it was conveniently located in the research institute attached to my own department. WREN emerged from a grant-funded conference called "Inside Out" that brought together women who had been incarcerated, people from agencies that provide services to women in "reentry," and Arizona Department of Corrections officials, including the director, Dora Schriro. According to the group's flyer, WREN was "created by and for women who have experienced incarceration and are now attempting to reestablish themselves in the community." These women "provide support, resources, information and educational opportunities for themselves, the community and women of all ages preparing for release." WREN's work included a class for women in the local jail and a speakers' bureau. In addition to watching video of the conference, I heard members of the group make presentations twice and attended a number of meetings.

As I listened to these women speak, I heard something that it would be going only a little too far to call a desire for prison. In using this phrase, I emphatically do not mean to locate criminality in the psyche of the criminal. No, I am fully persuaded by the work of Ruth Wilson Gilmore and other prison-abolitionist scholar-activists that crime, criminals, and prisons are socially constructed in the context of racializing political economic projects, although I think it is important to note that the WREN women were explicitly uninterested in such an analysis. As one said at the beginning of her presentation on a panel: "I'm not necessarily here to dispute whether incarceration is good, bad, or effective. I really do not know and for me there really is no point to looking at this aspect and saying, 'if this hadn't happened.'"

I use the phrase "desire for prison" because I heard prison located as a crucial turning point, the time and place in which these narrators kicked a drug addiction, got born again, learned job skills. I heard prison described as a site where one can (though might not, if one does not have the right attitude) get everything fixed, from one's soul to one's teeth. That is, I heard prison narrated as a necessary and valuable time during and after which the narrator took up a version of "entrepreneurial subjectivity" and began to build a life: worked the twelve steps, got a minimum-wage job but stuck with it, got some training and got a promotion, went back to school, got her kids back and started to provide good parenting.

These women not only narrated their own experience in this way, but they also promoted this view of prison as, potentially, the "beginning of the rest of your life" through their jail classes. Against the stigma of criminality and predictions of failure, one explained that she tries to model, as well as describe, the steps toward successful reentry: "I give women hope based on my own success; I'm a productive member of society today." This success is based largely on "taking responsibility." One panelist said, "I wasn't so much a drug-addict as a self-addict. . . . You have to take responsibility. Not 'I got caught' but 'I did this.'" And another stated, "I teach women that they are accountable to themselves and then they can be accountable to their families."

Their narratives imply and sometimes explicitly include descriptions of past lives in which the narrators made bad decisions. For instance, one of the panelists declared, "I made some very poor choices and these choices had consequences." In other words, the past life is implicitly one of irresponsibility as opposed to the present life of responsibility. Another panelist said, "I was a wild child of the '60s and '70s and now I've become establishment."

Initially, I found what I am calling a desire for prison, or, more accurately, the absence of a critique of prison, surprising and disappointing. I eventually realized that it would be unreasonable to expect that disempowered, disenfranchised, and extraordinarily vulnerable subjects, such as people with felony records, would resist the dominant discourse of entrepreneurial subjectivity when I cannot think of anyone but a few anarchist students who even try. And as it turns out, I am not the first scholar to experience naive disappointment at the participation in dominant discourse of those subject to the criminal justice system. One of the essays that emerged from a participatory action research collaboration between university-based scholars (led by Michelle Fine and María Elena Torre) and women in prison at Bedford Hills Correctional Facility describes the women's struggle to produce "counterstories" and similarly notes that inmates described prison as a site of rehabilitation, producing "new selves" that are "'improved,' 'working,' 'motivated,'" and "productive" (Torre et al. 2001, 157–58; see also Fine et al. 2003). This language, as the researchers point out, is required by parole boards as well as by other authorities and even family members.

And certainly, those in prison over the past few decades have been at least as subject to the discourse of personal responsibility and entrepreneurial subjectivity as those of us on the outside. In the Arizona state prison system, during the same period that I was going to the WREN presentations, Director Schriro was implementing a program she called Parallel Universe. As described in a November 2004 special issue of the Arizona Department of Corrections newsletter, Parallel Universe prepares felons for reentry from the very beginning of their incarceration, "introducing them in prison to real world requirements and rewards" (*ADC Post* 2004, 4). Premised on the idea that "felons tend to blame everyone else" and are "unlikely to assume responsibility for their behavior," in this program "inmates make decisions and accept responsibility for the decisions that they make at work and during leisure hours," and "they develop empathy for others through victim-focused activities. . . . they participate in charitable activities, community service and restorative justice programs during non-work hours" (4); such participation is also described as "an important way to accelerate accepting responsibility" (6).

The Bedford Hills researchers ultimately recognized that what sounded at first like narratives of redemption were rather "strategic and sincere points of entry into a hostile public conversation, paving the way for an expression of their power to think, speak and act as fully engaged citizens" (Torre et al. 2001, 160). Likewise, I came to recognize the embrace of responsibility by the WREN members not simply as submission to dominant norms, but rather as an effort to appropriate the magical powers of the term *responsibility,* a bold, against-the-odds, against-the-stereotypes claiming of agency and control over their present and future.

Observing the WREN members' embrace of the responsible entrepreneurial norm led me to recognize that part of the persuasive force of the discourse of entrepreneurial subjectivity more generally is precisely that it suggests that individuals have a great deal of agency. So, in reading the desire for prison expressed by the WREN members as a desire for access to entrepreneurial subjectivity, I cast them not as typical of those who have been incarcerated, but rather as exemplary of those of us who live in the "free" world. That is, as they narrate themselves, they appear to embody the ideal poles of responsible life building and irresponsible refusal—*ideal* in that, as I have learned from Berlant to recognize, very little of life actually occurs at either pole.

Despite their lack of interest in a critique of incarceration and their apparent embrace of responsible entrepreneurial subjectivity, these narrators are impassioned in their description of another sort of contradiction, one that can and does provide the ground for their social change activism. Their own agentive efforts to build a life are always articulated as requiring a supplement: God, good luck, and support group companions are given a lot of credit for their successes. So, for instance, one woman claimed, "God opens doors for me and I walk through them." And the WREN members are very clear about why such a supplement is needed: as several former prisoners argued vociferously at the conference, prison does not, in fact, provide adequate education or relevant job training. And "society" refuses to give women a chance:

> If a woman has committed a crime and pays her debt to the courts and society, wouldn't it be reasonable for her to expect the opportunity to grow within the community? Society has set up every obstacle possible to ensure failure for women with previous convictions. . . . a woman ends up with a job at a fast-food restaurant at $6.50 an hour, meanwhile she has a child at home, rent, and bills to pay just like everyone else. She is driven to live in the same poverty-stricken neighborhood because of income and the lack of housing available for felons.

That is, their desire for prison is in large part a desire for prison to be something other, or more, than what it is. But neither prison nor conditions of life after prison enable them to fully assume entrepreneurial subjectivity; its promise of rewards is rarely fulfilled, more often frustrated. While in WREN's own logic this contradiction between what is "reasonable" and what is reality produces a reformist and social service–oriented effort to hold the liberal state to its own promises of opportunity and equality while "taking care of our own," it also suggests that the conditions, constraints, and outcomes of the gap between promise and reality—legally mandated or privately enacted exclusions from social welfare programs, housing, education, and jobs that force these women to live life as a frustrating struggle for even basic survival, that track them back toward the past rather than toward a future—mean that the norm of entrepreneurial subjectivity is likely to be inhabited in the mode of failure.

But maybe such failure is not without systemic, even dialectical, consequences—especially now that it has become clear that the promises of entrepreneurial subjectivity have led to disappointment not only for those with criminal records but also for vast numbers of people unexpectedly unemployed and unhoused. In an August 2007 article in *The Nation* titled "Smashing Capitalism," Barbara Ehrenreich wrote:

> Somewhere in the Hamptons a high-roller is cursing his cleaning lady and
> shaking his fists at the lawn guys. The American poor, who are usually
> tactful enough to remain invisible to the multi-millionaire class, suddenly
> leaped onto the scene and started smashing the global financial system. . . .
> First they stopped paying their mortgages. . . . Then, in a diabolically clever
> move, they stopped shopping.

At that time, way back before Lehman failed and AIG was bailed
out, it seemed like a big deal that CEOs Stan O'Neal of Merrill Lynch
and Chuck Prince of Citigroup were being forced out. Ehrenreich recognizes, of course, that this was not a deliberate revolution; in suggesting/
fantasizing that the poor are anticapitalist agents, she is both constructing a good old-fashioned dialectical narrative—arguing that the
exploitative and predatory behavior of the high rollers has come home
to roost—and contesting the construction of personal indebtedness,
which, like crime, drug use, unemployment, and obesity, has been at
least until recently, and is maybe even still now, cast as a problem of
irresponsibility.

But Ehrenreich admits that her narrative does not work; she closes
by saying, "The poor have risen up and spoken; only it sounds less like
a shout of protest than a low, strangled, cry of pain." And when I turned
to the *Businessweek* article titled "The Poverty Business" (Grow and
Epstein 2007), Ehrenreich's source regarding the diverse efforts to ex-
ploit the poor by lending to them, I found that it opened with a description of a borrower who was not simply duped—although she does
claim to have not understood the terms of her car loan—but whose
borrowing disrupts the opposition between irresponsibility and entrepreneurial subjectivity, in that buying a car was part of her effort to
construct a properly enterprising self. According to the *Businessweek*
article:

> Roxanne Tsosie decided in late 2005 to pull her life together. . . . She landed
> a job as a home-health-care aid for the elderly and infirm. It paid $15,000
> a year and required that she have a car to make her rounds of Albuquerque
> and its rambling desert suburbs. . . . A friend told her about a used-car place.

The rest of the story about Tsosie is predictable:

> She agreed to a purchase price of $7,922, borrowing the full amount at a
> sky-high 24.9%. . . . she thought she had signed up for $150 monthly install-
> ments. The paperwork indicated she owed that amount every other week.
> She soon realized she couldn't manage the payments. Dejected, she agreed

to give the car back, having already paid $900. "It kind of knocked me down," Tsosie says. "I felt I'd never get anywhere."

Her story certainly exemplifies the "reproduction of predictable life" in a zone where "life building and the attrition of human life . . . are indistinguishable" (Berlant 2007b, 754). But the contradictions associated with deployments of credit and debt that seem one day to be responsible investment and look like irresponsible debt the next are not limited to the poor.

Elizabeth Warren and Amelia Warren Tyagi's best-selling book *The Two-Income Trap* (2003) is an interesting hybrid text, drawing on legitimate academic research but also taking the kinds of liberties that give statistics a bad name. It is half self-help book (aimed, I think, at that same "mass affluent" class to whom the *New York Times* addresses itself), half a pop policy book, intended to galvanize liberals to participate in debates over issues, like bankruptcy law, that might seem a bit dry. The trap it describes is one in which what it calls middle-class families spend every last penny of two incomes and thus have no cushion for job loss, a health crisis, a divorce, or any other unexpected event that might decrease income or increase expenses. It engages in direct debate with Juliet Schor's books of the same genre, *The Overworked American* (1991) and *The Overspent American* (1998). Warren and Tyagi cast Schor's argument as "the Over-Consumption Myth," a myth we find comforting:

> If families are in trouble because they squander their money, then those of us who shop at Costco and cook our own pasta have nothing to worry about. Moreover, if families are to blame for their own failures, then the rest of us bear no responsibility for helping those who are in trouble. Their fault, their problem. (19)

In contrast to the "individual responsibility" thesis associated with the "over-consumption myth," Warren and Tyagi identify a confluence of social dynamics as well as specific policies and laws, such as the deregulation of the credit industry, that have produced what they call "the two-income trap."

A central component of their argument is the claim that the cost of "necessities" such as housing, health care, and education has increased. But their discussion of what counts as a necessity with regard to housing is revealing:

> Why would the average parent spend so much money on a home? . . .
>
> . . . For many parents, the answer came down to two words so powerful that families would pursue them to the brink of bankruptcy: *safety* and *education*. Families put Mom to work, used up the family's economic reserves, and took on crushing debt loads in sacrifice to these two gods, all in the hope of offering their children the best possible start in life. . . .
>
> Everyone has heard the all-too-familiar news stories about kids who can't read, gang violence in the schools, classrooms without textbooks . . . evils associated with poverty. (22–23)

Warren and Tyagi try to distinguish this desire for safety and education from racism, citing studies that "found that, for similar homes, school quality was *the single most important determinant of neighborhood prices*—more important than racial composition of the neighborhood, commute distance, crime rate, or proximity to a hazardous waste site" (24). I am not so sure it is possible—or rather, I *am* sure it is *not* possible—to distinguish and separate race from the other components of human capital in which families are "investing" by undertaking mortgages that they cannot afford.[23] That is, "the evils associated with poverty" that Warren and Tyagi name are images associated with racialized "ghettos"; distancing from *racialized* poverty that has been located in specific residential areas by particular histories of policy and practice (Harvey 1974) then appears to be a key strategy for constituting the social creditworthiness that will enable greater "liquidity," the ability to move freely from one present to the next unburdened by a disabling past.

Describing the decision-making process of divorced women who, according to Warren and Tyagi's research, are especially at risk for bankruptcy, the authors again identify the zone in which the imaginary of the responsible entrepreneurial subject drives indebtedness that is simultaneously "irresponsible" and "irrational":

> Mothers . . . are guided by more than a steely eye on the balance sheet. They strongly resist pulling their children out of familiar schools and neighborhoods at the same moment that their family life is disintegrating. . . . They are haunted by the nameless dread that if they relinquish that precious bit of real estate, they will be letting go of the middle-class aspirations they hold for their children. (109)

"Haunted by nameless dread"—the attachment that Warren and Tyagi's "mothers" have to their homes, which is to say to burdensome mortgages that might drive them into bankruptcy—seems precisely characterized by Berlant (2007a, 33) in "Cruel Optimism":

> "Cruel Optimism" names a relation of attachment to compromised conditions of possibility whose realization is discovered either to be impossible, sheer fantasy, or *too* possible, and toxic. What's cruel about these attachments . . . is that the subjects who have *x* in their lives might not well endure the loss of their object or scene of desire, even though its presence threatens their well-being, because . . . the continuity of the form of it provides something of the continuity of the subject's sense of what it means to keep on living on and to look forward to being in the world.

And so here, as I close this chapter, I return to my beginning, to the question of how life is for those of us who are not Bartleby but rather keep on keeping on, for better and worse, attached to conditions of possibility that are bad for us and often even worse for others, as is the attachment of whiteness of Warren and Tyagi's "mothers." Berlant's project in "Cruel Optimism" and "Slow Death" resonates with Wendy Brown's effort, across much of her work and specifically in the essay "The Desire to Be Punished" in *Politics out of History* (2001, 47), "to reflect on the ways that problematic—disappointed, illicit, or otherwise unlivable—attachments function as a historically specific constraint upon emancipatory practices." Among the places they diverge is that Brown finally does see these attachments as only masochistic and self-harming, while Berlant sustains the ambivalence of the attachments as both enabling and disabling. Brown would have us loosen the attachment, and gain some freedom, by grieving the ungrieved loss that keeps us melancholically bound to the object. But as Berlant (2007a) makes clear in her reading of the John Ashbury poem in "Cruel Optimism," she recognizes that such an undertaking—and the related kinds of psychic risk taking proposed by those who would have us embrace or at least take a peek at the "radically open field of significatory possibilities" (Chow 2002, 110) that Lacanians call *the Real*—has conditions of possibility, of privilege, not widely or evenly available:

> It matters who wrote this poem, a confident person. He finds possibility in a moment of suspension and requires neither the logic of the market to secure his value, nor the intimate recognition of anything municipally normal or domestic to assure that he has boundaries. (40)

So I do not close with an inspirational flourish aiming to incite what Berlant (1997, 223) has called "acts of Diva Citizenship," important as those individual acts can sometimes be. Rather, I close with a keen sense of the need for collective intervention, collective counter-accounting, against the socially meaningful and structuring attributions (which are also distributions) of credits and debts, of possible presents and burdensome pasts, that constrain too many people to go on trying in the face of failure.

Stop now.

4 ACCOUNTING FOR GENDER

Norms and Pathologies of Personal Finance

In neoliberalism . . . *Homo œconomicus* is an entrepreneur of himself.
—Michel Foucault, *The Birth of Biopolitics*

Provocation

Students at my university offered the following comments during focus groups I helped to facilitate on the topic of personal financial attitudes and behaviors:[1]

> I trust my mother [for advice on financial issues]. My dad likes to think he built the business on his own, but my mom, she saved all the money; my father says here's $50 for the day and she says here's $5 for the month. (10/12/09, #3)

> I'm a shopaholic, so it hurts my heart to just see money sitting away. My mom says I have a huge problem. . . . My mom is very good with money—she has three kids, we've lived off one salary, and we've never been eating ramen at night . . . and she's always taught me to save. Though that hasn't worked out in my case. (10/13/09, #3)

> . . . that's 'cause I'm a guy. That's what I learned in marketing class, guys specifically target one object and that's what they are going to buy, and, this is a large generalization but this is what marketing class teaches us. (10/16/09, #6)

The first of these statements suggests that the speaker sees her parents as playing different roles in managing family finances and indicates the existence of gendered divisions, roles, and expectations in relation to personal finance. The second captures two different and potentially contradictory stereotypes of the relation of women to money—the "shopaholic" on one hand and, on the other, the competent, savvy, even wily, household manager. The third raises a crucial question about the production and reproduction of these gendered relations to money, not only through popular media or socialization in a familial context but also through the production and distribution of legitimate "knowledge." This chapter is a response to these provocations.

I examine the constitution of gendered norms for personal financial attitudes and behaviors through the production and circulation of knowledge, especially statistical articulation of populations, across the domains of popular culture, marketing research, and legitimate social science. I thus address a nexus of two central features of neoliberalism: governmentality and financialization. I find that gendered norms play a key role in articulating neoliberal norms more broadly. Specifically, negative, pathologized, portrayals of women as impulsive shopaholics on one hand and paralyzed noninvestors on the other indicate the boundaries of responsible entrepreneurial subjectivity. At the same time, these portrayals, found across a range of discursive sites, proffer images of proper femininity and masculinity, to be achieved through the enactment of different configurations of financial attitudes and behaviors. Noting the diversity and internal contradictions implicit in responsible entrepreneurial subjectivity (really subjectivities), I conclude with a consideration of the implications of the recent financial crisis and concomitant shifts in the evaluation of gendered behaviors.

Object and Method: Neoliberalism and Subjectivity

Entrepreneurial subjects are made, not born. Over the past few decades, as numerous scholars have demonstrated, so-called *entrepreneurial subjectivity* (Gordon 1991, 44) has been promoted and incited through political rhetoric and through changes in policies and institutional practices. Foucault identifies entrepreneurial subjectivity as a component of neoliberalism; and Wendy Brown (2003, 15) specifies that neoliberalism "normatively constructs and interpellates individuals as entrepreneurial actors in every sphere of life. It figures individuals as rational, calculating creatures whose moral autonomy is measured by their capacity for 'self-care.'" Neoliberalism might be characterized as not only (though still crucially) a free market approach to the economy or the political movement on behalf of a regime of accumulation aimed at the "upward redistribution" of wealth (Duggan 2003, xiv; Harvey

2005), but also "a method of thought, a grid of economic and socio-logical analysis" (Foucault 2008, 218). This "method of thought" has entailed a shift in locus of responsibility for social welfare provision from the state to the market, "the private sector," on one hand and to individual and domestic activity, "the private sphere," on the other (Clarke 2004, 32–33; Duggan 2003). It has likewise entailed a "shift in the locus of social governance" toward "'community' and 'family,'" as Wendy Larner (2000, 244) puts it (see also Dean 1997; Rose 1999), while "extending and disseminating market values to all institutions and social action" (Brown 2003, 7),[2] thus eroding liberal democratic institutions (Brown 2003, 4). Lauren Berlant (1997, 4) describes the displacement of any meaningful public sphere of political engagement over the course of the 1980s and 1990s by what she calls the "intimate public sphere," in which citizenship is the proper public performance of personal life, family values displayed on television. The publicly performed, private (sphere), intimate, familial life activity with which I will be concerned here is personal/familial finance. Personal finance is the now private (sector) responsibility, imposed on everyone, to look after one's own financial well-being in the absence/reduction of social welfare provision.[3]

In seeking to understand the making of entrepreneurial subjects, or, more specifically, subjects of personal finance, my object of investigation is not one particular government program or artifact but rather a diffuse "cultural project," to use Lisa Duggan's (2003, 12) phrase, that explicitly deploys and revitalizes existing gender norms as it promotes entrepreneurial subjectivity. Duggan uses the term "project" as Michael Omi and Howard Winant (1994, 56) do when they define "racial projects" as "simultaneously an interpretation, representation, or explanation of racial dynamics, and an effort to reorganize and redistribute resources along particular racial lines." Duggan (2003, xii) demonstrates the central role that "cultural projects," especially racial and sexual projects, have played in neoliberal efforts to recruit participation in this regime of capital accumulation. Describing neoliberalism as a pro-business social movement (xi),[4] Duggan notes not only the more and less explicitly racist, antifeminist, and antiqueer strategies used to mobilize a white, working-class electorate against its own interests (38–39) but also, like John Clarke (2007), the co-optation and incorporation of formerly radical social movements as depoliticized, reformist claimants to equal individual rights (50–51).

The cultural project that I sketch here does not emerge coherently from a central location, a political party, or a government agency; rather, it emerges in the resonances across a variety of discursive sites. Crucially, this includes discourse produced by corporations in and for the capitalist marketplace, such as market research and popular media (e.g., television shows and associated websites, and mass-market books).[5] My method is to "read" a variety of texts to identify the ways their consistency indicates that they are shaped by and shaping of a pervasive ideology. I use the term *ideology* advisedly, in the Althusserian sense, to suggest a social imaginary, within which subjects locate themselves, see themselves, and become attached to particular configurations of selfhood as to their very being, and thus to particular roles in economic processes (Berlant 2011, 24, 52–53; Žižek 1989).[6]

As Clive Barnett et al. (2008, 626) assert, "Key actors here [in the project of 'responsibilization'] include capital [corporations], but also a whole range of non-state actors such as charities, non-governmental organizations (NGOs) and campaign groups." That is, as is evident from the materials I will present below, capitalist actors directly engage in the processes of constituting subjects and social formations. They engage in practices of governmentality—statistical production of and intervention in populations—with the support not only of states but also of nonstate actors, such as academic social scientists.

The processes of statistical accounting and thus production of populations do not only enable the management of those populations through programs and policies. Although such processes may seem to simply abstract from and thus disregard particular embodied subjects, they also operate at an ideological level, inviting subjects to recognize themselves as members of those populations, to "become statistics" through their own practices. As Kathleen Woodward (1999, 180) argues:

> Statistics hail us. . . . The statistic and the anecdote—two fragments par excellence—are the pervasive conventions of media culture. Statistics often open what is called a "story" in print, broadcast, or internet news, to be followed by an anecdote—or vice versa.

We are bombarded with statistics as the normative mode of representation of anything and everything, and "statistical probabilities seem to implicate us as individuals in scenarios of financial ruin and of disaster by disease and weather" (Woodward 2009, 209). Interpellated and implicated by a one-two punch of number and narrative, Woodward suggests, we experience and respond to risk. This is an important insight, since being a risk taker and/or risk manager is a central component of entrepreneurial subjectivity. But I will be more concerned with what Woodward calls "difference demographics" (195) than with probabilities—what percentage of women versus men do x or achieve y or experience z. And thus I attend to the constitution of subjects and their attitudes and behaviors more broadly.

As I will show, "women" have been constituted as a key population group identified for intervention in the process of making people into *entrepreneurial* subjects, here in the rather literal sense of investors in and managers of their own personal financial futures. Oddly, while feminist scholars have examined the implications of the simultaneous contraction of the welfare state and intensified regulation of poor women (Smith 2002; Kingfisher 2002b), little critical attention has been paid to gender in relation to the promotion of entrepreneurialism and the financialization of daily life (Martin 2002). Of course, beyond the specific context of critiques of neoliberalism, feminist scholars have examined gender and consumption in U.S. and European contexts extensively, noting that women have been figured as having a special relationship with consumption, as both commodities and consumers (Roberts 1998; Deutsch 2010). Neoliberal gendered financial programs such as microcredit schemes in the "Global South" have received important feminist analysis (Bergeron 2003; Bedford 2009). And there is a recent but growing literature on women financiers (Roth 2006; Fisher 2012; Hall 2011). However, there is relatively little feminist scholarship on gender and *personal* finance in the "Global North." That is not to say that there has been no knowledge production on this topic; as I will explore below, it has emerged from other sites.

So, after some additional preliminaries, I proceed to conjure the gendered norms of personal finance in the contemporary period by way of a practice Berlant (1997, 86) has called "reading conjuncturally." That is, I will follow Berlant in "track[ing] and link[ing] a variety of . . . domains" (86) in which knowledge about gender and finance is produced and circulated. Those domains include academic social science, social science–like knowledge created as market research, and mass-mediated financial advice offered through television shows, magazines, books, and websites. And, like Berlant, "I assume throughout that gender categories are best seen as spaces of transformation, nodal points that are supposed to produce general social intelligibility while encrusted with constantly changing noncoherent meanings" (86).

My approach thus takes any particular concrete representation or performance of gender to be the product of a process, the emergent outcome of multiple social and historical determinations. It is markedly different from the studies of gender and finance I will discuss below, in that I am not interested in putting people into categories (these are men, these are women) in order to substantiate "scientifically" the differences we already expect to find between them. Such "scientific" claims work to affirm the social categorizations with which the researchers began and which were borrowed from dominant discourse (or "common sense") in the first place. Rather—and this is what I mean by "feminist" scholarship—observed categorization and differentiation are the questions, not the answers; that is, they are the starting point for exploring "why these [categories and the] relationships [between them] are constructed as they are, how they work, or how they change" (Scott 1986, 1057). Or, such categories may be understood as answers to the extent that they have a constitutive, performative, function themselves, contributing to "the ongoing accretion of associations these categories collect" (Berlant 1997, 86–87).

Preliminary Specifications

Scholars have identified two important aspects of the normative subjectivity solicited in the practices of the neoliberal regime of accumulation: *personal responsibility* and *entrepreneurialism*. Personal responsibility, developed in the context of neoliberalism to indicate moral praiseworthiness in the form of independent self-sufficiency, is defined against welfare dependency but also against irresponsibility as a lack of appropriate future-oriented self-discipline. (And potential blameworthiness is always hanging over those whose efforts at self-sufficiency and independence might fail. See Kingfisher 2002a, 27.) It has received scholarly attention and critique in relation to the dismantling of the welfare state. Entrepreneurialism, while implied by responsibility, has distinct entailments, with its emphasis on agency, activeness, and "personal initiative" (Ehrenberg 2010, 4); it has received most attention in relation to the "financialization of daily life" (Martin 2002). It is no accident that personal responsibility and entrepreneurialism have been emphasized in somewhat different class contexts (that of welfare recipients on one hand and that of personal finance consumers, such as mortgage holders, insurance buyers, or retirement investors, on the other). In fact, neoliberal discourses have articulated diverse normative subjectivities that operate in a complex relation to each other (Larner 2000; Dean 1997). While practices of privatization and rhetorics of responsibility are meant to compel some subjects (those supposedly irresponsible, dependent welfare recipients) to old-fashioned labor and saving, as I discussed in chapter 3, other comparatively affluent subjects are invited to believe they are laboring and saving when they are really undertaking high-risk investing (Martin 2002).

In *The Weariness of the Self,* Alain Ehrenberg (2010, 9) articulates neoliberal subjectivity through an examination of the changing meanings of depression: "Depression teaches us about our current experience as an individual because it is the pathology of a society whose norm is responsibility *and initiative*" (emphasis added). He describes the emergence, in concert with neoliberalism, of a particular conceptualization of depression "as an *illness of responsibility,* in which the dominant feeling is that of failure. The depressed individual is unable to measure up; he is tired of having to become himself" (4; emphasis added). But also, Ehrenberg explains, in this period we came to understand the depressed person as the "*the inadequate individual* with regard to *the norms of action*" (xvi; emphasis added). I turn to Ehrenberg's exploration of the ways neoliberalism has played out in the discourse of psychology because that psychological discourse turns out to be particularly pertinent in relation to the gendering of entrepreneurial subjectivity and personal finance (but for a more expansive exploration of depression as a political feeling, see Cvetkovich 2012). That is, gendered differences are described as psychological differences or problems. Such psychologizing is a crucial strategy of subjectification, of realizing the neoliberal project by installing in particular individuals the self who might (or might not) be personally responsible and entrepreneurial. Ehrenberg's work is particularly helpful in thinking about the relation of subjects to norms because it assumes and implies that dominant norms are not simply fulfilled, but rather may also be experienced as aspirational models or ideals that are lived in the mode of failure.

While neoliberal depression often takes the form of inability to act, as Ehrenberg (167) argues, another "pathology of action" (also considered by modern psychiatry to be a dimension of depression) has simultaneously come to the fore, and that is *impulsiveness.* Depression is composed of "indecision, hesitation, avoidance, along with physical, emotional, or cognitive blockage, on the one hand; *inability to wait or accept constraints, risk-taking, instability, and irritability on the other*" (170; emphasis added). Evaluating *inaction* appears to be straightforward in this context: "In a culture of performance and individual action, in which energy breakdowns can cost dearly, and in which we always have to be running at top speed and efficiency, inhibition is pure dysfunction, an inadequacy" (217). But, given the possibility of actions that are "impulsive," that are really just another depressive symptom, the evaluation of *action* is a bit more complicated. Where is the line between the responsible action required of the entrepreneurial subject of neoliberalism and the impulsive (irresponsible) action that is a symptom of the illness that provides the negative definition of that subject?

Of course, there is no "line"; rather, in keeping with neoliberal governmentality, there is "the specification of an optimal mean within a tolerable bandwidth of variation" (Gordon 1991, 20). In other words, there is a *norm,* more prescriptive than descriptive, toward which people are guided through an extensive popular pedagogy. (In using the term *pedagogy,* I do not actually mean to suggest a fully conscious process of teaching and learning—despite the fact that some of the popular texts I will discuss below are explicitly pedagogical, such as personal finance advice books, websites, and television shows—but rather the cultural project of subjectification, as I have indicated above.) Negative portrayals of women as impulsive shopaholics on one hand and paralyzed noninvestors on the other are deployed to indicate the boundaries of the "tolerable bandwidth" even as they also proffer images of proper femininity and masculinity, to be achieved through the performance of different (and differently valued) configurations of financial attitudes and behaviors.

Engaging in personal financial self-management is one of the most important activities expected of the responsible entrepreneurial subject (Martin 2002; Langley 2008). The centrality of personal finance is evident in that we have come to understand the phrase *identity theft* as referring to the theft of one's credit, the theft of one's access to resources through the formal financial system. In addition, we have been encouraged to internalize our credit scores, our credit identities, as indexes of our credibility and character as persons more broadly. As Donncha Marron (2009, 184) argues, "A FICO [credit] score is made salient for the individual as a unifying thread, weaving past and current actions into a cohesive sense of self; an attribution that has a dynamism and a sense of movement, and for which the individual is made responsible. . . . In certain ways, the individual is encouraged to view it as intrinsic to them."

This identification of credit and credibility is underscored by a series

Screen shots from CreditReport.com advertisements featuring "Stan" and "Lisa."

of television advertisements that ran in 2009 for CreditReport.com, a credit monitoring subscription service. The service offers help to those whose credit scores might misrepresent their human (and starkly, divergently gendered) worth. In one advertisement, Stan, who appears by clothing and setting to be a construction worker, says, "My credit score's not great. It's 580. So creditors think I'm lazy. I don't think so. I lost my job last year and now I work two jobs to cover my bills. . . . At CreditReport.com, I'm not a number. I'm Stan."[7] In another ad, Lisa, who is visibly pregnant and standing in front of a suburban house, says, "I plan for everything. But not a 612 credit score. It makes creditors think I'm unreliable. . . . At CreditReport.com, I'm not a number, I'm Lisa."[8] But even while these advertisements deploy and enhance our identification of character with credit score, their defense of the person with/against the low score also indicates a shift in rhetoric—and, maybe, in norms—brought on by the ongoing economic crisis.

"Stan" and "Lisa" might not be fully responsible for their "entrepreneurial abilities"; their being might not be fully expressed by their score (Marron 2009, 184). This slight opening of a space between person and credit identity acknowledges, while it also manages, the inherent, crisis-inducing contradictions of neoliberal entrepreneurial subjectivity as it does its work as a technology of capital accumulation. Like factory workers' labor in Karl Marx's analysis of capitalism, who cheapen their own labor power as their productivity increases, entrepreneurial subjects' efforts will almost inevitably be self-undermining. The recession has created the conditions of possibility for popular recognition that individual entrepreneurial subjects' personal failures are political, as the feminist slogan would have it, that there are social patterns to the failures, that maybe the effort is not worthwhile. As I will discuss in conclusion, some of the newer popular representations of gendered financial attitudes and behaviors work to manage this potential crack in subjective attachment; and they indicate that the dominant discourse of entrepreneurial subjectivity is undergoing a transformation.

Formations of Gender and Finance

The images that appear in the quotes from university students with which I began this essay—the self-important dad as family CEO, the money-wise mom, and the expert shopper-spender daughter—all reiterate figures from the modern history of gendered financial roles. This history yields a repertoire of possibilities from which one might draw in mobilizing gender on behalf of neoliberalism in the twenty-first century. The deployment of gender in the promotion of neoliberalism can arguably be said to have begun in the United States with Daniel Patrick Moynihan's famously pathologizing report *The Negro Family: The Case for National Action* (1965). The Moynihan Report, as it is commonly called, is rife with charts and graphs representing statistical comparisons of "whites" and "nonwhites" or "whites" and "negroes." Moynihan argues that at the center of "the tangle of pathology" characteristic of the "culture of poverty"[9] is the "matriarchal structure which, because it is so out of line with the rest of America, seriously retards the progress of the group as a whole, and imposes a crushing burden on the Negro male. . . . Ours is a society which presumes male leadership in private and public affairs" (29).

In contrast with more recent discourse, which is explicitly focused on the inadequacies of Black men and fathers, "what comes out of and is supported by the Moynihan Report is alarm at the existence of two problems: the single black female parent . . . and the black female over-achiever" (Lubiano 1992, 333). Moynihan's critique of Black women and mothers is focused on their supposed excessiveness. The Black lady is too educated and earns too much money; even the so-called welfare queen, as head of household, is in many ways portrayed as too powerful.

The norm of male dominance against which Moynihan measures this pathology was itself coming under pressure by the mid-1960s. Although the Moynihan Report is not usually thought of as specifically engaging what we now call "personal finance," the gender roles and hierarchies it invokes did have specific implications for roles in managing household and personal finance. According to that mid-twentieth-century norm, as Paul C. Luken and Suzanne Vaughan (2005, 1622) articulate it, "women [are] managers of homes. . . . [and] men . . . are to provide houses for wives to manage. The husband becomes the pre-sider over and financier of the household while the wife becomes the manager and purchaser."[10] For some, this norm of financial roles was relatively new, as Luken and Vaughan point out in their analysis of an early twentieth-century government-sponsored marketing campaign promoting homeownership called "Own Your Own Home" (OYOH):

> The OYOH textual practices organize women and men's relation to homes and instruct families in the proper manner of living in the emerging "modern," urban and industrial America of the early 20th century. . . . Many of the traditional tasks of women and men had been commodified and their production transferred to factories. The OYOH ad copy . . . speaks of women's homemaking and mothering work as impelled by a constant antediluvian dynamic "since the world began" and "since time immemorial," while at the same time articulating its imagery to connect with "modern" discourses on the middle-class wife as domestic scientist and effective "business woman" administering the "home finances." (1621–22)

However, the wifely role of household financial manager was new only for the middle and upper classes. Previously, in those privileged classes, money management had been men's work. The shift came, Viviana A. Zelizer (1997, 38–39) explains, because

> as the consumer economy multiplied the attractiveness of goods while, at the same time, the discretionary income of American households rose, the

proper allocation and disposition of family income became an urgent and contested matter. Spending well became as critical as earning enough.

This new concern coincided with the commodification of processes of household accounting itself, for, as Zelizer continues, women "bought the account ledgers and budget books recommended by experts to carefully register their expenses" (39). Nonetheless, according to Zelizer, for these wealthier women it was a long-term struggle to actually get full access to and control over the money they were now responsible for managing, rather than receiving it as an occasional gift, a dole they had to beg for, or even a regular allowance (41–53).

Meanwhile, by contrast, for working-class households it was already the norm to manage "their limited and often uncertain incomes by appointing wives to be the family's cashier. Husbands and children handed their paychecks over to the wives, who were expected to administer the collective income" (38). A number of scholars have noted that this pattern continued through the twentieth century: when managing household finances was a painful chore, it was women's work. Lillian Rubin's 1976 study *Worlds of Pain* (1992, 107) concluded that in 75 percent of working-class families women were responsible for bill paying, while in 75 percent of professional middle-class families men assumed the task.[11] And Deborah Thorne's (2001, 170–82) study of families entering bankruptcy in the late 1990s finds that the wives are overwhelmingly responsible for the impossible job of bill paying prior to the bankruptcy and then for the bankruptcy filing itself. Men tend to participate, according to Thorne, when some particular task related to finances can be an occasion for performing efficacy, such as telling a bill collector to "go talk to my lawyer" after the bankruptcy filing (181).

The Moynihan Report thus seems to be a phenomenon of a very particular moment in mobilizing a recent, and passing, gendered and classed norm dictating that women have a specific and limited role as household financial managers, but not primary breadwinners, to enable the demonization of poor people, particularly women of color, such that they appear responsible for their own poverty due to their abnormality. Clearly, the welfare queen had to be dethroned, normalized by being denied state support and instead made "independent" through financial reliance on male partners and low-wage labor. Therefore, as many others have described, the Moynihan Report laid down some cornerstones of the rhetorical strategies used in the dismantling of the welfare state over the next three decades (Goode 2002).[12] And even as such strategies were used to build consent for particular policies, they simultaneously articulated an ideal norm of familial structure and behavior. In a familiar, even a bit old-fashioned, rendition of this statistical prescription, former U.S. senator and presidential candidate Rick Santorum made this statement in a speech delivered at the Republican National Convention on August 28, 2012:

> Graduate from high school, work hard, and get married before you have children and the chance you will ever be in poverty is just 2 percent.
>
> Yet if you don't do these three things you're thirty-eight times more likely to end up in poverty![13]

"The Tangle of Pathology"

The subject of the "culture of poverty" discourse as imagined by Moynihan and Santorum is a subject of labor and (non)consumption, encouraged, even compelled, to save her- or himself by working and saving toward deferred gratifications in accord with the Protestant ethic described by Max Weber. But, as discussed in chapter 3, the entrepreneurial subject has been distinguished as the subject of personal finance and risk management. I receive my own daily dose of pedagogy with regard to these financialized, entrepreneurial norms and expectations by reading the *New York Times*. The need for the extensive advice offered there as well as the financial products that are described is explicitly cast as the consequence of a changed world, a world in which one cannot count on social security, pensions, or inheritance but must instead take responsibility for oneself. In an article titled "On Their Own: Save Yourself," for instance, David Leonhardt (2006) attests:

> When my wife and I talk about paying for our retirement, we assume that we will be pretty much on our own. We are both 33, and it's hard to have a lot of confidence that Social Security and traditional pensions will do for us what they did for our grandparents. . . .
>
> . . . President Bush has said that Social Security is "headed toward bankruptcy." United Airlines and Bethlehem Steel have reneged on some promises to their retirees. . . . So my wife and I do not expect much.

As this quote makes clear, class- and sexuality-based normative assumptions about kinship and life course are often evident in the advice provided by *New York Times* writers. And gender is sometimes addressed explicitly, as in a September 2011 Your Money column titled "For the Recently Widowed, Some Big Financial Pitfalls to Avoid," by *Times* personal finance adviser Ron Lieber:

> Women live longer than men, and they're likely to outlive their male spouses, given that decades ago, many women married men a few years older. Plus, gender roles being what they were, men often took on most of the household finances.
>
> As a result, many widows aren't as familiar with investing, insurance and taxes as their dead husbands were.[14]

As indicated by the listed financial projects, the gender norms in evidence here are those of a comfortable class.

In news stories (rather than advice columns), the *Times* has recognized that vulnerability to financial exploitation has varied by race and gender. In a January 2008 news article headlined "Baltimore Finds Subprime Crisis Snags Women," John Leland (2008) reports: "Though women and men have roughly the same credit scores, the Consumer Federation of America found that women were 32 percent more likely to receive subprime loans than men. The disparity existed within every income and ethnic group." In fact, the Consumer Federation study found that the disparity between men and women increases as income goes up (Fishbein and Woodall 2006).[15] Explanations of the disparity focus on patterns of reverse redlining, in which only subprime lenders are present and available in certain neighborhoods, and predatory practices of the lenders, in which certain customers are "steered" into particular products. But like the advice for widows, these explanations depend on a presumption of specific vulnerabilities in the targets: Leland (2008) points out that "even at high-income levels, mortgage brokers may assume that women are less confident to negotiate or shop around, and so offer them higher rates." He continues, "A survey in 2006 by Prudential Financial found that two-thirds of women graded themselves at C or lower in their knowledge of financial services or products."

In contrast with the established norm in which women were supposed to be competent household managers, here we get a hint that the current norm for women, across class and racial differences, is *incompetence* with regard to personal finances. (Alternately, one could interpret this portrait as entirely in keeping with—merely a reiteration and extension of—the norm that limits women's financial arena to household management and assigns the financing of that household to men.) In the popular elaborations of the failings and foibles of women with regard to personal finance, to which I turn next, women's attitudes and behaviors clearly fall outside the boundaries of proper entrepreneurialism. Moreover, as a statistically defined population, "women" are explicitly pathologized, represented as displaying the symptoms of neoliberal depression.

Hyperactivity: The Shopaholic

Perhaps we should not be surprised that in the contemporary period the special relationship women have long been thought to have with consumption—Mary Louise Roberts (1998) traces the phenomenon to the eighteenth century—(re)appears as a pathology. Specifically, it has morphed into a pathology of personal financial management: expert shopping becomes hyperactive compulsive spending, which becomes failure to manage a household budget competently, which then becomes overindebtedness.[16] As Hannah Seligson (2010) points out in "The Shopaholic Myth," an entire industry of financial advice for women depends on the idea that "we're all a paycheck away from being like Carrie Bradshaw [the main character in the *Sex and the City* television and film series] and blowing $40,000 on Manolo Blahniks [high-fashion shoes] instead of saving for a down payment on an apartment. We all have an inner Rebecca Bloomwood, the protagonist in the *Shopaholic* series. We need help." Seligson says that "studies show" that women do not really shop very differently from men. But actual behavior of men and women is less the point than the more general project of mobilizing gender on behalf of the pedagogy of personal responsibility and entrepreneurial subjectivity.

The term *shopaholic*—constructed on the model of *alcoholic* to indicate a disease of addiction (a disease that can never quite shed its connotation of moral failure)—seems to have been popularized, if not invented, by the series of so-called chick-lit books by Sophie Kinsella that began with *Confessions of a Shopaholic* (2001), which was turned into a 2009 movie of the same title. The main character in the film, Rebecca "Becky" Bloomwood, is a connoisseur of fashion who cannot resist actually acquiring a collection of fine clothes and accessories that is far beyond her means, creating a debt that ultimately threatens the personal relationships she values. Becky's special expertise in fashion is explicitly contrasted with her lack of expertise in financial matters, a lack that she performs when she accidentally interviews for a job at a business magazine rather than the fashion magazine to which she aspires. Initially, the movie suggests that business and finance are a boy thing, while fashion and shopping are a girl thing. It deliberately blurs these boundaries just a bit—there is a role for Becky at the business magazine, and the male editor of that magazine turns out to know a thing or two about fashion himself. And ultimately, the job gives Becky Bloomwood the ability to learn a lesson, put her human connections first, sell off her material objects to pay down her debt, and become personally financially responsible for herself.[17]

The double pathological core of shopaholism as a women's emotional problem and as a failure with regard to personal financial management was substantially elaborated in a series of episodes of *The Oprah Winfrey Show*. In 2006, before the current financial crisis hit the news, the program aired five shows and mounted an elaborate website promoting Oprah's "debt diet."[18] The series claims to address what the featured experts call an "epidemic" of indebtedness: "70% of Americans are living paycheck to paycheck." It follows three middle-class families (one African American and two white)—the Bradleys, the Egglestons, and the Widlunds—who have become overindebted. Each family is assigned a personal finance expert who is the author of a personal finance advice book: Glinda Bridgforth assists the Widlunds, Jean Chatzky works with the Bradleys, and David Bach helps the Egglestons. (More recently Oprah has joined forces with Suze Orman, now the most prominent financial adviser on Oprah's website, about whom more below.) Glinda, Jean, and Dave put their assigned families on the "diet" and on a path not only out of debt but also toward wealth.

The moral of the story lies in the causes of indebtedness for these families. No one on the series is in debt because of a lost job, a broken marriage, or a health crisis—the usual precipitators of personal bankruptcy (Warren and Tyagi 2003, 81). In fact, each family has an annual combined income in the neighborhood of $100,000. As we learn about each of the families, and as is indicated by the metaphor of dieting, we find that their debt is largely the result of overindulgence[19]—specifically, overspending by the wives. They, like Marnie Widlund, are mothers who can't say no to their kids, who simply stop opening their bills, and who hide their compulsive shopping from their husbands. Or, like Lisa Bradley, who forged her husband's signature to buy a new truck, they seek to live up to lifestyle images they cannot afford. Oprah has some sympathy with Lisa's need to spend money to manage her image in that, as an African American woman, she takes her side against Chatzky when it comes to spending money on hair straightening. But more generally, Oprah does not recognize indebtedness as a result of materially and subjectively consequential efforts by these families to distinguish themselves from raced or classed "others." She psychologizes and individualizes, diagnosing their problems as emotional, as due to "a lack of responsibility . . . denial, living a lie." Meanwhile, the personal finance experts force the wives to face the bills, give up luxuries, and turn over financial control to their more rational husbands.

The story of the Egglestons initially portrays them as sharing a dysfunctional philosophy of careless spending, but it turns out that their carelessness takes different forms, with different implications. Dan is disengaged, while Sally actively spends too much: "'The whole thing just makes me feel really stupid,' says Sally. 'I feel bad that I got my family into this.'" So a key step in their process is for Dan to get more involved; as Sally notes, "'Dan was so not a part of the bills or the finances, and [now] he's talking in language I've never heard him talk before.'"

Likewise, Chatzky's prescription for the Bradleys involves adjusting the gendered power dynamic:

> "Steven's in charge," Jean tells Lisa. "And he's going to pay the bills. You are going to get an allowance and he is going to give you $20 a day." Lisa begrudgingly agrees to Jean's plan. "I'm going to the bank today to get rid of my womanhood," says Lisa. "So I'm transferring all of my money from my savings account into Steve's checking account, so that he can be the man now and manage the money and take control of Lisa Bradley."

This series, and the shopaholic narratives more broadly, mobilize a long-standing association of women/femininity with emotion and men/masculinity with reason to promote personal financial responsibility and entrepreneurial subjectivity (earning more money is part of the solution for all of the couples).[20] Overactive women must be brought under control by men who are asked to step up into more active entrepreneurial roles in providing financially for their families.

But the ongoing complexity of gendered stereotypes around personal finance is notable here: it is (mostly) women who mediate the financial responsibilization of these families and Oprah's audiences—Oprah, Jean, and Glinda. Outdoing them all is Suze Orman, who spends each episode of her own long-running CNBC television series scolding, finger wagging, grading financial plans, and, most famously, evaluating spending requests as "approved" or "denied." Although Orman refers to her female callers as "girlfriend," her physical, tonal, and rhetorical performance inscribes her somewhere between a schoolteacher and an irritated mother of teens.

Hypoactivity: From Worry to Paralysis

If Oprah's debt diet entails reining in hyperactive shopaholism by restoring more "traditional" gendered power dynamics, much of the social scientific literature, and the popular financial advice for women that spins off from it, works in the other direction, proposing to empower women by freeing them from the other symptom of depression: anxious paralysis. In *The Financial Psychology of Worry and Women,* behavioral finance scholar Victor Ricciardi (2008) provides a useful literature review. He gathers research showing that financial decisions are shaped not only by cognition but also by affect, indicating, for instance, that worry increases one's perception of risk (16). He specifically discusses studies on worrying and money that cast such worry as a psychological problem. Dubbed "money sickness syndrome," it is "produced by the *feeling* of not having control of their money or limited knowledge of their financial circumstance" (7–8) and is not a response to inadequate material resources. Ricciardi then turns to gender, assembling a vast array of studies from across the social sciences—he cites about fifty—showing that women worry more than men, not just about money but about everything (19–23).

When Ricciardi turns to the literature on gender, affect, and finance, he turns not primarily to academic social science—he says that there has not been much research (24)—but rather to studies conducted by or for the financial services industry. Specifically, he references the Experian credit agency and the 1997 Dreyfus Gender Investment Comparison Survey, which, as he says, was referenced in a conference sponsored by NEFE and AARP called "Frozen in the Headlights: The Dynamics of Women and Money" and in a paper of the same title by Anthes and Most (2000).[21] As he demonstrates in his Table 1, reproduced here, in the decade following the Dreyfus study many other investment firms, nonprofit organizations with links to or particular interest in personal finance, and diverse popular finance magazines reproduced the finding that women worry about money. These types of studies continue to proliferate.[22]

The worry and insecurity identified in studies conducted by the financial services industry constitutes "women" as a great market for advice about overcoming fear, procrastination, and avoidance. The "Frozen in the Headlights" paper is particularly interesting in this regard: more than many authors of texts on this topic, Anthes and Most clearly identify substantial material obstacles to wealth for women that are primarily due to gender roles and discrimination. They observe that women earn less than men and consequently receive smaller retirement benefits and that women are more likely than men to have jobs without health benefits while simultaneously having greater responsibility for caretaking of both children and aging parents, which costs time that might be spent earning and gaining promotions as well as money that might be saved and invested. And yet Anthes and Most's core argument is not that systemic issues, such as health care provision, and social structures, such as gender roles and hierarchies, need to change. Rather, it is that, "like men," women must "become more responsible for their own financial well-being" by overcoming "financial anxiety, financial illiteracy and financial ill-preparedness" by "develop[ing] a whole new relationship with money, a new attitude" (130). Anthes and Most thus set up the space for an advice and services industry to enter.

Following a similar formula, financial self-help books targeted to women—by Suze Orman, among others—likewise attest to women's insecurities about money and personal finance. As Ricciardi (2008, 29–30) represents them, in these texts the term *worry* is supplemented by words with somewhat less constructive connotations: not just *insecurity* but also *anxiety, fear,* and *phobia,* leading to *procrastination* and *avoidance,* or even, as the "Frozen in the Headlights" title indicates, *paralysis.* Here it is not irresponsible or compulsive hyperactivity that is pathologized. Rather, passivity and inactivity are the disease.

In *Women and Money,* Orman (2007, 1) bends over backward to explain why she is even writing the book, since "women can invest, save, and handle debt." The problem is that women do not take action: "You refuse to own your power, to act in *your* best interest" (3). She cites the same kinds of studies that Ricciardi reviews (and in this case quotes the same passage):

> Ninety percent of women who participated in a 2006 survey commissioned by Allianz Insurance rated themselves as feeling insecure when it came to their finances. *Ninety* percent! In the same survey, nearly half the respondents said that the prospect of ending up a bag lady had crossed

Table 1. Nonacademic research studies on women, worrying, and financial decisions

Year	Study Sponsor(s)	Sample Research Group
1996	*Money Magazine*	1,218 household financial decision makers

Key finding of the study: The study disclosed that women are more anxious than men since "more than half of women surveyed (55%) say paying an unexpected $1,000 bill would pose a big problem, vs. only 33% of men" (Belsky [1996, p. 24]).

2001	Million Dollar Round Table	1,000 adult Americans (520 women)

Key finding of the study: This endeavor revealed seventy percent of the women in the survey disclosed some concerns or worries about the issue of retirement planning. The greatest worry among the women was not having enough money during their retirement years to maintain their existing style of living in which, forty-one percent of the women identified this issue as a significant concern (Anonymous [2001]).

2002	Gallup Poll	1,003 adults, aged 18 and older

Key finding of the study: This survey found forty-nine percent of women versus forty-two percent of men reported being "moderately or very worried" regarding having enough money to cover medical expenses caused by a serious accident or poor health (Jacobe [2002]).

2003	Prudential Financial	359 adults (ages 45 to 60 years)

Key finding of the study: This study documented that forty-seven percent of females reported worrying about having to delay retirement compared to thirty-two percent of males reported that belief (Anonymous [2003]).

2003	*Money Magazine* International Communications Research	500 adult women

Key finding of the study: This survey measured the top money concerns for women and found the five major financial worries were money management, retirement investments, healthcare expenses, overwhelming debt, and purchasing a home (Chatzky and Freedman [2003]).

2004	Gallup Poll	3,035 adults (1,588 women, 1,447 men)

Key finding of the study: This national survey reported females of different income categories worry at greater levels when compared to males in terms of financial matters such as retirement issues, credit card debt, healthcare coverage, and mortgage loans (Arora [2004]).

2005	Visa USA, Consumer Federation of America	1,031 adult women

Key finding of the study: This endeavor demonstrated that forty-nine percent of women disclosed worrying about their personal finances and more than one third of all females reported they "lost sleep" as a result of this worrying (Anonymous [2005a]).

2006	American Psychological Association (APA) National Women's Health Resource Center iVillage	1,600 adults

Key finding of the study: This extensive research survey found 28 percent of women compared to 19 percent of men identified money as a very important source of stress (Anonymous [2006]).

2006	*Health* magazine	940 adult women (ages 25 to 54)

Key finding of the study: This study reported "one-third of the 940 women surveyed said their financial situation was their number-one worry, topping appearance/weight (20%), job (12%), and health (11%)" (Delaney [2006]).

2007	ShareBuilder Securities Corporation	1057 adult males and 967 adult females

Key finding of the study: This national endeavor found more women (36 percent of the sample) stated they worry about retirement issues "all the time" and this compared to a lower degree of men with 29 percent reporting a high degree of concern about their retirement (Anonymous [2007b]).

Nonacademic research studies on women, worrying, and financial decisions (Ricciardi 2008, 36–37).

> their minds. A 2006 Prudential financial poll found that only 1 percent of the women surveyed gave themselves an A in rating their knowledge of financial products and services. (8)

Orman offers a miscellany of pop sociology and behavioral psychology explanations: the issue "has much to do with our history and traditions, both societal and familial"; "we'll have to look at this on a behavioral level, too, since traits that are fundamental to our nature clearly affect how we approach money as well. . . . It's a generally accepted belief that nurturing comes as a basic instinct to women" (11). But finally it is a matter of desire: "I know and you know that women still don't want to take responsibility when it comes to their money" (9). So her task is to "motivate us to *want* to act" and get us "over the blocks" (4). After telling numerous stories of women who undermine or undervalue themselves, she offers a positive image of "wealthy women" and then finally, in chapter 6, moves on to the practical advice, "The Save Yourself Plan" that encourages action, because "at the end of the day you have to stop talking and *just start doing*" (57; emphasis added).

The pedagogy of normative entrepreneurial subjectivity through these divergent gendered pathologies brings together an array of rhetorical techniques. Narratives that put a "face" on the situation, inviting identification (or disidentification), are interwoven with representations of statistical norms that hail us in our efforts and failures as properly belonging (or not) to a legible kind of humanness (Woodward 1999, 180–81; Berlant 1997, 187). The central role of statistics in reproducing gender stereotypes has provoked a critical response in the form of an investigation of the validity of the scientific claims themselves. Feminist economist Julie A. Nelson (2012, 7–8) takes this approach when addressing findings regarding gender and risk:

> What does the statement that "women are more risk averse than men" actually mean . . . ? It communicates the idea that risk aversion is an intrinsic sex-linked trait: Women are associated with greater risk-aversion, and risk-aversion is in turn equated with womanliness. . . . Such an interpretation, however, *does not, in fact, correspond at all* to any of the research on which the statement is based, due to the empirical importance of intra-sex variability. . . . Not all women act the same way, nor do all men.

Nelson argues that it is important to ask about the *extent* of any difference,[23] or, rather, *similarity,* to see the substantial overlap between men and women on any characteristic. The failure of various speakers to notice the overlap and refrain from such overgeneralizing and essentializing claims suggests that they "*look for* difference, and make the empirical results conform to societal preconceptions" (9).

While this kind of intervention against bad science is valuable, I am more concerned with understanding the constitutive and ideological work that this production and circulation of statistical knowledge accomplishes. By taking a Butlerian approach to the endlessly reconfirmed "fact" of gender difference—women worry more than men—rather than debunking the finding itself, we can understand its pervasiveness to suggest that being a woman is predicated upon being a worrier. That is, I suspect that worrying is constitutive of femininity, is a part of the norm or script reiterated, performed, and thus performatively installed, or brought into being, as an "inner truth" of the self.

EXAMPLE

1

We want to explore whether the outcome of the study—the score on a test—is affected by the test-taker's gender.

Therefore:
Gender is the **explanatory**
Test score is the **response**

Illustration in "Module 2 The Role-Type Classification (1 of 2)" in Carnegie Mellon Open Learning Initiative introductory-level course in probability and statistics.

In the online Carnegie Mellon Open Learning Initiative (OLI) introductory-level course in probability and statistics, gender is the first example of an explanatory variable (elsewhere called an "independent" variable), which the course defines as "the variable that claims to explain, predict or affect the response."[24]

But what if we treat worrying as the "explanatory" variable and gender as the "response" variable, with higher worrying predicting higher likelihood of woman-ness? In this view, the strong correlation between worrying and the checking of the F box on the survey suggests that worrying is necessary to the proper performance of woman-ness, even in the filling out of surveys. That is, the remarkable persistence of the findings is evidence that there is not simply a statistical norm that provides descriptive information about a population (and that might be traced to some essential, even biological, difference between genders), but rather that there is a prescriptive social norm of femininity that includes worrying. Of course, this prescription, the "cause" of the observed association between gender and worrying—the "lurking variable" in the language of the OLI course—is not gender norms as exclusively an idea/ideal but, per Anthes and Most, as a material practice: given gender inequality in income and gendered divisions of labor, those assigned to women's work and income are likewise assigned to worry. The point here is that, in the scientific production and popular circulation of the feminine pathologies of personal finance, the prescriptive norm is not merely indexed by the survey research; it is promoted by the research and its popular mediations.

The Contradictions

> Thankfully, my dad has not been laid off, so my family still has the same main source of income. The biggest loss we have suffered in the past year is that all the money he's put into his 401K over the past seven years has evaporated. I find that pretty unbelievable—it would have been better if he had spent it, rather than invested it, which goes against so much that I have learned in economics! (Shim and Serido 2010b)

These words were written by a young woman in response to the final question on the APLUS Wave 1.5 Economic Impact Study, conducted in the spring of 2009, which sought to capture the immediate effects of the 2008 financial crisis. The only qualitative, open-ended question in the survey, it asked: "What are some ways that the current economic situation has affected you or your life as a college student?" Most of the 429 students who answered the question mentioned increased tuition costs and reduced university offerings due to budget cuts, reduced financial support from parents, increased difficulty in getting and keeping jobs, and greater efforts to reduce spending. And, not surprisingly, those who described these material impacts with reference to worry, stress, or fear were more likely to self-identify as female than as male. The response I have quoted here is nearly unique in offering a transformed perspective on financial common sense, noting a provocation to unlearn "so much." But if we have learned nothing else from the financial crisis, we should have learned to take the outlier, the thin end of the bell curve, the so-called black swan, seriously. This singular response raises a crucial question: To what extent has the crisis led to a questioning of financial common sense and, more fundamentally, to a crack in the ideology of responsible entrepreneurial subjectivity?

In fact, the pedagogy and ideology of responsible entrepreneurial action, shored up by pathologized, feminized hyperactivity on one hand and the equally pathologized, feminized specter of paralysis on the other, have run afoul of the economic crisis. Even activities most conservatively recommended for responsible entrepreneurial subjects—investing in homeownership, education, retirement accounts—backfired for vast numbers of people. Efforts since the 1980s to promote homeownership, rationalized as a way to increase "wealth and opportunity for historically disadvantaged populations" (Saegert, Fields, and Libman 2009, 301), we now know were just the newest strategy for massive asset stripping from those very populations (Kochhar, Fry, and Taylor 2011). It has turned out that the subjects "*active* in making choices in order to further their own interests and those of their family" (Gordon 1991, 44) are the subjects most vulnerable to exploitation. The public revelation of what was, of course, for many people a long-term, ongoing but privatized experience of contradiction, of the self-undermining outcomes of entrepreneurial subjectivity, raises the question of the stability of that dominant norm. Does our popular culture continue to promote the same behavior in the same way, in spite of the havoc it has wrought? And, given my account of the ways the performativity of gender has been instrumentalized for capital accumulation, are gendered norms deployed in the same ways?

As it turns out, the financial crisis has produced a reversal of judgment with regard to gender. A range of scholarly and popular representations now proclaim that had women been running Wall Street (or the City of London),[25] they would likely not have stacked up risks in the ways that ultimately produced tremendous financial losses and destabilized the global economy, by contrast with testosterone-driven irrationally risk-seeking and competitive men, whose hormones get the better of them (Lofton 2011, 33). (In fact, it is precisely this claim that Nelson is responding to in her critique of essentializing interpretations of findings of gender difference discussed above.) In a *New York Times* op-ed titled "The Biology of Bubble and Crash," John Coates (2012) popularizes his scientific findings (Coates and Herbert 2008), findings that also prompted Linda McDowell's (2010) recent revision of her arguments about the gendered culture of the City of London. McDowell's prior claim was that a "particular masculinized set of performances is more highly valorized" (653). On the basis of Coates and Herbert's work, which McDowell first encountered because it "received significant exposure and discussion in the broadsheet press and, in the UK, on a BBC Radio 4 programme" (655), she incorporates a biological explanation for apparently gendered patterns of behaviors. As she herself points out, it is rather remarkable for a feminist to "attribute social behavior to biological mechanisms . . . [as] it was not so long ago that 'female irrationality,' attributed to the female body and its hormonal cycles, was used as a reason to exclude women from positions of power" (655).

So now, in the ostensible interests of inclusion, the mass mediation of the financial industry has piled essentializing bioscientific claims onto essentializing social scientific claims. I say "ostensible" because, as Melissa Fisher (2012, 155–56) points out, the ranks of women on Wall Street have been disproportionately cut during the financial crisis. Moreover, pioneering female financiers had long since deployed essentializing gendered notions of feminine risk aversion and savvy shopping to gain access, with complex and contradictory outcomes (98). The reversal of judgment reaffirms not only gender stereotypes but gender hierarchy as well.

This same, now positive, image of women has also been applied to *personal* finance; some of the feminine attitudes and behaviors previously portrayed as pathological are now promoted as wise. In March 2010, in an article titled "How Men's Overconfidence Hurts Them as Investors," accompanied online by an audio report, "The Feminine Advantage in Investing," Jeff Sommer of the *Times* reported on a study conducted by Vanguard, a large mutual fund company. The study of 2.7 million holders of Vanguard individual retirement accounts "found that during the financial crisis of 2008 and 2009, men were much more likely than women to sell their shares at stock market lows. Those sales presumably meant big losses—and missing the start of the market rally." In addition, the *Times* article draws on a 2001 academic article by Brad M. Barber and Terrance Odean titled "Boys Will Be Boys." According to Sommer, Barber and Odean found that "men traded stocks nearly 50 percent more often than women . . . [which] drove up the men's costs and lowered their returns." Men are the "shopaholics" when it comes to investing.[26]

It is striking how much attention Barber and Odean's ten-year-old publication gained in the aftermath of the financial crisis, many reporting on the findings as if they were new (Fisher 2009; Swan 2011; Bitti 2011). It became a springboard not only for this *Times* article but also for a column on the Motley Fool investment website titled "Warren Buffett Invests like a Girl" (DiCosmo 2008), itself mentioned in another *Times* article, "At Last, Buffett's Key to Success" (Mitchell 2008). The author of the Motley Fool column, LouAnn Lofton, developed the concept into a book titled *Warren Buffett Invests like a Girl: And Why You Should Too* (2011). Seligson's 2010 *Slate* article that, as mentioned above, seeks to bust "the shopaholic myth" turns to "Boys Will

Be Boys" to make a positive claim for women's financial competence: "When it comes to investing, women may actually be savvier" because they trade less often and choose less risky products. Where previously it was pathological to be anxious and worried, now we learn that "pessimists tend to be more realistic. . . . Women, thanks partly to the fact that they lack the same confidence levels as men, tend to react more realistically" (Lofton 2011, 23). Uncertainty has become a positively valued willingness to "put in more time and effort researching" (34). And inactivity becomes the cost-saving and wise ability to "be patient and wait it out" in the face of a financial panic, rather than "freak out and sell," thus locking in losses (21–22).

What is the import of this new configuration of gendered representations? The *Times* article dismisses its own argument, reasserting responsible entrepreneurial norms by suggesting that women may have just gotten lucky; their passivity, which might otherwise appear irresponsible, worked out for them only because of the unusual decadelong decline of the stock market. They will not be budged from their neoliberal commitments so quickly. But even if we are willing to take on board the reevaluation of ideal behaviors, here again at the personal finance level, gender norms can be seen as reaffirmed. The ever-present, wise woman household manager reappears to get us through hard times. Meanwhile, in a chapter titled "Embrace Feminine Influences," Lofton situates this woman in the appropriately limited role of helpmate, tempering masculine impulses; she reports that Buffett "surrounded himself with a cadre of smart, strong women over the years. Perhaps the influence of those women has resulted in his feminine side shining forth" (109). Again here, the reversal actually reaffirms gender norms and heteronorms. Moreover, given the presumption that one is already an active investor, this promotion of feminine inactivity is just a financial industry stop-loss strategy, sustaining material class relations and hierarchies: the inactivity being recommended is the (in)activity of keeping your money *in* the market.[27]

Nonetheless, the amount of maneuvering the financial services industry undertakes to keep people attached to their capitalist identifications through their gender subjectivities is striking. So I wonder what's going on with "Lisa" and "Stan" and the insightful undergraduate with whom I began this last section. Does the advocacy of inaction have an excess, or a "tail," in statistics talk? Might the failures of action and the advocacy of inaction be conditions of possibility for people to detach from their subjection to the given statistically constituted imaginaries? The crisis itself has been characterized by inaction in the form of debt nonpayment: people with no choice and people with some choice have walked away from mortgages and defaulted on student debt. Such practices, even when they involve conscious rejection of the norm of moral obligation to pay, are not necessarily ideologically or politically transformative.

On the other hand, these inactions have been made meaningful by the Occupy movement. Marieke de Goede (2011) notes that the "ambition [of Occupy] to *stay,* to extend its presence, to remain immobile, interrupts the constant drive to commodification and circulation of investment capital." While such an effort is, as de Goede says, "impossible," I find more promising the possibilities that emerge from the effort to refigure debt default as an appropriation of the power to foreclose, as a "strike"—the slogan "Strike debt" invokes both a collective work stoppage and the graphic act of striking a debt from an accounting book, crossing it out. And maybe most potently, displacing the prescriptive normal curve, they have articulated populations and hailed subjects through an alternative statistical imaginary: "We are the 99 percent." In ending with this image, I do not mean to endorse or propose the displacement of gender by class; rather, I mean to recognize these strategic interventions in the regimes of financial and statistical accounting as a point of departure.

5 ACCOUNTING FOR INTERDISCIPLINARITY

Contesting Value in the Academy

If management teaches us to run things, where do we want to go
and how should we organize ourselves to get there?

—Randy Martin, *Under New Management*

The university of the future will be inclusive of broad swaths of the
population, actively engaged in the issues that concern them, relatively open to commercial influence, and fundamentally interdisciplinary in its approach to both teaching and research.

—"The University of the Future," *Nature*

THIS CHAPTER WAS ORIGINALLY WRITTEN during my service
as chair of the University of Arizona Strategic Planning and Budget
Advisory Committee (SPBAC). A "shared governance" committee, including vice presidents, deans, staff, academic professionals, and student leaders as well as faculty (a majority of voting members), SPBAC
is responsible for participating in institutional governance, primarily
through the annual crafting of the five-year strategic plan, but also
by providing budget advice, which generally means advice on how to
handle relentless budget cuts.[1] Identifying performance measures for
both internal and external accountability is a routine part of the strategic planning process; in relation to the severe budget cuts imposed
while I was chair, the stakes seemed to go up because the selected performance measures could, we committee members imagined, be used
to make consequential decisions about which programs and departments should be cut more or even eliminated entirely. In this chapter, I explore the changing meaning and role of *interdisciplinarity* en
route to a broader discussion of the impact of the complex and dynamic

demands for accounting and accountability and the possibilities for transformative engagement.

I undertook the original writing of this piece, amid the crazy busyness of the SPBAC chair job, in an effort to bring the critical tools available to me as a scholar to bear on the practices in which I was engaged, with which I was complicit. I hoped not only to work out a personal strategy for this participation—to figure out what to say in the next meeting—but also to help mobilize the broader discussion and engagement that might provide ballast for those of us who, in such roles, find our power as individuals to be severely limited. If I learned any one most important lesson from my participation, it is that without a faculty collective or movement to hold us accountable, the handful of faculty in "leadership" roles are quickly absorbed into the administrative team, working in alliance with the president, the provost, and their vices on behalf of the institution as entrepreneurial subject, all of us speaking and spoken by the dominant neoliberal discourse of university management. While a great deal of insightful scholarship has been published in the past few years in what has been called "critical university studies,"[2] the need to develop a collective strategy of engagement and intervention remains urgent. Randy Martin (2011b, x) proposes that, rather than "take flight from the managerial imperative—assuming, of course, there is somewhere else to go, . . . [we] look inside this calculus and see how it might be figured otherwise." Having inhabited "the calculus," I share my experience here because I am persuaded that informed engagement is relevant not just for those few of us who "choose" administrative or shared governance roles but for many of us. As Eli Meyerhoff, Elizabeth Johnson, and Bruce Braun (2011, 493) put it, "Even radical faculty who seek to enact transformations *outside* the university find themselves performing *within* the university as managers not only of their own labor, but of that of their students and their colleagues." And all of us need to be the social movement that keeps the pressure on our "leaders."

The Business of Interdisciplinarity

"In science, interdisciplinarity is the way business is done." Mike Cusanovich, former University of Arizona (UA) vice president for research, former interim provost, and then director of Arizona Research Labs, made this statement several years ago at an informal meeting called to discuss a possible conference on interdisciplinarity. What he meant most explicitly is that interdisciplinarity is the norm; as he later explained, "As a consequence of technology and the complexities of the problems scientists face, no one individual can have the necessary expertise to address the important questions" (personal communication). This view is affirmed by the editorial in *Nature* (2007, 949) quoted in this chapter's second epigraph, which also asserts, "Many argue that in a host of areas—ranging from computational biology and materials science to pharmacology and climate science—much of the most important research is now interdisciplinary." One might also read Cusanovich's statement as having a second meaning: that interdisciplinarity is the way *business* is done. In the wake of the Bayh–Dole Act of 1980, which allowed universities to patent and become owners of intellectual property produced in the course of research funded by federal grants, and in the context of financial constraints that have led universities to eagerly seek new revenue sources,[3] including those research grants, direct industry sponsorship of research, and income from the licensing of that intellectual property, interdisciplinarity has become an official priority at many research universities. But what is meant by interdisciplinarity in the context of university administrative discourse?

First, as Cusanovich suggests, interdisciplinarity means "collaboration" among scholars with different disciplinary training and expertise. But in administrative discourse it also means cross-sectoral collaboration between nonprofit universities and for-profit corporations. So, in working on UA's Strategic Plan, I learned that local business and political leaders were explicitly enthusiastic about interdisciplinarity on the model of UA's BIO5 Institute. The mission of BIO5, as stated on the institute's website, is as follows:

> BIO5 brings together scientists from five disciplines—agriculture, medicine, pharmacy, basic science and engineering—to treat disease, feed humanity and preserve livable environments. BIO5 creates science, industry and education partnerships to engage in leading-edge research, to translate innovations to the market and to inspire and train the next generation of scientists.[4]

Here, interdisciplinarity does not only mean collaboration but also has a special relationship with "applied" research, where application is understood to occur through commodification: "BIO5 teams with the UA

Office of Technology Transfer to facilitate connections between researchers and industry that translate university research to the marketplace where it can directly and more quickly impact people."[5]

The strategic plans of several major public research universities similarly suggest that interdisciplinarity is a priority, that interdisciplinarity involves collaboration across fields but also across institutional sites and economic sectors, and that its purpose is to produce knowledge that can be commodified, often framed in terms of application to societal problems or challenges, not always quite so explicitly as translation to the market. For instance, one of four main sections of the University of Minnesota–Twin Cities' *Transforming the U for the 21st Century: Strategic Positioning Report to the Board of Regents* (2007), titled "Exceptional Innovation," is focused on interdisciplinarity. A sidebar in this section features a graphic that shows "disciplines" leading to "new knowledge," intersected by "institutes," with an arrow leading to "real world issues" (35).

Likewise, Purdue's strategic plan, titled "New Synergies" (2008, 5), features interdisciplinarity as part of its overall vision statement: "Purdue University will set the pace for new interdisciplinary synergies that serve citizens worldwide with profound scientific, technological, social, and humanitarian impact on advancing societal prosperity and quality of life."

While the issue of revenue is sometimes downplayed in the prose, it becomes clear in the performance measures associated with these strategic plans. For instance, the University of North Carolina at Chapel Hill Academic Plan (2003) has six major "Priorities," the second of which is "Further integrate interdisciplinary research, education and public service" (21). The Progress Report on the Academic Plan (2004) measured "funding generated by centrally supported interdisciplinary initiatives" (18).

My fantasy of interdisciplinarity—from my perspective as a cultural studies, women's studies, queer studies scholar—far from being "the way business is done," has always been "no business as usual" (meaning, "interdisciplinarity is the way capitalism is critiqued and disrupted"). And the ongoing downsizing and financial impoverishment of the humanities in general and, to some extent, our interdisciplinary fields (though the funding dynamics for women's studies and ethnic studies are not the same as those for the traditional humanities disciplines) make it easy to believe that our work takes place at some

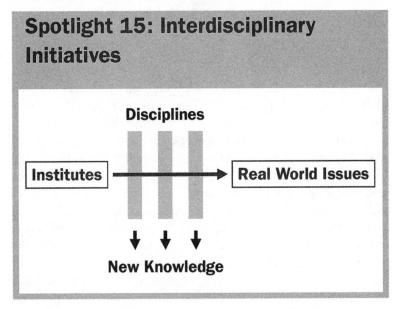

Spotlight 15: Interdisciplinary Initiatives

Disciplines

Institutes ⟶ **Real World Issues**

⬇ ⬇ ⬇

New Knowledge

Sidebar in University of Minnesota (2007, 35) *Strategic Positioning Report.*

distance from the market, a belief affirmed in the groundbreaking research of Sheila Slaughter, with Larry Leslie in *Academic Capitalism* (1997) and with Gary Rhoades in *Academic Capitalism and the New Economy* (2004), which traces the shifts since the 1980s in resources (human and financial) across fields and institutional units according to proximity to the market (the spatial metaphor is theirs).

(No doubt you are already irritated by my reference to *our* work. I choose this term deliberately, although I am uncertain of the referent and will discuss differences among *us* shortly. I do so in order to invoke the sense of "us and them" that too often structures our relations with our science colleagues, a sense that I would suggest needs to be disrupted.)

Where, according to the strategic plans I have mentioned, practical application is identical with commodification, by contrast, it is precisely in the moment of claiming practical application that Stuart Hall (1990, 18), describing the imaginary of early cultural studies at Birmingham, notes—with what? regret? pride?—that distance from the market:

We tried, in our extremely marginal way up there on the eighth floor in the Arts Faculty Building, to think of ourselves as a tiny piece of a hegemonic struggle. Just one tiny bit. We didn't have the illusion we were where the game really was. But we knew that the questions we were asking were of central relevance to the questions through which hegemony is either established or contested.

The fantasy that cultural studies is distant from the market has been most famously challenged by Bill Readings. In *The University in Ruins* (1996), he identifies "excellence," a management discourse that circulated widely in the academy in the 1990s and early 2000s, as a rationale of bureaucratic accounting that is indifferent to particular cultural content, concerned only with performance indicators that abstract from and make equivalent (commensurable) any particular content. He argues that where the university once functioned to create a national culture, it now supports globalization through this empty discourse of excellence. And he argues that the institutionalization of cultural studies, a field that he defines as coherent insofar as it exists to contest the centering of high national cultures, has been made possible by excellence—the loss of any cultural center to contest—and in effect subtends that discourse.

Whereas Readings clearly means for us to be scandalized by the resemblance between and participation of cultural studies and/in globalization, Ira Livingston, in his book *Between Science and Literature* (2006), offers us a different possible response. Livingston notes that new theories of nature developed in biology and physics—theories of autopoiesis, of complex self-organizing systems—are often presented in metaphors borrowed from and underwriting globalizing capitalism (138–40). One might, and Livingston does, point out that the resemblance among contemporary conceptualizations of economic, biological, and physical phenomena as complex, open, self-organizing systems extends to the concepts produced by interdisciplinary humanities scholarship, which has "increasingly recognized the interdependence of identities . . . and . . . begun to treat them as emergent and internally heterogeneous constellations in ongoing ecologies" (110). Livingston's argument suggests that we are "where the game really is" to a much greater extent than Hall thought (or most of us feel—but we might want to make a distinction between being "distant" from the market and being *in* a failing business). But rather than trying to "restore the sense of scandal" (138) regarding what is, Livingston asserts, an irresistible epistemic shift toward a paradigm that sees both science and capitalism as "participating in what they represent" (139), in which "we come to recognize self-organization because we as a global species have attained it to some critical degree" (140), he proposes instead that we "argue about its terms" (141). And I propose that rather than get hung up on "complicity," we extend his nonscandalized reaction to the recognition that interdisciplinarity is, after all, business as usual and forge ahead with our critical analysis and intervention.

In fact, we might need to recognize that our implication in the game implies responsibilities to actively take up the hegemonic struggle; we are not made innocent by our marginal location on the eighth floor of our local ivory tower. Livingston argues that being in the game is not the same as changing it: "The interrelationality and plurality of all formations are good places to start and ongoing axioms in an argument, not the payoffs of one" (110). Those payoffs, he says, "had better be sought in the creative and counterhegemonic possibilities of their pluralities and contradictions" (110).

Livingston's approach itself resembles Marx's argument in the "1857 Introduction" to the *Grundrisse* (discussed at length in chapter 1). There, Marx (1973, 104) seeks to explain the ability of Adam Smith to conceive of "labor in general" precisely by suggesting that the generalization has been achieved in reality:

> As a rule, the most general abstractions arise only in the midst of the richest possible concrete development, where one thing appears as common to many, to all. . . . On the other side, this abstraction of labour . . . corresponds to a form of society in which individuals can with ease transfer from one labour to another, and where the specific kind is a matter of chance for them, hence of indifference.

But then, Marx neither simply accepts the notion of labor in general as a natural empirical category nor rejects the notion of "abstract labor" because it has been enabled by capitalism itself. As I argued in chapter 1, Marx rejects the version of abstraction that involves stripping away history and specificity to identify a common core. Likewise, he rejects a version of empiricism that conceives of the concrete as "given [and] observable" in favor of a notion of "complex" or "differentiated" "unities," which are a "rich totality of many determinations and relations" (Hall 2003, 129). The task then becomes a different kind of abstraction, the grasping of the "abstract determinations [that] lead towards a reproduction of the concrete by way of thought" (Hall 2003, 129). This methodology, which among other things enables the identification of contradictions, rather than interdisciplinarity per se (or challenging national cultures), is the distinctive meaningful feature of cultural studies as a critical enterprise. As I have been arguing in various ways throughout this book, such critical abstraction provides a strategy for both understanding and intervening in the ways we do business and the ways we account for ourselves. But I am getting a bit ahead of myself.

University strategic plans, like the mission statement of BIO5, consistently claim that interdisciplinarity is meant to solve "societal grand challenges" (Purdue University 2008, 14). Bringing knowledge to market as private property is often presented as the *only* path by which knowledge can be "applied" in the "real world," a cause for concern, especially but not only because much of the research behind this intellectual property is paid for by the federal government, and thus this commodification entails an enclosure of public goods; likewise, one might have concern regarding the faith, apparent in many of these projects and programs, that technology is, by itself, sufficient to solve these great problems. However, it is also worth noting the proliferation of programs related to the environment, sustainability, and climate change that explicitly bring together physical, biological, and social sciences, emphasizing the importance of "ecological, economic, and socio-cultural factors" to, for instance, "the complex problems of sustainability of arid lands."[6]

The claim that this work will feed the hungry, preserve the environment, improve health care, and so on suggests that our interdisciplinary science colleagues share some of the concerns of the scholars in interdisciplinary humanities/social science fields. That is, we too like to think that our work addresses "real-world issues" and great social problems, although (and this is no small difference) we tend to articulate those problems in terms of generative systems of meaning and power (gender, race, and so on) rather than the immediate empirical manifestations—poverty, illness, environmental degradation. On the other hand, at least one side of a debate within our fields values "translating" (or immediately producing) our knowledge for use in practices and policies to address precisely those empirical manifestations. I sometimes think that we may not have adequately explored potentials for alliance and collaboration, although the epistemological difference is a huge challenge to any collaboration. And while I acknowledge that it is hard to imagine (and, for some of us, to desire) "selling" our work for practical use, I note that the project of "translation" is not always obvious even in technoscience fields: the University of Arizona held a symposium on translational environmental research (TER), titled "Making the Connection," that aimed to "build capacity" through, for instance, a session called "Paired Researcher and Stakeholder Point–Counterpoint: How Does TER Really Work?"

However, it has been not so much in attempts at translation or application as by virtue of our interdisciplinarity itself that some of us have imagined we might change the game, wanting to believe that our scholarly practice is itself a political practice insofar as transforming the structure of knowledge contributes to transforming the social hierarchies sustained by knowledge production. One of our central projects has been to show how social hierarchies are created and sustained through the interplay of economic, political, and social/cultural processes, describing, among other things, how the separation of those domains (and the division of knowledge production about them into distinct disciplines) works to naturalize those hierarchies.

Hall (1990, 12) casts the project of cultural studies as, originally, an attempt "to address the manifest break-up of traditional culture, especially traditional class cultures . . . [and] the fluidity and the undermining impact of the mass media." He casts this set of concerns as directly opposed to the then-dominant perspective in the humanities: "The humanities . . . were conducted in the light, or in the wake, of the Arnoldian project. What they were handling in literary work and history were the histories and touchstones of the National culture, transmitted to a select number of people" (13). So, according to Hall, the initial project had to include the demystification of the disciplines, to show "the regulative nature and role the humanities were playing in relation to the national culture" (15). But then, in developing a positive agenda—the study of the "concept of culture," "contemporary cultural forms," "the political questions, the relationships, complex as they are, between culture and politics"—the cultural studies project involved not "a coalition of colleagues from different departments" but "a series of raids on other disciplinary terrains. Fending off what sociologists regarded sociology to be, we raided sociology. Fending off the defenders of the humanities tradition, we raided the humanities. We appropriated bits of anthropology while insisting that we were not in the humanistic anthropological project and so on" (16).

I do not, by the way, mean to suggest that interdisciplinarity in the sciences is by contrast with "ours" merely "a coalition of colleagues from different departments" or that the scientific disciplines have not themselves been transformed. A quick review of the websites of various interdisciplinary scientific endeavors at my university suggests that they too entail politically significant transformations of the structure of knowledge and, implicitly, the social categories upheld by those knowledge structures.[7] Meanwhile, although the notion that interdisciplinarity implies the transformation of disciplines and not merely collaboration between disciplines is central to some of "us," "we" are riven by differences, including—but by no means limited to—the extent to which we are invested in a critique and transformation of the disciplines (not to mention the identities and social hierarchies that some of us think are upheld by the disciplines). It is no accident that I have, so far, located my argument in Stuart Hall. While I might, of course, have found scholars of women's studies or ethnic studies or queer studies to cite on behalf of my fantasy of interdisciplinarity, I would feel truly presumptuous (or, rather, simply incorrect) making broad epistemological claims for women's studies or ethnic studies. I experienced those differences between us as a practical constraint in one of my earlier university-level service projects:

During a previous bout of downsizing and reorganization, called Focused Excellence, the president and provost, for the most part, took it upon themselves to discern where to cut or invest; however, in four areas they put faculty committees to work to sort out what to do. Of the four, only the one I cochaired, the Cultural, Ethnic, Gender and Area Studies Study Team, was outside the sciences. (The CEGA Team, as we called it, included representatives from Mexican American studies, Latin American studies, American Indian studies, Middle East studies, Africana studies, and, in my body, both women's studies and LGBT studies, plus a few others whose representational role was less clear.) And while the other three teams were meant to develop new interdisciplinary initiatives (and one did lay some of the ground for the BIO5 Institute discussed above), ours was, I have always assumed, meant to negotiate/neutralize politically difficult waters in the hope that we might voluntarily come forward with some sort of money-saving proposal for combining units.

Initially, I took the formation of the team to be an extraordinary opportunity. In my experience, the units represented on the team en-

gaged in notably little collaboration; the fact that we were going to have to work together seemed to open the possibility for moving beyond political and historical divides, such as that between area studies, rooted in Cold War government funding and still international in orientation, and U.S. ethnic studies, rooted in political struggles oriented to the nation-state, and—underwriting as well as crosscutting the others—the fundamental political and epistemological differences between those of us oriented toward applied social science and those with some combination of roots in the humanities, poststructuralism, and left/progressive political commitments. As our work proceeded, we were, in fact, able to support each other in practical ways, putting the whole team behind the requests of particular units for lines and other resources and engaging in crucial information sharing and strategizing vis-à-vis policies that would affect us all (though there were holdouts to the last). However, we failed to bridge or even create spaces for bridging the historical, political, and epistemological fault lines among the units.

We produced a principled thirty-page report full of specific proposals for simultaneously respecting the autonomy of and strengthening the individual units while building structures for collaboration such as interdisciplinary programs and centers. We tried to make audience-based arguments, articulating our proposals in terms of "excellence," which we interpreted to mean being on the cutting edge intellectually, being nationally or internationally recognized (we especially emphasized our responsibilities as an Association of American Universities institution), and, of course, being fundable by foundations, government agencies, and private donors. (It is important to note that our interpretation attempted to shift the meaning of excellence away from the meaning Readings had identified and back toward traditional qualitative professional standards.) With a price tag of a mere two million dollars (one-twentieth the size of the proposals made by the science teams), ours was received as a doable modest proposal—until, nearly simultaneously with our receiving a very encouraging official response from the provost, the next round of budget cuts was announced. Adding insult to injury, at least from my perspective, while telling us that our proposals would have to be deferred to some future in which the budget would be better (i.e., never), the provost invited the CEGA Team to write itself into the margins of a health sciences funding request by adding some language about ethnic

*and gender health disparities and the cultural competencies needed
by health professionals.*

*The CEGA Team responded to this situation in several ways. First,
we took up the invitation to supplement the health sciences funding
request. Given that several of the units involved could benefit substantially were the request to be funded due to their own emphases on
applied social science of health, there was no way to say no.*

*At the same time, we responded by making an array of astoundingly
conservative arguments for the humanities (and I played a central role
in crafting this particular memo). We argued that money should not
be allowed to be the mission of the university, that we have an ethical
responsibility to pursue an educational and scholarly mission and to
find the money to do it; and we suggested that our mission could be
articulated in terms of the national security concerns that were a hot
issue both at the state level in the form of an anti-immigrant voter
initiative and at the national level in the form of a reckoning with the
"intelligence" failures that had enabled 9/11—I quoted Porter Goss,
then nominee to head the CIA, regarding the necessity of training in
languages and cultures. (Was it inevitable that in arguing for what I
called in this context "humanities and humanistic social sciences," I
would simultaneously invoke nationalist arguments?) But at the same
time, we tried to learn, really learn, that what is valued is money:
we rebudgeted our proposals at twenty million dollars. And we got
a commitment from the president that he would bring (some revised
politically palatable version of) our proposal forward as a state budget
request. This went nowhere, as such requests depend on support from
the governor (then a Democrat dealing with a Republican legislature), and our governor, we were told, was unwilling to take even a
politically sanitized version of our proposal to the Arizona legislature.*

Our flailing around for arguments on behalf of our proposals (and the
fact that we ultimately found that we were subject to a political arena)
raises the larger issue: To whom are we accountable and in what terms?

Modes of Accountability

There are three modes of accountability that are relevant to those of
us in interdisciplinary fields such as women's studies, ethnic studies,
and cultural studies. First, professional accountability: the formal peer

review processes that determine publication, tenure and promotion, and honors and awards but also, more informally, the respect of colleagues, our reputations, the impact of our scholarship on others in our fields. Second, political accountability: to various degrees we hold ourselves accountable for the extent to which we are contributing to a political movement, creating knowledge that is useful for policy, will change lives, change the perspectives of our students or a larger public. And third, as I have already suggested, institutional and public accountability with regard to money and productivity, which takes the form of an array of performance and financial measures that shape the institutional conditions within which we seek professional and political achievement. A component of what has been called "the new public management" (see, e.g., Pollitt 1995; Lorenz 2012), the neoliberal governance technology that pushes state agencies to operate like private businesses, in fact privatizes government functions, and manages through measurement of outcomes rather than substantive direction, this third mode has gained institutional, state, and public prominence and for that reason has taken up increasing space in the consciousness of the faculty as well.

The tensions between the first two modes of accountability—professional and political—have garnered substantial attention within women's studies and cultural studies.[8] Responding to an array of "laments" bemoaning a greater emphasis on professionalization as against feminist activism, supposedly brought on by the very success of women's studies in gaining institutional space and legitimacy, Robyn Wiegman (2000, 2002a, 2002b, 2004) has taken up the issue across several important essays.[9] Wiegman notes that the critiques of the institutionalization of women's studies call for accountability to real women, a call often staged against *theory* (engagement with which is cast as professional co-optation). Wiegman argues that this demand for accountability produces epistemological constraints, temporal and spatial. Building on Jane Newman's "The Present in Our Past: Presentism in the Genealogy of Feminism" (2002), Wiegman (2002b, 21) argues that the imperative to be accountable to the feminist movement requires that the measure of all knowledge be its present usefulness. This "presentism," she argues, is enacted "in the figure of the live, suffering woman for whom academic feminism bears its guilty obligation of justice; in the rhetorical gesture toward the priority of discerning the materiality of the everyday; in the live encounter between researcher and researched" (2002a, 13–14), which in turn has disciplinary implications, pushing us toward "humanistic and interpretative social scientific inquiry" (2002b, 29). (I would add that there is also a version of this political accountability that drives the field toward policy-ready *quantitative* social science.) And this in turn actually aligns our work with the "university's own instrumentalization of identity," which supports the efforts of the United States to "extend its imperial mission into a seemingly ethical globalizing human rights agenda (and with it various forms of economic 'development' . . .)" (2002b, 22). Likewise, she argues that "Women's Studies' own self-defined justification as the academic arm of the women's movement can function as a territorial one, foreclosing in the present the interdisciplinary extension of feminist knowledge into domains that will have no obvious connection to the field's self-narration (such as the sciences)" (2002a, 5).

Wiegman's analysis leads her to make the case that women's studies should pursue "a non-instrumentalized relation to knowledge production" (2002b, 33), that is, an argument for what we might call "basic science." Such an argument is difficult to make even in the sciences these days. And despite the fact that I completely endorse the effort to pry open a space for "basic science," I am—to the limited extent that I am able—undertaking an instrumental, present, and political project here.[10] But in doing so, I suggest a definition and temporality for *the political* that contrasts with the one Wiegman finds so constraining: rather than accountability to a (nostalgically remembered) political movement imagined to be by definition representational, one that would tie us to social scientific study of the live suffering woman now, this notion of the political is about ongoing struggle, requiring us, holding us accountable, to bring to bear an analysis on the conditions in which we find ourselves in order to shape effective intervention;[11] our strategies—representational, methodological, disciplinary—would be contingent on our informed assessment of those conditions.

In noting the implication of our work in U.S. imperialism, Wiegman implicitly directs our attention beyond the tension between professionalization and political engagement. While she mentions the engagement of women's studies with "the broader institutional demands about accountability and 'excellence'" (2002b, 19) as one of the provocations for the laments over professionalization, I think we might take it as a provocation to political struggle. With that in mind, I want to begin to explore the demands for accountability in somewhat more detail so we might start to plot a critical intervention in the accounting of our work.

First, it is crucial to recognize the enormous number and diversity of particular sets of metrics to which any given university finds itself accountable: data about the University of Arizona are collected by the federal government (the Integrated Postsecondary Education Data System established by the National Center for Education Statistics),[12] the College Board (the Common Data Set),[13] the state governor's office, the Arizona Board of Regents, and accrediting bodies for the university as a whole and for individual programs. And then, of course, there are the various purveyors of university rankings. While the most notorious of these is the *U.S. News & World Report* ranking system, always criticized for being largely based on reputation, others, thought to be more legitimate because based on quantifiable data, have gained currency: the National Research Council (NRC 2011) produced an "assessment" of doctoral programs based on the application of complex algorithms to an extensive set of data collected from participating institutions,[14] and the Center for Measuring University Performance produces a ranking of "the top American research universities" based on nine factors (informally referred to as the Lombardi measures):

Total research expenditures
Federal research expenditures
Endowment assets
Annual giving
National Academy members
Faculty awards in the arts, humanities, science, engineering, and health
Doctorates awarded
Postdoctoral appointees
SAT scores

In response to the threat of a federally mandated regime of accountability that seemed a clear and present danger in the context of the Department of Education, as led by George W. Bush's secretary of education, Margaret Spellings—something that would go beyond the existing data collection to a more public, comparative, and potentially consequential collection, analysis, and presentation of data, including, most importantly, some standardized mode of "learning outcomes assessment"[15]—the organizations of universities began to generate their own voluntary rubrics. These include the Voluntary System of Accountability,[16] which requires use of one or another of the recently developed and more or less palatable measures of the quality of undergraduate education, such as the Collegiate Learning Assessment (a test of critical reading and writing) and the National Survey of Student

Engagement (not a test but rather a survey that asks students the extent to which their experiences have included certain activities and practices that are educational "best practices").[17]

The values that are embodied in these various sets of measures differ from each other; and, in fact, one can discern a tension that parallels the tension between professional and political accountability for individual faculty members. In this context, political accountability is not an individually generated sense of obligation but a direct imposition. Federal and state governments and the governing boards have articulated the mission of higher education principally in terms of national economic competitiveness and economic development. So "key indicators" in the Arizona Board of Regents' "2020 Vision" system-wide strategic plan, which was developed initially to implement and elaborate a long-gone governor's pledge to double the number of bachelor's degrees produced by the state's universities annually by 2020, include the following: number of degrees awarded (bachelor's, master's, and doctoral, with the explicit rationale that those with degrees have higher lifetime earnings and are potentially attractive to high-tech employers), "degrees awarded in high demand fields" (which generally means science, technology, engineering, and math, or STEM, and health care, though this measure was not immediately defined), technology transfer (measured by "invention disclosures transacted"), "research expenditures," "impact of community engagement activities" (also not quickly defined), and "total income and expenditures related to service and engagement activities." These last three all assume that the expenditures employ people and buy things and thus multiply as they trickle out into the local economy. Although it is not one of Arizona's "key indicators," the value of research is often measured in terms of "return on investment," meaning either this multiplier effect or more specifically the extent to which dollars invested by the state leverage federal or industry dollars. If large dollar numbers are better in the various research metrics, small dollar numbers are better with regard to educational activities. Accessibility, affordability, and efficiency are central in this context, thus this plan measures community college transfers and degrees awarded to community college transfers (it is cheaper to let the community colleges provide the first two years of credits toward the bachelor's degree); number of bachelor's degrees awarded per hundred full-time-equivalent students (a time-to-degree measure, since, again, faster is cheaper); total educational expenditures per degree awarded; and cost of attendance as a percentage of Arizona median family income. Finally, the plan measures the institution's "financial health," using the "comprehensive financial index," calculated from four financial ratios based on the university's audited financial statements: primary reserve ratio, viability ratio, return on net assets ratio, and net operating revenues ratio.

Meanwhile, university administrators, like faculty, are concerned with their standing among peers and thus with rankings and the measures that contribute to the rankings they value; so, for instance, when discussing what measures should be included in our strategic plan, our president inevitably suggests starting with the Lombardi measures, which, it is important to note, place very high value on funded research and faculty accomplishments by contrast with the measures related to undergraduate education that are the focus for the various governments and governing boards. In this context, National Science Foundation rankings of universities by research expenditures often trump all other measures. The conflict between the values of administrators and those of political actors was evident as I observed a monumental battle waged by our administration to have "research"—or, more accurately, "research expenditures"[18]—be included in a meaningful way in the Arizona Board of Regents' system-wide strategic plan. Their efforts were motivated by the assumption that these measures would be integrated into a funding formula and would thus have financial implications.

But really, what is the impact of all this accounting and accountability?

As Michael Power has argued in *The Audit Society* (1997), auditing, which might be understood as the incitement to and evaluation of accountings, can fail in two opposite ways: it can distort the substantive activity of an organization (and it might depend on one's political perspective whether changes to the substantive activity constitute distortion or improvement), or the encounter over the accounts can take place in a kind of administrative shell at the surface of the organization that actually shields the daily work of most participants. In some ways it is clear that both of those things happen at the University of Arizona: a great deal of the strategic planning and measuring ultimately turns out to be a performance of management by the administration for the Board of Regents and other publics that have little impact on day-to-day life inside the institution, except for the drain of resources into that performance. On the other hand, the ongoing and ever-redoubled accounting efforts do insinuate themselves in various ways. Shore and Wright (2000, but see also 2004), in a Foucauldian argument drawing on Power's work, emphasize the shift from superficial performances of accounting to more meaningful subjectification of the institution as a whole, as it creates new procedures—record-keeping and control systems—to make itself an "auditable commodity" (72), and of the individuals within the institution, as they respond to the new panoptic technologies by "freely" regulating their own conduct to meet the measured goals (62). On the other hand, the incoherent proliferation of divergent sets of measures must undermine any intended disciplinary effectivity for both institutions and individuals, as I learned through my own efforts to govern by measurement:

When I started as a member of the University of Arizona Strategic Planning and Budget Advisory Committee, I immediately joined the "measures committee" and was struck by the disconnect between the regimes of accountability that I was familiar with as a faculty member—annual performance reviews, tenure and promotion reviews, student course evaluations—and the measures that we were discussing as the possible ways to evaluate the university as a whole. That is, none of the information that we all submitted in the form of CVs and narratives about our accomplishments served as usable data to be assessed cumulatively for the university as a whole—we simply had no mechanism for doing so; faculty CVs were not entered into a database for sorting and counting in any way. In some ways I was appalled and in others relieved to find that the regime of accountability was unable to see the real work of the faculty, that it was to a large extent irrational and ineffectual. We would measure those things for which we had data, for which we could show progress—not the things that mattered in relation to our stated mission and goals. Whether I was more appalled or more relieved in a given moment depended on who was to be held accountable: I wanted meaningful measures to hold the whole institution accountable for making progress on diversifying the faculty; and I wanted resource allocation to be made on some basis other than cronyism or mistaken prejudices about productivity and financial return on investment (for instance, good financial accounting can sometimes counteract the assumption that big-science indirect cost recovery subsidizes the rest of the university and show instead that big science is subsidized by other revenue sources, such as tuition). As one colleague put it, decisions based on data are an improvement over the "faith-based" decision making promoted by the George W. Bush administration.

As chair of SPBAC, I found myself trying to close the gaps between what faculty actually do and what is measured, between what we as an institution say we intend to do and what is measured. At the request of our new provost, SPBAC undertook a project that aimed to select a "robust" set of measures, such that we could measure every single goal in the strategic plan and reframe each goal as a numerical target (although even the provost understood, as I had come to understand, that measuring can be an enormously expensive undertaking, primarily in personnel time, and that the value of each new metric had to be weighed against the cost). Frustrated again and again by the lack of data to support measures of the things we claimed to value, and even though I knew better, I proposed that faculty submit at least portions of their annual performance reviews online so that the information could be dumped into a database that the university could then draw on to find out, for instance, how much "public service" our faculty do (we are a land-grant institution after all) or, as an indicator of "interdisciplinarity," how many joint and affiliate appointments our faculty have or how many are participating in grants with co–principal investigators from different departments. On the theory that what is counted is what counts, I found myself advocating for certain problematic measures simply as placeholders, as stakes in the ground for the significance of the objects imperfectly measured: so, desperate for some measure of teaching quality, against the better judgment of faculty colleagues and ultimately unsuccessfully, I proposed that we use teacher/course evaluation data. And specifically in order to preserve some of the professional power of faculty against the power of administrative management, in selecting measures, I advocated for a publications and citations measure because it refers back to peer evaluation, even though the most established publications and citations database uses only selected journals (not books) as its raw data and so undercounts in "book" fields while missing entirely the output of our colleagues in fine arts. No doubt, the commonly used measures stack things in favor of certain fields.

My sense that the institutional and state-mandated measures fail to see us, or at least fail to see us as we see ourselves, fail to value what we value, registers the discrepancy between that regime of accountability (incoherent and contradictory as it is) and the professional and political modes of accountability that are still more primary for most of *us*. The disjuncture can make these newer measures feel impactful when deployed inside the institution, frightening in their potential to shift resources; and thus they gain our attention, forcing us to seek ways to defend ourselves in their terms. Sheer quantities of research dollars, student credit hours, or degrees produced can become local-level measures used to rate the productivity or "cost-efficiency" of departments or degree programs against each other.[19] At the University of Arizona, the data collected for the new NRC rankings of doctoral programs were deployed (in conjunction with narrative self-evaluation and justification) for a review of all UA graduate programs, with an eye toward the potential elimination of programs that fared poorly in this assessment (rumor had it that a similarly consequential assessment took place at Ohio State University). And the emphasis on financial accountability likewise can be rolled down—many universities, including UA, now use some form of what is called "responsibility-centered management" or "responsibility-based budgeting," which, despite its name (suggesting that money would be distributed based on "responsibility"—that is, role in fulfilling the mission), starts with an accounting of who is bringing in money and only then taxes this income so as to redistribute resources to subsidize units perceived to be important but not adequately revenue generating, such as the library.[20]

As I have already illustrated in the CEGA Team story, this regime of accountability exacerbates existing differences—between "us" and the "sciences" and among us, between those whose work is visible in a given accounting scheme and those who appear unproductive by those measures, between those who produce research expenditures or commodifiable knowledge products and those who produce student credit hours and degrees (most often not the same scholars or academic units, though there is the occasional "double threat," such as the Psychology Department at UA, which brings in very substantial research dollars and provides vast quantities of undergraduate instruction). What began to seem obvious was that the only way the CEGA Team might have made a case for anything beyond fundable applied social science of health research (the one area of cultural, ethnic, gender, and area studies that registers in terms of research expenditures) would have been to claim that we would be increasing the efficiency and quantity of undergraduate degree production, and even then it would have been a weak claim, since we neither offer degrees in STEM fields nor train health care providers. Our knowledge production quite literally does not count.

How should we respond to this situation?

As many have noted, the most common impulse of humanities (or, more broadly, qualitative or interpretive) scholars in response to quantitative accounting is to refuse, to claim that qualities cannot or should not be counted (see, for instance, Scobey 2009). Readings (1996, 127–28) argues against the counting of "credit hours" because "the complex time of thought is not exhaustively accountable." Poovey (2001b, 12) proposes that the humanities should refuse commodification by refusing quantification, laying claim to goods that, she claims, are not quantifiable: "the goods of living culture, which embody and preserve human creativity." Against counting, they tend to place a great deal of political optimism on qualitative or narrative accounts of the "singular": "Singularity . . . recognizes the radical heterogeneity of individuals" (Readings 1996, 115). In discussing the evaluation of teaching quality, for instance, Readings suggests that in place of the usual course evaluations that ask students to rate various aspects of a course on a numerical scale, students should "be required to write evaluative essays that can themselves be read and that require further interpretation" (133). Readings offers this approach as a way of accepting the imperative to evaluation—"Those in the University are called upon to judge, and the administration will do it for them if they do not respond to the call" (130)—while "refus[ing] to equate accountability with accounting" (131).[21]

A less reactive, potentially more constructive version of this response has been developed using the postworkerist theorization of an "immeasurable" commons of human abilities and resources (for a useful set of critical engagements with this theory, see Dowling, Nunes, and Trott 2007). De Angelis and Harvie (2009, 4–5) helpfully summarize the argument (in order, then, to contest it):

> It has been argued, most famously by Hardt and Negri in *Empire,* that the production of *things*—material objects that can be counted, weighed, measured—is no longer hegemonic. Capital has invaded every aspect of human lives and production is increasingly immaterial, producing information, affects (the increased capacities of bodies to act) and percepts. . . . the skills, know-how and attitudes of workers are (re)produced by the relational

practices learnt and re-learnt in the home, from uncles and aunts, sisters and brothers, mothers, fathers and lovers. . . . Hence, cooperation is far more likely to be of a horizontal, rhizomatic nature, organised on the basis of networks, informal workgroups, peer-to-peer relationships, and even social ties, rather than directed by the boss standing at the apex of a hierarchy. The value produced by this labour is therefore "beyond measure," because the immaterial living labour producing value is identified with "general social activity," "a common power to act" that cannot be disciplined, regimented and structured by measuring devices such as clocks.

This theorization suggests that one might respond to the regimes of accounting and accountability not by a retreat into singularity but rather by resort to alternative spaces of collectivity, such as the space of "study" Stefano Harney and Fred Moten have evoked in the series of essays now collected as *The Undercommons: Fugitive Planning and Black Study* (2013). This vision of alternative collectivities is crucial. I propose that an alternative "we" might be constituted not beyond measurement but rather through its appropriation and transformation.

In the wake of my administrative engagements, I no longer feel comfortable with claims that "quality can't be counted," or that "what we do can't be measured." No doubt, my discomfort with these answers finds one of its sources in the immediate personal discomfort I felt when counting and measuring were demanded and what I wanted to do was to show that we measured up. That is, the refusal of accounting puts us in a rhetorically untenable situation; it can be dismissed as the arrogant sour grapes of those who *do not* measure up. Describing the closely related difficulty of defending scholarship that does not produce immediately applicable knowledge (knowledge that measures up by the appointed measures), Poovey (2001a, 420) says, "It is impossible to defend reviving the values that associate learning with curiosity and knowledge with freedom by any means that don't seem self-serving or nostalgic."

More important, the notion that qualities cannot be counted, quantified, commodified is wrong; commodification is a process through which qualitatively distinct products are made commensurable by being considered abstractly, as products of human labor according to Marx or as marginally useful (aka objects of demand) in neoclassical economic theory and thus exchangeable (for instance, human labor is made commensurable with money). Against the hopeful claims for immeasurability, De Angelis and Harvie point out that "an army of . . .

accountants, bureaucrats, political strategists and others is engaged in a struggle to commensurate heterogeneous concrete human activities on the basis of equal quantities of human labor in the abstract, that is, to link work and value" (2009, 5–6). They take academic labor as a perfect example of immaterial labor. Examining the array of creative technologies of data creation, assemblage, and analysis imposed in Britain (which is similar to what I have described here but far more centralized and coherent), they show that the immaterial can be successfully articulated with quantitative measures. However, they point out that subversive efforts such as "fabrication" and "mindless 'tick-boxing'" (14) can stymie any regime of total managerial control, creating instead a "struggle over *measure*" (15). And thus, rather than effective total control, the crucial issue for them is the extent to which the measures establish *norms* of productivity to which workers and institutions then actively aspire (18). The important implication is that we cannot assume ahead of time any autochthonous collective resistance, even among those (the most of us) for whom subscribing to the norms, to the measures, will be the self-undermining effort of the entrepreneurial subject.

I propose struggling with measure not only because it is possible but also because that struggle responds to responsibilities and opportunities. Gayatri Chakravorty Spivak (2003, 44–45) offers one of the most savage critiques of empiricist knowledge production: in the context of a critique of international "development" efforts aimed at women, she argues that the production of the "generalized name of 'woman,'" which involves the suppression of "singularity in order to establish a 'fact,'" works to "ensure predictability in the field of women" and to create a "common currency" that enables entities such as the United Nations and the World Bank to "operate in the field of gender." Elsewhere she states, baldly, that "positivist empiricism" is "the justifying foundation of advanced capitalist neocolonialism" (Spivak 1999, 255). But she also encourages us to make use of this critique with some caution: "A just world must entail normalization; the promise of justice must attend . . . to the anguish that knowledge must suppress difference as well as differance, that a fully just world is impossible, forever deferred and different from our projections, the undecidable in the face of which we must risk the decision that we can hear the other" (1999, 199). Spivak learns from Derrida that "responsible action" requires accounting, requires deploying the "calculus" of "accountable reason," even while we keep "always in view" that "if responsible action is fully formulated or justified within the system of the calculus, it cannot retain its accountability to the trace of the other" (1999, 427–28). Instead of *replacing* accounting with accountability as Readings suggests, we might *supplement* accounting with accountability, push accounting to its limits as we also stake a claim to goals, to values, not currently articulated within the regimes of accounting to which we are subject.

If Spivak invokes our responsibilities, our opportunities come into view through an analysis of the determinations constituting the current conjuncture. But it might be important to first recognize that the current conjuncture is not so different from previous conjunctures as we might imagine. While faculty may experience the new public management as an alarming development, invading their time and psyches—once upon a time, didn't we faculty just go about our business, trying to get our research done and our classes taught, leaving it to our department heads to deal with bureaucratic reporting requirements and negotiations with deans for money and faculty positions?[22]—accountability is nothing new in the academy. Hoskin and Macve (1988) note in their narrative of "the genesis of accountability"—by which they mean the deployment in large corporations of integrated financial and performance measurement that ultimately makes humans calculable—that accountability got its start in medieval universities, where new techniques for "gridding" information "plus the use of the formal examination" were first developed. And then, Hoskin and Macve claim, nineteenth-century universities were the site of the next significant development with "the introduction of written examinations and mathematical marking systems" (37). They credit the development of managerial accounting systems in the United States largely to regimes implemented at West Point Military Academy (regimes modeled on the École Polytechnique), which included extensive marking and grading (sorting into hierarchies) not only of the students' performance (45–49) and personal finances (49n12) but also those of the instructors (59). This history suggests that rather than ignore accounting to the extent that we can, inhabitants of universities are well positioned to impactfully engage the ongoing political struggle over accounting systems that are always in flux.

Taking up this opportunity in the current conjuncture, we might note, as Christopher Newfield does in *Unmaking the Public University* (2008), that while the higher education mission and the forms of accountability demanded by state actors are often articulated in terms of expanding the availability of affordable education, in fact the driver has been an attempt to control the democratizing force of the expansion of higher education that took place between the end of World War II and the early 1970s. Newfield says that the "culture wars" attacks on universities of the 1970s–90s, which focused on so-called political correctness, affirmative action, and the introduction of "multicultural" content in both curriculum and research, worked in tandem with the discourse of market fundamentalism that gained dominance during the same period to delegitimate the whole notion of racial and economic equality, narrow the mission of universities to economic rather than general social and human development (thus specifically devaluing cultural as opposed to technical knowledge), and undermine the credibility of higher education (that is, the professional authority of the faculty). This enabled funding cuts—real reductions in resources for the middle class as the cost of education was shifted from the state to individual consumers of education in the form of tuition—and, I would add, opened the way for the relentless performance and financial auditing to which we are now subject (per Power and Shore and Wright, audit performs and extends mistrust; see Shore and Wright 2000, 77). That is, Newfield suggests that the three forms of accountability I identified earlier—professional, political, and managerial—have been played off against each other, with political attacks, deployed to undermine professional credibility (and thus confidence in the existing systems of accountability, which depended substantially on qualitative peer evaluation), legitimating new modes of managerial and financial accountability that are a Trojan horse for a political project of privatization and exclusion. Recognizing the current regime of accountability as the not-inevitable outcome of struggle and strategy—a cultural-economic project—suggests that we too might intervene, manipulate the modes of accounting and accountability, appropriate for ourselves the interpellating power of quantitative representation, and reshape what counts and who gets to count.

What would this look like? One implicit suggestion in Newfield's narrative is that we should/could reappropriate the demands for affordable, accessible higher education and for economic development. Rather than rejecting accounting per se, retreating to professional accountability, or holding ourselves accountable to an originary moment of identity-based social movement, we might engage in a broader contestation over the scope and goals of higher education by affirming the democratizing and developmental goals our states and governing boards have articulated but holding them accountable to those goals in ways they did not necessarily intend or envision. And that is where I landed in an earlier version of this essay:

Trying to think through how to deal internally and externally with the impending budget cuts, a colleague proposed that in order to really galvanize ourselves to fight, we might need to abandon "craven" economic development arguments for more heartfelt arguments in support of the value of knowledge itself, noting that economic development is not really what moves us and that if all we are about is workforce development, that really could be done more cheaply. But he recognized the inevitable problems—we would come across as elitist, pompous, arrogant, and, in true academic form, would wind up wanting to surround our affirmation of knowledge with caveats about its link to power. In response I wrote the following:

> I don't think that an argument for the value of knowledge per se will get us anywhere in the present political moment. However, we might ask some questions/make some arguments about the definition and scope of "economic development": If, for a moment, we accept the notion that economic development refers only to for-profit business development, we might still ask if technoscience knowledge is sufficient in itself to drive economic development. What range of knowledge, skills and personal attributes are necessary to invent a new product or service, one that will actually meet the needs and desires of humans in their cultural, social, psychological complexity and diversity, believe you can build a business around it, sell the idea to investors, gather, organize and manage the people needed to produce your great new thing, communicate what it is, how it works and why it is desirable to consumers . . .
>
> And, is "economic development" a means or an end? If it is a means, providing the material basis for something more than itself (let's say relationships with—pick your favorite—other people, the god of your choice, nature, arts, the wondrous new gadgets developed by other people who are doing "economic development," etc.), then those other areas might need some attention from educational institutions as well.
>
> Who is meant to benefit from "economic development"? Is this about a few entrepreneurs making fortunes, while everyone else is a low-paid cog in the machine? At the national level, we've been hearing a lot about access and affordability regarding higher ed. Shouldn't we be holding our elected officials accountable on this front? (The rhetoric has been about holding the universities accountable, but the politicians must be held to account as well.)

And, I would ask the question deferred above: Are for-profit corpora-
tions the only kind of activity/organization needed for economic develop-
ment, or might we need expertise in public policy, social service provision,
education itself? That is, might economic development mean more than
business development? While our legislative leaders don't care about any
of this—they seem quite explicitly committed to reducing access to educa-
tion (and the political and economic power that comes with it), preferring
to incarcerate those that, if educated, might threaten them—a broader
public might actually care.

But I was never entirely comfortable with that as an ending or as a
strategy. Rather than answering my colleague's question about how to
galvanize *us*, I spoke from inside the political constraints of the moment,
letting those constraints limit my own imagination of the speakable to
a liberal humanism that erases meaningful conflicts and contradictions
(though those are signaled at the end by my reference to incarceration).
It has always struck me as more symptom than solution.

Writing my way through this book has made some other thoughts possible, though every one has dangers and impurities. For instance, we
might start by taking the idea of pushing accounting to and beyond its
limits quite literally. On one hand, as I suggested in chapter 4, knowl-
edgeable intervention in the "bad science" that simply reproduces existing social categories and hierarchies is a first step. I have mentioned
above that, as Newfield (2008, esp. chaps. 12 and 13) has shown, good
financial accounting can counteract our assumptions about who is really
responsible for various costs and revenues. Similarly, a national study
of higher education finance demonstrated that in contrast to the pre-
sumptions underlying the public outcry over the rising costs of higher
education, in fact costs have remained remarkably stable (especially at
public institutions)—tuition has gone up because states have shifted
the burden of those costs onto individual students (Wellman et al.
2008). And as the study I discussed at the end of chapter 2 regarding
the impact of diminished financial aid on student engagement suggests,
accountings can be (though they most often are not) designed to reveal
social conflict and contradiction.

Recognizing the interpellating power of numerical representations,
discussed in chapter 4, the possible creation of social accountings raises
the question of how and whether we might take the risk of deploying
such accounts, not to fetishize, to provoke fear or some condescend-
ing sympathy regarding a crisis experienced by others, but rather to

galvanize *us,* as my colleague suggested. Moving beyond interrupting bad science and the lone acts of subversion that De Angelis and Harvie describe, we might engage in *collective* "struggles over measure" to demand that the best, most creative sciences of measurement be brought to bear to count the things that *we* think ought to count. As nothing seems "beyond measure" for capital, we might appropriate such creativity toward different ends.

Both Newfield and Martin have put substantial effort into envisioning transformative engagements with (rather than rejections of) accounting and accountability. One component of their interventions takes as its premise that our problem is not so much that our products have been commodified as that they have failed as commodities. We invest in producing, but the product does not sell—the market for our knowledge is relatively small—one might even say that, in this historical context, it has little socially recognized use value; without use value, no exchange occurs, and the product does not become commensurable with other valuable commodities, with money.[23] Reacting against the typical "humanities" responses described above, Newfield and Martin have both suggested that the substance of knowledge production and dissemination in the humanities needs to be renovated; it needs to integrate strategies developed at its interdisciplinary cutting edges that reconsider objects, methods, and audience, so as to produce in a way that has impact, that has value (by some measure, if not the existing measures). Newfield (2008, 147) argues that literary studies (and other humanities fields) have partially accepted "the 'market' as the arbitrator of the shape of the profession" insofar as they have accepted as *fact* reduced demand for their products (primarily publications, especially books, and Ph.D.s, which is to say professors). However, he points out that they have failed to learn the other half of "the lesson of business," which is "how to manage markets—how to discover hidden demands, how to create demand for products one thinks are important, how to adapt the market to one's output, how to subordinate markets to the needs of one's 'customers,' not to mention the wider society" (148–49). He suggests that humanities fields and literary studies in particular might have but did not reposition themselves to be and be seen as socially relevant (145).

In "Taking an Administrative Turn," Martin (2011a) radicalizes and elaborates this vision. Calling for "a different charge for the humanities as well as a more steadfast engagement with the administrative decisions" (156)—and apparently taking the hint from Livingston or Marx—he appropriates the complicity of interdisciplinarity with capitalism, pointing to the similarity between interdisciplinarity and financial derivatives. Financial derivatives (but also derivative products in other fields, in the arts for instance) involve "a transmission of some value from a source to something else" (158); invented as a risk management tool, a way to hedge against unknown future price fluctuations, a financial derivative is a contract that references some set of goods or assets—by, for instance, insuring (or betting on) their future price—but generally does not exchange or use those goods directly. So the number of derivatives relative to any commodity is potentially limitless, and derivatives become mobile, commensurable, exchangeable financial instruments in themselves. Likewise, Martin says,

> interdisciplinarity has certainly become expansive, even obligatory, over the past decades as a way of enhancing flexibility and embracing risk. . . . But what if the relation is more than metaphorical, what if the derivative displays a social logic—by no means exclusive of all modes of reason or exhaustive of every approach to explanation—that discloses the very sociality by which the value of our labors might be more fully recognized and placed in circulation? (159)

Against the claims for the *intrinsic* value of humanities objects and scholarship, Martin advocates instead for critical interdisciplinary studies that—in an echo of Stuart Hall's (1990, 16) suggestion that we conduct "a series of raids on other disciplinary terrains"—derive value from multiple elsewheres. These interdisciplinary studies would, like financial derivatives, be valuable as sites of "engagement, affiliation, activism, and organizing," as technologies of abstraction that enable us "to recognize ways in which the concrete particularities, the specific engagements, commitments, and interventions we tender and expend might be interconnected" (159), to see "the value of our work in the midst of volatility" (160), and to engage "the future not simply as contingent, uncertain, or indeterminate but also as actionable in the present" (160).[24]

Brilliantly claiming the liquidity of the financier on behalf of critical knowledge production, Martin's vision is savvy and inspiring. And it addresses many of the issues I have raised across this book: it proposes to intervene directly in the articulation of abstraction and particularity, and in the social processes of value formation, rather than accepting fetishes produced by those processes. Moreover, engagement, affiliation, interconnection, and organization are most certainly measurable, if we have a will to measure them. While universities employ extraordinarily sophisticated quantitative researchers in their institutional research offices, these researchers are rarely asked or allowed to do anything beyond simple counting—they are kept too busy assembling data and responding to various governmental demands by putting the best face (graph) on the institution to actually analyze anything. So, in our strategic planning process, when I proposed that we measure interdisciplinarity through a social network analysis that would map (in one of those now-familiar spiderweb-type graphs) and count meaningful inter/connections (such as faculty members' service on graduate committees beyond their own departments or as co-principal investigators on grants outside their home units), this was rejected as too difficult. But it might have been worth struggling harder, as I suspect that *we* would do very well in such a measure. Similar techniques would be useful in making visible the impact of our work in relation to "real-world issues" as well. And, most important, could we galvanize new collectivities? Might we activate, by measuring, relationships that could be more potent than they are?

The question is whether we can take inspiration from Martin's appropriation of the derivative not simply to ensure and expand *our* value but to imagine a mode of accounting *for* justice, on behalf of justice. It seems to me that the trajectory of this book has enabled some optimism about accounting for justice but also posed a daunting challenge. Can we articulate an accounting against criminalization, against incarceration, against the production—through, for example, the intertwined and divergent accountings of debt and crime, discussed in chapter 2, that critical abstraction enables us to recognize—of social hierarchy in general and racial formation in particular?

This is an immediate challenge for us here in Arizona, at the University of Arizona in Tucson; we are living and working in the wake of the passage of laws (Arizona's anti-immigrant law, SB 1070, and anti–ethnic studies law, HB 2281, were both passed in 2010) that enhance the school-to-prison pipeline by dismantling high school programs statistically "proven" to disrupt it by improving "pass" rates on mandatory statewide tests (Cabrera, Milem, and Marx 2012) and, likewise, enlarge the immigration-to-detention pipeline by extending and intertwining criminalization and policing, meanwhile producing "attrition through enforcement."[25] For high school students whose educational options have been foreclosed or for those more relentlessly and rigorously held accountable to immigration status databases, these laws have direct material impact; for many others the impacts are more indirect but still palpable and disabling to participants and participation in the multiple and overlapping spaces, institutions, collectivities, and jurisdictions across which our lives are strung.

And yet university leaders, faced with all-too-serious financial and political pressures, deny that any of this is *our* problem: the K–12 school district is not within our purview; there is no evidence of an impact of the state legislation on our campus climate; the decline in incoming graduate students of color is not statistically significant. Some frustrated faculty members take such statements as provocation to produce irrefutable (that is, statistical) proofs of the impacts on us, on our recruitment and retention of students, faculty, and administrators or on our climate. But such proofs might not be easy to construct: relatively little time has passed, the *n*s are small because in many categories we had few people of color already, and we have no information about those who simply never applied for jobs or to Ph.D. programs here; meanwhile, the climate might very well be fine for many members of the white majority. And even if some creative accounting did show direct impacts on the university, such proofs might not in themselves move the handful of university leaders to whom they would be addressed, who are constrained by endless demands to demonstrate creditworthiness through the regimes of accounting and accountability I have described, regimes to which they (if not all of us) are most certainly fully subject.

Once again it seems that intertwined but differentiated regimes of accounting particularize us differently. So when I walk into the next meeting with my colleagues—and I end where I began, with the urgency of the impending meeting—I might propose a more, shall I say, *interdisciplinary* approach. The stubborn numbers may refuse to speak, refuse to name a "crisis." Might we recognize those who have gone missing from our classrooms and our faculty meetings and our provosts' offices[26] by accounting for that silence, as derivative, the form of appearance of determining conflicts and connections? Might *we* be hailed in the process?

ACKNOWLEDGMENTS

This work has been in progress for a long time. Along the way, this book and I have benefited from the intellectual, personal, and financial generosity of many people and organizations; precisely due to the extended time and space over which this project ranged, gaps in memory and perception will no doubt leave gaps in these acknowledgments, though it is truly my wish to extend full credit for all of the amazing support I received. If you are not named here but should be, I apologize.

This book is dedicated to Sandy Soto, and she also deserves my first thanks. As my partner in life and work throughout the years during which this project unfolded, Sandy has supported my administrative engagements (though I know she sometimes experienced that part of my work as fingernails on a blackboard) and (with greater pleasure, I hope) participated in many of my intellectual adventures. Her specific contributions to this book run the gamut from arguing with me about ideas to pointing out *Frontline* episodes on credit (featuring Elizabeth Warren before Warren was famous) to copyediting chapters in the final push to finish the manuscript.

This project began in conversations with Zoe Hammer, whose dissertation about and activism against "the border prison system" compelled my attention to the phenomenon of mass incarceration. Zoe introduced me to Ruth Wilson Gilmore and Julia C. Oparah (formerly Sudbury), both great sources of inspiration and wisdom. My first chance to embark on this work was provided by the seminar on "community" at the School of American Research organized by Gerald Creed; Gerald put together an amazing group, and I thank all of the participants in that seminar, including especially Mary Weismantel and Elizabeth Chin, who engaged me in importantly formative conversations. For that seminar I wrote the first draft of the essay later published in *The Seductions of Community* as "A Debt to Society," which ultimately became the kernel of chapters 1 and 2 of this book. I am grateful for the guidance I received from Gerald and the anonymous reviewers of that article. Emily M. Schmidt provided excellent research assistance.

Davina Cooper's invitation to be a visiting scholar in the AHRC Research Centre for Law, Gender, and Sexuality at the University of Kent offered an important opportunity to write an early version of material in chapters 2 and 3 and to receive valuable feedback on that material.

Ranu Samantrai provided the provocation to write "Accounting for Interdisciplinarity" by inviting me to contribute to *Interdisciplinarity and Social Justice* while I was in the throes of my work as chair of the University of Arizona Strategic Planning and Budget Advisory Committee. To my colleagues on that committee I owe a profound debt for their confidence, mentorship, and wisdom, and for taking me seriously when I was more junior and less experienced than they were, all of which enabled me to succeed. Wanda Howell, chair of the faculty, nominated me for that position, thus inviting me to become an intimate partner in crime through two crazy years of upheaval. I am deeply grateful for the extraordinary opportunity she gave me and for her wonderful companionship through it all. I thank then-president Robert Shelton, who gave me and the committee meaningful room to contribute, and then-provost Eugene Sander, for his encouragement and for just being himself. Many thanks to Chris Newfield not only for his indispensable scholarship, informed by his work in a similar role, but also for taking a phone call when I needed practical political advice. Likewise, Randy Martin has been there, an ally in administrative adventure through his scholarship and conversation.

Corey Knox, my colleague here at the University of Arizona's Southwest Institute for Research on Women (SIROW), in collaboration with the late, great Michele Convie, organized the Inside Out conference that led to the formation of the Women's Re-entry Network. I am deeply grateful to Corey, Michele, and the other members of WREN who allowed me to hang out with and learn from them. I also want to thank Patricia Manning (formerly of SIROW), from whom I have learned a great deal about the prison industrial complex and who invited me to participate in the Alternatives to Violence Project program she led in prisons in the Tucson area; I only wish I had been able to take her up on the invitation more fully.

Chapter 3 was largely written during my tenure as a Distinguished Visiting Fellow at Queen Mary University of London. I will be forever grateful to Nicholas Ridout for the invitation to apply. Being there was an amazing treat; among those who made it fun and productive were Tim Edkins, Lois Weaver, Tracy Davis, and Stefano Harney. That time in the United Kingdom was an opportunity to deepen my conversations with John Howard, Anne-Marie Fortier, Cindy Weber, Anna-Maria Murtola, and Campbell Jones. Particular thanks to Anne-Marie and Anna-Maria for opportunities to present and get feedback on the work in progress. Wendy Larner's invitation to participate in a seminar at the University of Bristol spurred a spin-off of chapter 3 that ultimately took on its own life as an essay on gender and personal finance that appears here as chapter 4. The seminar introduced me not only to Wendy and her work but also to Sarah Hall and her work and to Paul Langley's work (and, consequently, to Paul himself, at an amazing conference on finance sponsored by the Centre for Research on Socio-Cultural Change at the University of Manchester).

Chapter 4 was inspired and made possible by collaboration and conversation with Joyce Serido, which was itself made possible by Soyeon Shim. Their openness to including and engaging with an outsider to their APLUS project has been truly extraordinary. Although my work here departs from the main trajectory of their project, moving in theoretical, political, and methodological directions unfamiliar to them and with which each would, in her own way and for her own reasons, at least in part likely disagree, I am deeply grateful for the access and education they provided.

This work has emerged in the context of a number of ongoing conversations with colleagues at the University of Arizona, some sustained through the multiyear research cluster Sexuality, Subjectivity, and Political Cultures, sponsored by the Institute for LGBT Studies. Members of that group at various times included Paul Allatson, Maribel Alvarez, Laura Briggs, Araceli Esparza, Caryl Flinn, Anne-Marie Fortier, Adam Geary, Laura Gutiérrez, Elizabeth Lapovsky Kennedy, Adela Licona, Eithne Luibhéid, Sallie A. Marston, V. Spike Peterson, Hai Ren, and Sandy Soto. Visitors sponsored by that research cluster, including Lauren Berlant, Ann Cvetkovich, Lisa Duggan, John Howard, Saba Mahmood, Alicia Schmidt Camacho, and Cindy Weber, provided extraordinary intellectual stimulation. In addition, two independent study reading courses with gender and women's studies graduate students, one with Shannon Randall and the other with Angela Stoutenburgh, were transformative for me and for this book.

Conversations with colleagues and friends far and near have been more important than we knew in the moment: I thank Fiona Allon, Kate Bedford, Bruce Burgett, Patricia T. Clough, Elizabeth Freeman, Christina B. Hanhardt, Gillian Harkins, Rosemary Hennessy, Janet Jakobsen, Caren Kaplan, Leigh Claire La Berge, Adela C. Licona, Ira Livingston, Leerom Medovoi, José Esteban Muñoz, Diane M. Nelson, Tavia Nyong'o, Geeta Patel, Stephen T. Russell, Nayan Shah, Susan J. Shaw, Andrea Smith, Alexandra Tracy-Ramirez, and Robyn Wiegman.

I received direct and helpful feedback from reviewers for the University of Minnesota Press and for *Social Politics,* as well as from Bret Benjamin, Lisa Duggan, Adam M. Geary, David Kazanjian, Elizabeth Lapovsky Kennedy, Wendy Larner, Heather Lukes, Molly McGarry, Andreas Philippopoulos-Mihalopoulos, María Josefina Saldaña-Portillo, Sandy Soto, and Susan Stryker. Laura Gronewold provided invaluable assistance with the manuscript in the final push. At the University of Minnesota Press, Erin Warholm-Wohlenhaus and Rachel Moeller have been a pleasure to work with, and Richard Morrison kept the pressure on in the nicest possible way. I am very grateful to copy editor Judy Selhorst for a light hand and careful eye.

My parents, Ellen and Larry Joseph, continue to make my life possible in all sorts of ways that I do notice and appreciate. Galen Joseph, Harlan David Joseph, Susan Gloria Joseph, Nancy and Jim Katzoff, Trudy Rosen, Nina Thomas, David and Michelle Joseph, Pearl Joseph, and Irma Soto all have contributed to my life and this work. Pipo Chico, Prince of Pipolandia, tried his best to be (un)helpful. And I have not forgotten the comforts and pleasures provided by Rafa and Sophie, even with the arrival of Chuch, whose paw is resting on my computer as I type this sentence. Last but certainly not least, a hearty *salud* to the Pasc@s, Frank Galarte, Pancha Castañeda González, Laura, and Sandy, for good company on the treacherous ride through the daily grind.

NOTES

Introduction

1. Lazzarato is quoting Deleuze (1995, 81, 89). See also Mahmud (2012).

2. I use the word *criminal* too many times throughout the book to set it off in quotes every time. But I want to be clear that I do not take "criminal" to be a kind of person or an individual who has individually undertaken to violate the law. Rather, I understand so-called criminals to be the products of processes of criminalization that deploy technologies of lawmaking, policing, charging, sentencing, incarceration, and more in order to racialize, manage economic crisis, and suppress social conflict and change.

3. This type of work might be said to have been launched by editors Burchell, Gordon, and Miller in *The Foucault Effect* (1991). Nikolas Rose and Peter Miller, among many others, have produced extensive scholarship in this vein.

4. This sentence is obviously dependent on Mary Poovey's (1998, xii) exploration of "the modern fact" as a phenomenon that "simultaneously describe[s] discrete particulars *and* contribute[s] to systematic knowledge." Her discussion of the procedures of double-entry bookkeeping, specifically, informs my analysis. I will return to this topic in chapter 1.

5. See also Woodward (2009). Universities use "social norming" campaigns—posters displayed all over campus that read, for instance, "80% of [University of Arizona] students typically party one night a week or less"—to shape student behavior, based on the theory that this kind of Althusserian interpellation actually works.

6. See Liberty Mutual's website at http://responsibility-project.libertymutual .com.

7. Rick Santelli's February 19, 2009, appearance on the floor of the Chicago Mercantile Exchange has been credited with inspiring the tea party movement. Santelli argued against President Obama's proposed stimulus and mortgage modifications, instead suggesting a "referendum to see if we really want to subsidize the losers' mortgages." He then turned to the traders on the floor around him and asked, "How many of you people want to pay for your neighbors' mortgage?" Fellow

traders responded with a good loud round of booing and hooting. A few sentences later, Santelli proposed a "Chicago Tea Party." See Heritage Foundation, "CNBC's Rick Santelli's Chicago Tea Party," http://www.youtube.com/watch?v=zp-Jw -5Kx8k (accessed April 2013).

8. Numerous scholars make this argument, including Angela Davis in *Are Prisons Obsolete?* (2003) and Loïc Wacquant in "Race as Civic Felony" (2005).

9. Two articles appeared that year in the *New York Times* under the headline "The Subprime Landscape from Detroit to Ithaca": "What's behind the Race Gap?" (Bajaj and Fessenden 2007) and "College Towns Escape the Pain" (Fessenden 2007).

10. Thinking of Althusser's (1971, 132–33) distinction between the workers who learn submission and those who, as agents of exploitation, learn how to "'handle' the workers correctly. . . . To manipulate the ruling ideology," I recognize that as a tenured faculty member, I am not so much proletarianized as managerialized. (For more on this issue, see Rhoades 1998; Martin 2011.)

11. Wendy Brown gives a productive Foucauldian turn to Marx's argument in her essay "Rights and Losses" (1995).

12. In "National Brands/National Body," Berlant (1991, 112–13) describes the "peculiar dialectic between embodiment and abstraction," in which "the American subject is privileged to suppress the fact of his historical situation in the abstract 'person': but then, in return, the nation provides a kind of prophylaxis . . . as it promises to protect his privileges and local body . . . the implicit whiteness and maleness is thus itself protected. . . . Needless to say, American women and African-Americans have never had the privilege to suppress the body."

13. For an excellent review of the feminist critiques of quantitative knowledge production, see McLafferty (1995).

14. See Gordon (1991) and other essays in Burchell, Gordon, and Miller (1991).

15. As I discuss in chapter 5, my stance is meant to be aligned/allied with Randy Martin's position, advanced in *Under New Management* (2011b).

1. Accounting for Debt

1. This quote comes from a January 2013 press release titled "Strike Debt Bay Area Announces Oakland's First Debtors' Assembly." See the Strike Debt Bay Area website at http://www.strikedebtbayarea.org (accessed January 2013) and the main Strike Debt site at http://strikedebt.org (accessed January 2013).

2. From the Strike Debt Bay Area website, http://www.strikedebtbayarea.org (accessed March 2013).

3. Case No. 1:08-cv-00062-JFM, Second Amended Complaint for Declaratory and Injunctive Relief and Damages, Mayor and City Council of Baltimore, City Hall, 100 N. Holliday St., Baltimore, MD 21202, Plaintiff, v. Wells Fargo Bank, N.A., 464 California Street, San Francisco, CA 94104, and Wells Fargo Financial Leasing, Inc., 207 9th Street, Des Moines, IA 50307, Defendants, 22–23. (The Jacobson and Paschal declarations referred to in this quote are attachments A

and B of this complaint. Additional in-text citations will refer to this document as *Baltimore v. Wells Fargo.*)

4. The second half of the book, to which I admittedly give less attention here, presents the narrative of debt in the period referenced in Graeber's subtitle, *The First 5,000 Years.* As Chris Hann (2012, 447–48) puts it, "Experts are likely to chafe" at the claim made there, that these five thousand years can be divided into four periods (each of the first three of more than twelve hundred years) in which parallel trends and processes occurred across the globe and in which grand cycles between the dominance of bullion or coin and the dominance of credit can be perceived and linked to military violence (in the case of hard currency) and to peace and stability (in the case of credit). I am not an expert in the history or anthropology of most of those five thousand years, so I will leave it to the experts to evaluate Graeber's evidence. The point of this narrative, as Luban (2012, 105) puts it, is to suggest, "insofar as we are shifting from a period of bullion to one of credit [since our departure from the gold standard in 1971], . . . the era of great state-based military empires—above all, the current American imperium—is coming to an end." He further notes that this should open the opportunity for a shift to "localized communities of trust and mutual aid, coupled perhaps with new global institutions to protect debtors" (105). This prophetic vision depends on the theory of debt laid out in the first half of Graeber's book.

5. Graeber explicitly promotes an anarchist perspective. See, for instance, his *Fragments of an Anarchist Anthropology* (2004), a pamphlet intended to call forth anarchist scholarship.

6. Graeber's time frame of five thousand years makes sense when one realizes that he is rejecting both Marx and, implicitly, Foucault. Like advocates of restorative justice such as Howard Zehr (1990, 333–35), who call for a shift from a regime of justice extracting payment of "debts to society" to one requiring compensation to community, Graeber is less interested in the emergence of disciplinary strategies than he is in the capture of social processes by state apparatuses; he notes in particular the "devastating" impact on "communal solidarity" of the capture of the management of debts by the courts.

7. While I use Toscano here because of his particular focus on abstraction, I do want to point out that he is by no means alone in reading Marx as an anti-empiricist. Rosemary Hennessy (2000, 95; 2003, 59–60) has been persistent in making this argument.

8. Graeber (2011, 267–68) mentions abstraction not only with reference to the physical extraction of human beings for enslavement but also with reference to the distortion of our values by exchange: "I've also argued that any system of exchange is always necessarily founded on something else, something that, in its social manifestation at least, is ultimately communism. With all those things that we treat as eternal, that we assume will always be there—our mother's love, true friendship, sociality, humanity, belonging, the existence of the cosmos—no calculation is necessary, or even ultimately possible; insofar as there is give and take, they follow completely different principles. What, then, happens to such

absolute and unlimited phenomena when one tries to imagine the world as a set of transactions—as exchange? Generally, one of two things. We either ignore or deify them. (Mothers, and caregiving women in general, are a classic case in point.) Or we do both. What we treat as eternal in our actual relations with one another vanishes and reappears as an abstraction, an absolute."

9. See also Toscano's (2008, 276) discussion of Finelli on this point. Marx is careful to distinguish this construction of the concrete in thought from the emergence of the concrete in reality, since the concrete in reality is always structurally, interdependently positioned in a web of relations, while in thought the determining relations are abstracted, in the sense of being separated/isolated from that web of relations. According to Marx (1973, 101): "The simplest economic category, say e.g. exchange value, presupposes population, moreover a population producing in specific relations. . . . It can never exist other than as an abstract, one-sided relation within an already given, concrete, living whole. As a category, by contrast, exchange value leads an antediluvian existence."

10. Davis's speech was transcribed by R. K. Chin and is available on YouTube; see "Angela Davis Address to the Movement" (2011), http://www.youtube.com/watch?v=HlvfPizooII. For Davis's question-and-answer session following the speech, see "General Assembly Q&A with Angela Davis" (2011), http://www.youtube.com/watch?v=cmxWyhIPzgM.

11. See Fukuyama's *Trust: The Social Virtues and the Creation of Prosperity* (1994). See also the interactive feature provided online by the Pew Research Center for the People & the Press (http://www.people-press.org), "Public Trust in Government: 1958–2013."

12. Throughout *A Culture of Credit* (2006), Olegario traces the development of credit reporting technologies in the nineteenth-century United States, about which I will have more to say in the next chapter.

13. These articles appeared in the print version of the *New York Times* on Sunday, November 4, 2007, in the Week in Review section, page D16.

14. Scholars have published numerous overviews of the development of critical accounting and debates within accounting history. My account here is drawn primarily from Fleischman and Radcliffe (2005) and Walker (2005), but see also Miller (1994), Jones and Dugdale (2001), Previts and Merino (1998), and Quattrone (2005).

2. Accounting for Justice

1. In addition to the two million people incarcerated, nearly five million are under the noncustodial supervision of the criminal justice system. This fact has received far less attention from scholars and activists—and will not receive adequate attention here—although I think that any adequate critique of the contemporary criminal justice apparatus does need to account for its vast reach beyond prison walls.

2. "The master's tools" is Audre Lorde's famous phrase, but my hesitation here

owes more to Lauren Berlant's (2007b) effort to turn our attention from "crisis" to "slow death."

3. Solinger is best known for the traveling exhibition and then book, *Wake Up Little Susie: Single Pregnancy and Race before Roe v. Wade* (2000).

4. Solinger, in exhibit brochure for *Interrupted Life: Incarcerated Mothers in the United States: A Traveling Public Art Installation,* by WAKEUP/Arts; see also Solinger (2007).

5. See Real Cost of Prisons Project, http://www.realcostofprisons.org/comics .html. It is interesting to note that this website has a ticker that tracks real-time incarceration statistics.

6. This is a story recounted by many scholars. See, for instance, Colvin (1997), Meranze (1996), Beaumont and Tocqueville (1964), and Davis (2003, esp. chap. 3).

7. Mann (2002) and Coleman (1974) both offer versions of this story.

8. Olegario (2006) explicitly addresses the role of "sex and race," noting, for instance, that women were thought to lack "energy," a key component of the character of the creditworthy. However, Olegario's evaluation of the impact of gender and race is limited by the fact that she is studying the credit reports themselves, which include those of only relatively few women and people of color who were operating as individual business proprietors; the reports do not reflect those foreclosed from credit and thus business by their status as wives or slaves (108–13).

9. Lauer is quoting Meagher (1876).

10. Hoskin and Macve defend their position in their essay "Knowing More as Knowing Less?" (2000).

11. The first words of this law state that its purpose is "to protect investors by improving the accuracy and reliability of corporate disclosures." The text of the law is available on the U.S. Government Printing Office website, http://www .gpo.gov.

12. On the other hand, in a more Foucauldian mode, it is crucial to remember the productivity of the criminal justice apparatus: a conviction is a life sentence (except where it is a death sentence), constituting and managing the subject of a life, if a life of limited agency and endless exploitability.

13. Derrida (1992) makes this clear at the end of the second part of the essay (see esp. 62), which is a reading of Walter Benjamin's "Critique of Violence" (1978).

14. Kay Pranis (2001, 6–8), restorative justice planner for the Minnesota Department of Corrections from 1994 to 2003 (according to her bio at http://www .livingjusticepress.org), explicitly promotes the power of storytelling as a tool for building relationships and thus community. Interestingly, storytelling is central not only to the process of restorative justice but also to the representation and promotion of restorative justice. Much of the restorative justice literature itself makes substantial use of stories to convey how the process works: Braithwaite's (2002) book is full of boxes containing narrative examples; Zehr's (1990) book opens with a number of stories of restorative justice in action; even the U.S. Department of Justice bulletin prepared by Bazemore and Umbreit (2001) provides a boxed sidebar story as an example of each type of restorative justice procedure.

15. It also includes an industry of English-language academic and nonacademic publications circulating across these various locations (which provides the text that I am reading; I have not conducted my own ethnographic research on restorative justice processes).

16. This stance is inspired in significant part by Andrea Smith's efforts (learning from Sarah Deer) to promote community accountability strategies while acknowledging an array of contradictions and resisting the widespread co-optation of restorative justice by state justice regimes fundamentally enabled, as she points out, by settler colonialism (see Smith 2010a).

17. Their willingness to mobilize idealized examples from such a diverse array of cultures, past and present, should give one pause. See, for instance, Braithwaite (2002) and Zehr (1990, esp. chap. 7).

3. Accounting for Time

1. Gordon is quoted in Rose (1999, 142n13). Rose is referencing Gordon (1991).

2. *New York Times* columnist Nicholas D. Kristof's piece "The Larger Shame" uses "wretchedness coming across our television screens from Louisiana" as a jumping-off point for drawing attention to persistent and worsening poverty in the United States. And yet the point of view of the column, which speaks of "our shock and guilt," opens it to Berlant's critique: "So the best monument to the catastrophe in New Orleans would be a serious national effort to address the poverty that afflicts the entire country. And in our shock and guilt, that may be politically feasible. Rich Lowry of *The National Review,* in defending Mr. [George W.] Bush, offered an excellent suggestion: 'a grand right–left bargain that includes greater attention to out-of-wedlock births from the Left in exchange for the Right's support for more urban spending.' That would be the best legacy possible for Katrina."

3. Armin Beverungen and Stephen Dunne (2007) provide a helpful survey and evaluation of the obsession with Bartleby.

4. The reading was reported on the website GalleyCat (see Yin 2011). Additional online commentators include Lauren Klein (2011), Michele Hardesty (2011), and Hannah Gersen (2011). And now Edelman (2013) has weighed in as well.

5. In addition, Williams turns to Geronimus to back up her argument, writing, "Geronimus . . . demonstrates quantitatively: (1) that women who are poor do better to have their babies young, before the dire effects of poverty take a toll on their health; (2) that young mothers have usually had sufficient child care experience with younger kin . . . ; (3) that when one of two sisters has a baby as a teenager she does no worse educationally or economically than her sister who does not; and (4) that infants born to teen mothers do better than other poor children, both at birth and by educational measures later on" (350). Geronimus's more recent work with J. Phillip Thompson reinforces and expands on these arguments with a larger research agenda regarding health over the life course for poor people of color. As an alternative to "the dominant cultural scenario for the life course [that] entrains the proper objects of attachment (first to parents and then to spouse and other peers) and identity development (always as an individual, first in the context of

a nuclear family of origin and later in the context of peers), and . . . outlines the cadence of life-course demands along the axes of dependence and responsibility" (Geronimus and Thompson 2004, 253), she develops the concept of *weathering*: "That is, people's health reflects the cumulative impact of their experiences from conception to their current age" (257). And Geronimus draws on the theory of "John Henryism" to suggest that weathering is exacerbated by greater efforts to succeed in the face of the greater challenges posed by a racist environment. Geronimus offers, in effect, scientific evidence for what Berlant calls *attrition,* the wearing away that is simultaneous with building a life. (Geronimus and Thompson's essay includes bibliographic information for much of Geronimus's earlier work.)

6. The naming of federal laws is one symptom of a neoliberal obsession with "responsibility" that has endured from Ronald Reagan to Barack Obama, including not only the Personal Responsibility and Work Opportunity Reconciliation Act of 1996 but also the 1982 Tax Equity and Fiscal Responsibility Act, the 1996 Illegal Immigration Reform and Immigrant Responsibility Act, and now the Credit Card Accountability Responsibility and Disclosure Act of 2009, among others.

7. For a feminist analysis of the Personal Responsibility and Work Opportunity Reconciliation Action of 1996, see Anna Marie Smith (2002).

8. Kate Bedford (2009) has argued that this approach, in which so-called entrepreneurial subjectivity is produced through manipulation of kinship and gender, is a global phenomenon promoted by the World Bank.

9. Many thanks to Joyce Serido for pointing out to me that the subject of hard work and planning that I was describing as entrepreneurial subjectivity did not sound anything like the kind of subjectivity required of business entrepreneurs, which is all about confident risk taking, not a slow and deliberate process of building toward a future.

10. In "Financial Advice for the 'Mass Affluent,'" Glenn Rifkin (2006) describes this group as "the 22 million American households with $100,000 to $1 million in assets, excluding real estate, that can be invested. . . . 'The mass affluent group is so critical to America,' Mr. Grooms said. 'It sounds as if they have a lot of money, but this is really middle-class Americans who have done some responsible saving over the past 30 years.'"

11. It is not entirely clear to me whether the wealthy are meant to read Sullivan's column or if this is rather an opportunity for voyeurism and fantasy. I suspect the latter.

12. David Leonhardt wrote about this in a 2006 *New York Times* article titled "Save Yourself": "When my wife and I talk about paying for our retirement, we assume that we will be pretty much on our own. We are both 33, and it's hard to have a lot of confidence that Social Security and traditional pensions will do for us what they did for our grandparents.

"So at a time when the national savings rate has fallen below zero—that is, Americans spent more than they earned last year for the first time since 1933—my family has gone the other way. Laura and I have become addicted to retirement savings even though we are decades from retirement. . . .

"I don't really think Social Security will be gone when I retire, and I expect to get some kind of small pension. But it seems foolish to ignore what's going on. President Bush has said that Social Security is 'headed toward bankruptcy.' United Airlines and Bethlehem Steel have reneged on some promises to their retirees. I.B.M., Verizon and General Motors have said that future retirees should expect smaller pensions. So my wife and I do not expect much.

"Apparently we are part of a small movement of new savers. Hidden by the statistics on average savings, a growing group of Americans in their 30's and 40's are acting like disciples of Ben Franklin. You can find this group in the Federal Reserve's latest study on family finances or just by talking to people around the country.

"Of course, the new generation of savers is not exactly a cross section of the population. We tend to make good salaries, be healthy—or at least well insured—and often have relatives who can help us out now and later. We're saving not only because we think we need to but also, simply, because we can."

Leonhardt's article goes on to explore the class divergence in retirement income expectations and savings more fully.

13. I am quoting from the inside cover of the brochure, published by the U.S. Department of Housing and Urban Development. The program described in the brochure was developed during the George W. Bush administration in 2002–3; the brochure calls the program "A Public/Private Partnership to Increase Minority Homeownership by 5.5 Million by the End of the Decade." My thanks to Shannon Randall for alerting me to this program and this document.

14. Smith borrows the term *ethopolitics* from Flint (2003).

15. Smith (2008, 532) points out that "this 'housing-wealth effect'—drawing on housing equity to raise consumption above the levels driven by earned incomes alone—may be what bailed out the Anglo-American economies, and particularly that of the UK, through recent world recession." The same argument has been made in some mainstream news venues as well. The central role of consumption in sustaining the economy (which certainly got a boost when George W. Bush told Americans to go shopping after 9/11) has produced an explicit sense of contradiction in the current economic crisis in which, again, while some people feel that the lesson to be learned is to save more and spend less, others want to do their part to rescue the larger economy by shopping.

16. The texts of this act and of other federal laws mentioned here are available online from numerous sources, including the U.S. Government Printing Office website, http://www.gpo.gov.

17. Ho (2009) cites Andreas Langenohl's (2008) study of financial professionals, which consisted of thirty guided interviews conducted in Frankfurt in 2003–4, in order to suggest that despite valorizing instant transformation in conjunction with the market, bankers themselves see short-term accounting as problematic: "Whereas the short-term logic is regularly held responsible for 'irrational' developments on the markets (for instance, herd behavior or bubbles) and is put into relation with existential emotions such as greed and fear, the long-term logic is attributed a normative, law-like value" (Langenohl 2008, 18).

18. The "long-term" perspective that is to be imposed on the bankers is clearly different from the "long run" in which the market is always right, since that long run is now, while the long term might be two years or five years from now.

19. Stories featuring Brent White debating the morality of "walking away" from a mortgage appeared in the *Wall Street Journal, Chicago Tribune, Los Angeles Times, Washington Post,* and *New York Times,* as well as on *Good Morning America* and programs on CNN and MSNBC, among others.

20. See the 2007 special issue of *GLQ* on temporality (vol. 13, nos. 2–3).

21. See Karyn Ball's "Death-Driven Futures, or You Can't Spell *Deconstruction* without Enron" (2007) for an analysis of Enron's financial/accounting strategies through the Derridean notion of *differance* as well as a variety of *death drives.* Most pertinent with regard to "meaningless circulation," according to Ball, might have been Enron's "'wash and round-trip trades' in which there was no genuine counterparty. In effect, Enron 'appears to have essentially been trading with itself' to inflate its revenues and asset values without generating actual cash" (20).

22. The drama over the accounting rules takes place in the staid form of statements called Financial Accounting Standards Board Staff Positions, in this case, FASB Staff Position FAS 157-4, "Determining Fair Value When the Volume and Level of Activity for the Asset or Liability Have Significantly Decreased and Identifying Transactions That Are Not Orderly" (available at http://www.fasb.org).

23. In "Class-Monopoly Rent, Finance Capital and the Urban Revolution," David Harvey (1974, 242) argues that "rents," which is to say profits in a real estate context, are enabled by social as well as economic divisions that trap the poor in particular urban neighborhoods, while upper-income groups are not trapped by their limited income but rather by "their sense of social status and prestige." Such status and prestige allows them to be exploited by speculator developers due to their "need" to buy in the "right" neighborhoods.

4. Accounting for Gender

1. The focus groups were undertaken in preparation for Wave 2 of a longitudinal survey-based study of financial attitudes and behaviors initiated by colleagues in the School of Family and Consumer Sciences. To my knowledge there has been no published analysis of the focus groups, and this chapter certainly does not constitute such an analysis. The larger research project—Arizona Pathways to Life Success for University Students (APLUS)—has been led by Soyeon Shim (former principal investigator) and Joyce Serido (formerly co–principal investigator and project manager, now principal investigator). Serido designed (with some input from me), organized, and cofacilitated the focus groups. Funding for the APLUS project has been provided by the National Endowment for Financial Education (NEFE) and more recently by Citi Foundation. An overview of the project and the results of the Wave 1 survey are described in Shim et al. (2010). The results

of Wave 1.5, which surveyed a subset of the study participants with the intention of understanding the impact of the recession of 2007–9, are reported in Shim and Serido (2010a, 2010b). Wave 2 results are reported in Shim and Serido (2011). See also Serido et al. (2010).

2. Scholars working in a more Marxist framework have also noted a revived reliance on family and community as sites of production in the context of post-Fordism and flexible accumulation (Harvey 1990; Joseph 2002).

3. Leyshon, Thrift, and Pratt (1998) note the conjuncture of the growth in personal finance products with the dismantling of the welfare state.

4. Duggan's analysis is similar to that of Soss, Fording, and Schram (2011, 28), who describe a "conservative resurgence" brought about by "well-organized political actors."

5. Clark, Thrift, and Tickell (2004) describe the increasingly important role played by the mass media in financial markets and the growing phenomenon of finance as popular entertainment.

6. I long ago refused to choose between discourse and ideology, between Foucault and Marx. As the through line of my work is the effort to understand the ways that social formations are constituted and transformed by capitalism as it transforms and reinvents itself, I am no doubt more fundamentally Marxist in my orientation. But I find "discourse" and "subjection" to be indispensable concepts for understanding and naming technologies by which social formations emerge as lived realities and change. And for me, the two frameworks come together as demonstrated by numerous feminists (Butler, Berlant, Chow) who, in different ways, engage with and develop theories of subjective attachments to capitalism overdetermined by Foucauldian subjection and the psychoanalytic Marxisms of Althusser and Žižek (see my discussion of these theorists in chapter 3).

7. See "Creditreport.com Stan 'Lazy,'" http://www.youtube.com/watch?v=7GEL7rapVgM (accessed March 2013).

8. See "New CreditReport.com Television Ad," http://www.youtube.com/watch?v=u60J-zSuL2c (accessed March 2013).

9. While Oscar Lewis actually developed the "culture of poverty" concept, it was popularized and racialized for a U.S. audience by the Moynihan Report (Goode 2002, 70). The importance of this document in political discourse in the United States is indicated by Wahneema Lubiano's (1992) persuasive claim that it played a key role in shaping the controversial confirmation hearings surrounding Clarence Thomas's 1991 appointment to the U.S. Supreme Court.

10. Many thanks to Shannon Randall, a Ph.D. student in gender and women's studies at the University of Arizona, who introduced me to the Luken and Vaughan article and who read and discussed it and others on this topic with me.

11. This finding is discussed in Thorne (2001, 170n5).

12. In the United States, the 1996 Personal Responsibility and Work Opportunity Reconciliation Act, which President Bill Clinton claimed "end[ed] welfare as we know it" (quoted in Vobejda 1996), promoted and coerced "personal responsibility." It linked intervention in (and regulation of) kinship and gender relations—

requiring women to identify the biological fathers of their children to qualify for benefits, limiting the number of children eligible for benefits, and funding various programs promoting marriage—to the coercive promotion (by time and other limits on the provision of income support) of "personal responsibility" through work (Smith 2002; Goode 2002; Soss et al. 2011). That is, although the policy would seem to promote traditional gendered divisions of financial labor, in which the biological fathers of children provide financial resources for the mothers to spend in caring for their families, in fact the law forced mothers into the low-wage workforce. We see here the articulation of neoliberal and neoconservative approaches that Larner (2000) identifies in the New Zealand context, in which personal responsibility and entrepreneurialism are to be imposed (at least on some populations) through close governmental monitoring and manipulation of familial relations. Others have called this "neoliberal paternalism" (Soss et al. 2011). One might also read it as a situation in which social relations serve as a supplement to economic processes (Joseph 2002).

13. This statement struck me as plagiarized from Juan Williams (2006), but it may just represent a kind of shared common sense.

14. Discussion of this article on the accompanying *Times* blog included comments highly critical of Lieber's "characterization of women as financially helpless."

15. David Koeppel (2008) also discussed this CFA report on MSN Money in an article titled "Single Women Slammed by Housing Mess." One of the experts quoted in the article is Anita F. Hill, once famous for her role in the confirmation hearings for U.S. Supreme Court Justice Clarence Thomas: "'Even women with similar incomes as men were more likely to get subprime loans,' says Anita Hill, a professor of law, social policy and women's studies at Brandeis University in Waltham, Mass. '... and African-American women were even more likely. Women were advised they weren't qualified for prime loans, and in many cases that was erroneous information.'"

16. I say "overindebtedness" because, as Donncha Marron (2010) has argued, indebtedness per se has not been framed as pathological. In fact, as many scholars have pointed out, in a period of flat or declining wages for working people, demand and thus profit have been supported by greatly expanded access to credit. So use of credit in itself could hardly be cast as always already a disease.

17. Many thanks to Laura Gronewold for introducing me to chick lit in general and the *Shopaholic* series in particular. See Gronewold (2012).

18. Initially the website offered various lessons and worksheets to help viewers personally undertake the "debt diet"; now the site actually provides the content of the series of shows. Except where noted, quotes presented below are drawn from the website, at http://www.oprah.com/money.

19. For example, "the Widlunds' budget includes many unessential expenses—'fat' that can be trimmed during their debt diet. Marnie estimates that the family spends about $150 a week on take-out and another $200 each weekend on entertainment. Marnie's obsession with crafts is also digging them deeper into debt. Marnie admits she buys on impulse." And, of course, Marnie overindulges their teenage daughters: "'My love for them probably clouds my judgment,' Marnie

says." These folks need more than a financial adviser, they need psychological help; Oprah diagnoses Marnie as "living her life unconsciously." Oprah brings in psychotherapist Dr. Robin Smith, whose diagnosis is that "Mark is giving up his power—and Marnie is causing him to shut down." According to the website, "Dr. Robin says Mark needs to take the power back."

20. Nelson (2012, 22) discusses the ways that classical economic theorists such as John Stuart Mill built masculine-associated traits of autonomy, self-interestedness, and rationality (defined as calculation) into the conceptualization of "economic man" and the domain and methodology of economics as a "scientific" field of study (see also Nelson 1996). The deployment of a particular gendered conceptualization of disengaged, asocial calculative rationality to distinguish not only appropriate economic actors but also, more broadly, those eligible for participation in public life, for citizenship and self-determination, was, of course, pervasive across the work of the key philosophers of liberalism.

21. His citation is to "Women More Cautious about Running Up Debt (Experian Credit Monitoring Service Study)," *ERT Weekly,* September 15, 2005. I have not been able to locate the actual study by Experian, or this article, or the Dreyfus survey.

22. For instance, the 2006 Prudential Financial study mentioned in the *Times* article on the Baltimore subprime mortgage crisis discussed above is actually one in an ongoing series. The most recent is *Financial Experience and Behaviors among Women* (2012). According to the Prudential website, this 2012–13 biennial study reveals that "women are more in control of their finances then ever," but "they are facing significant challenges with financial decision making."

23. Nelson (2012, 16) recommends using "'Cohen's *d*' . . . (as one measure of) 'effect size.'"

24. It is worth noting, however, that this course includes a section called "Causation and Lurking Variables (1 of 5)" that offers a strong warning: "Association does not imply causation" (Carnegie Mellon University 2012). (Note: Each page of this course states, "This work is licensed under a Creative Commons Attribution-NonCommercial-ShareAlike 3.0 Unported License," and includes a link to the license, which states, "You are free to: Share—copy and redistribute the material in any medium or format.")

25. Melissa Fisher describes this phenomenon in *Wall Street Women* (2012). See also Hall (2011, 408).

26. Barber and Odean's study, despite the article's title, ostensibly uses gender only as a *proxy* for confidence, depending on prior findings of an association between gender and confidence (no doubt overstated and essentialized in precisely the way Nelson critiques) in order to show that "overconfidence" leads to overactive trading and unnecessary financial losses. While Barber and Odean's findings have been widely represented as showing the relationship between gender and confidence, that is their starting assumption; what they actually examine are relative levels of *activity*.

27. Many thanks to Bret Benjamin for pointing this out.

5. Accounting for Interdisciplinarity

1. The university also has a Faculty Senate with more traditional *academic* governance responsibilities.

2. See, for instance, Martin's numerous essays and his recent book on the academy (Martin 2011b). See also Bousquet (2008), Newfield (2008), Arsenjuk and Koerner (2009), and, of course, Slaughter and Leslie (1997) and Slaughter and Rhoades (2004).

3. The trajectory of university funding has been detailed by a number of scholars. Poovey provides a good quick summary in "The Twenty-First-Century University and the Market" (2001, esp. 3–5). See also Wellman, Desrochers, and Lenihan (2008, esp. 19–22).

4. University of Arizona, BIO5 Institute, http://bio5.arizona.edu (accessed January 2009).

5. Ibid.

6. University of Arizona, Graduate Interdisciplinary Program in Arid Lands Resource Sciences, "About ALRS," http://alrs.arisona.edu/about-alrs (accessed December 2008).

7. So for instance, from the website for the UA Department of Biochemistry and Molecular Biophysics (http://www.biochem.arizona.edu): "Biochemistry is, by definition, the study of the molecular basis of life processes. . . . [Students of today must be well prepared in . . . chemistry, physics, mathematics and biology.] With recent developments in microanalytical chemical techniques, including DNA chip technology and related methods, mass spectrometry of biological molecules, and other nanoscale bioanalytical methods, coupled with the developing genome databases and computational methods to interrogate the databases, the future promises to be even more exciting than the past." And from the Cognitive Science Program (http://cogsci.web.arizona.edu): "Cognitive Science is a model inter-disciplinary program in that it is the interdisciplinary study of the mind, encompassing the study of intelligent behavior as well as the brain mechanisms and computations underlying that behavior. The field is at the intersection of several other disciplines, including philosophy (knowledge representation, logic), psychology (basic human cognition, perception and performance), computer science (computational theory, artificial intelligence and robotics), linguistics (theories of language structure) and cognitive neuroscience (brain mechanisms for intelligent behavior). Typical research areas of cognitive science include judgment and decision making, language comprehension and production, language acquisition, visual recognition of objects and events, attention, learning and memory, goal directed movement in complex environments and consciousness."

8. This tension seems to have been one of the prime motivations for the volume *Interdisciplinarity and Social Justice: Revisioning Academic Accountability* (Parker, Samantrai, and Romero 2010), in which a previous version of this essay was published. In the book proposal that the editors shared when inviting me to contribute, they wrote that while interdisciplinary programs (explicitly, gender

and ethnic studies with the more recent additions of lesbian/gay/queer, environmental, cultural, postcolonial, and critical legal studies) were originally *accountable* to social justice movements and to "disenfranchised people," "perhaps they can no longer be said to be tethered to their political origins."

9. In "Academic Feminism against Itself," Wiegman (2002b) cites Gubar's "What Ails Feminist Criticism" (1998), Messer-Davidow's *Disciplining Feminism: From Social Activism to Academic Discourse* (2002), the special issue of *differences* titled "Women's Studies on the Edge" edited by Joan Wallach Scott (1997), and a number of the individual essays in that volume.

10. It strikes me that any binary opposition between instrumental and noninstrumental is unworkable. The deconstructive question: What is at stake in the distinction, in the categorization of some ends as the ones that "instrumental" knowledge production would promote?

11. I am deeply grateful to Elizabeth Lapovsky Kennedy and Adam Geary for suggesting that I clarify this point and to Kennedy for articulating this vision of *the political*.

12. As described on the website of the U.S. Department of Education's National Center for Education Statistics (http://nces.ed.gov; accessed December 2008), on the page listing "surveys and programs": "The Integrated Postsecondary Education Data System (IPEDS), established as the core postsecondary education data collection program for NCES, is a system of surveys designed to collect data from all primary providers of postsecondary education. IPEDS is a single, comprehensive system designed to encompass all institutions and educational organizations whose primary purpose is to provide postsecondary education. The IPEDS system is built around a series of interrelated surveys to collect institution-level data in such areas as enrollments, program completions, faculty, staff, finances, and academic libraries."

13. As described on the website of the UA Office of Institutional Research and Planning Support (http://oirps.arizona.edu; accessed December 2008): "The Common Data Set provides information on the following topics:

A. General Information about the University of Arizona
B. Enrollment and Persistence
C. First-Time, First-Year (Freshman) Admission
D. Transfer Admission
E. Academic Offerings and Policies
F. Student Life
G. Annual Expenses—tuition, fees, room and board
H. Financial Aid
I. Instructional Faculty and Class Size, Student to Faculty ratio
J. Undergraduate Degrees Conferred—by area of study."

14. The NRC report was delayed by many years and by a fair bit of wrangling and struggle over the metrics and the actual details of the data analysis. The fol-

lowing are the NRC metrics to which UA graduate programs were initially asked to respond:

Percent of faculty that is female
Percent minority faculty
Average number of annual Ph.D. graduates 2001–2006
Median time to degree for FT and PT Ph.D. students
Percent female Ph.D. students in 2005
Percent of minority Ph.D. students in 2005
6-year completion rate for male students (8-year for Humanities)
6-year completion rate for female students (8-year for Humanities)
Percent of students with individual work space
Percent of FT first-year students with full support
Percent of first-year students with external fellowship
Percent of first-year students with external traineeship
Citations for faculty publications
Faculty awards and honors
Placement of graduate students? Of Ph.D.s?
Percent of faculty who are principal investigators on grants
Faculty size

15. The Spellings "threat" was made fairly explicit in the so-called Spellings Commission Report, the official title of which is *A Test of Leadership: Charting the Future of U.S. Higher Education* (U.S. Department of Education 2006).

16. According to the Voluntary System of Accountability website (http://www .voluntarysystem.org; accessed April 2013): "The VSA is a voluntary initiative for 4-year public colleges and universities. Developed through a partnership between the American Association of State Colleges and Universities (AASCU) and the National Association of State Universities and Land-Grant Colleges (NASULGC), the VSA is designed to help institutions meet the following objectives: demonstrate accountability and stewardship to public; measure educational outcomes to identify effective educational practices; assemble information that is accessible, understandable, and comparable."

17. The political battles among the Department of Education (and its secretary, Margaret Spellings, who was also responsible for "No Child Left Behind"), the accrediting agencies, the colleges and universities, and Congress over the question of learning assessment (which is really a question of who gets to control assessment) were covered extensively in *Inside Higher Ed* and the *Chronicle of Higher Education* during my tenure as SPBAC chair.

18. I pushed for including a "publications and citations" measure, and it was there for a while. I am not sure when or why it vanished, but its disappearance affirms that what is relevant about research is that it is in itself and promotes (through tech transfer) economic activity, not that it produces new knowledge.

19. A faculty committee on which I participated developed a "cost-efficiency

ratio" that calculated the relation of state dollars invested to research expenditures and student credit hours (each as a portion of the university total).

20. Although "responsibility-based budgeting," or "responsibility-centered management," as we call it at UA, is of great relevance to the question of accounting and accountability, I have largely bracketed it here as it would quickly overtake the entire chapter. There is a growing literature on the topic; for brief introductions, see Hearn et al. (2006) and Fuller, Morton, and Korschgen (2005). Newfield (2008) offers a critique in his chapter titled "The Costs of Accounting."

21. In fact, in the world of student outcomes assessment, portfolios of student work including self-reflexive essays are something of a gold standard.

22. Liz Kennedy has quite correctly pointed out that for women's studies faculty, leaving the battles for resources to our department heads is a privilege of the second and third generation that was not available to the founders. The founding of women's studies required all hands on deck. Kennedy reads my argument here as suggesting that this may be another "all hands on deck" moment. Martin discusses the sense of lost autonomy (that we no longer have the "professional" latitude we once had) in the first chapter of *Under New Management* (2011).

23. Marx argues that commodities are composed of use value and value—*use value* being the concrete object with particular qualities for which uses have been developed in a given historical context and *value* being the quantity of abstract socially necessary labor that produced the object. For capital (a form of value) to circulate, it must be embodied in particular useful products (though in the twenty-first century those products may be far less "concrete" or object-like than Marx imagined).

24. If Martin is a bit utopian about the nature of the work in existing "critical interdisciplinary" spaces, as a goal, the establishment of creative and even unlikely interconnections is just right. Such connections have been for me one of the rewards of administrative work, which takes its participants into relationships far beyond what then comes to seem a very limited "interdisciplinary" field.

25. This phrase appears on the first page of SB 1070, 49th Leg., 2d Sess., Arizona Session Laws Ch. 113, in Section 1: Intent. The text of the bill is available on the Arizona State Legislature's website, http://www.azleg.gov.

26. The best evidence of a direct impact of the recent policy actions of the state emerged in the context of UA's recent national search for a new provost. What appear to have been sincere and relatively sophisticated efforts to create a "diverse" pool of viable candidates were frustrated by the reported unwillingness of those candidates to try to work in what they perceived as an unwelcoming political environment or to expose their families to Arizona schools and communities. Is this an anecdote or a case study?

BIBLIOGRAPHY

ADC Post. 2004. "Setting the Course to Flagship Status." Special edition. November.

Aho, James Alfred. 1985. "Rhetoric and the Invention of Double Entry Book-keeping." *Rhetorica* 3 (1): 21–43.

———. 2005. *Confession and Bookkeeping: The Religious, Moral, and Rhetorical Roots of Modern Accounting.* Albany: State University of New York Press.

Ahrens, Lois. 2008. *The Real Cost of Prisons Comix.* Oakland, Calif.: PM Press.

Alder, Christine. 2000. "Young Women Offenders and the Challenge for Restorative Justice." In *Restorative Justice: Philosophy to Practice,* edited by Heather Strang and John Braithwaite. Burlington, Vt.: Ashgate.

Althusser, Louis. 1971. "Ideology and Ideological State Apparatuses." In *Lenin and Philosophy, and Other Essays.* Translated by Ben Brewster. New York: Monthly Review Press.

Anderson, Benedict. 1983. *Imagined Communities: Reflections on the Origin and Spread of Nationalism.* London: Verso.

Anthes, William L., and Bruce W. Most. 2000. "Frozen in the Headlights: The Dynamics of Women and Money." *Journal of Financial Planning* 13 (9): 130–42.

Appelbaum, Binyamin. 2012. "Regulator Rebuffs Obama on Plan to Ease Housing Debt." *New York Times,* July 31. http://www.nytimes.com.

Arsenjuk, Luka, and Michelle Koerner, eds. 2009. "Study, Students, Universities." Special issue. *Polygraph,* no. 21.

Associated Press. 2010. "Greenspan: Modest Economic Recovery in a 'Pause.'" *Washington Times,* August 1. http://www.washingtontimes.com.

Bajaj, Vikas. 2007. "Bankers' Lesson from Mortgage Mess: Sell, Don't Hold." *New York Times,* November 5. http://www.nytimes.com.

Bajaj, Vikas, and Ford Fessenden. 2007. "What's behind the Race Gap?" *New York Times,* November 4. http://www.nytimes.com.

Ball, Karyn. 2007. "Death-Driven Futures, or You Can't Spell *Deconstruction* without Enron." *Cultural Critique* 65: 6–42.

Barber, Brad M., and Terrance Odean. 2001. "Boys Will Be Boys: Gender,

Overconfidence, and Common Stock Investment." *Quarterly Journal of Economics* 116 (1): 261–92.

Barnett, Clive, Nick Clarke, Paul Cloke, and Alice Malpass. 2008. "The Elusive Subjects of Neo-liberalism." *Cultural Studies* 22 (5): 624–53.

Baudrillard, Jean. 1975. *The Mirror of Production*. St. Louis, Mo.: Telos Press.

Bazemore, Gordon, and Mark Umbreit. 2001. *A Comparison of Four Restorative Conferencing Models*. Juvenile Justice Bulletin, NCJ 184738, February. Washington, D.C.: U.S. Department of Justice, Office of Juvenile Justice and Delinquency Prevention.

Beaumont, Gustave de, and Alexis de Tocqueville. 1964. *On the Penitentiary System in the United States and Its Application in France*. Carbondale: Southern Illinois University Press.

Beccaria, Cesare. 1963. *On Crimes and Punishments*. Translated by Henry Paolucci. Indianapolis: Bobbs-Merrill.

Beck, Allen J., and Lawrence A. Greenfeld. 1995. *Violent Offenders in State Prison: Sentences and Time Served*. Bureau of Justice Statistics Selected Findings, NCJ-154632, July. Washington, D.C.: U.S. Department of Justice, Office of Justice Programs.

Bedford, Kate. 2009. *Developing Partnerships: Gender, Sexuality, and the Reformed World Bank*. Minneapolis: University of Minnesota Press.

Beirne, Piers, ed. 1994. *The Origins and Growth of Criminology: Essays on Intellectual History, 1760–1945*. Aldershot, England: Dartmouth.

Benjamin, Walter. 1978. "Critique of Violence" (1955). In *Reflections: Essays, Aphorisms, Autobiographical Writings*. Edited by Peter Demetz, translated by Edmund Jephcott. New York: Harcourt Brace Jovanovich.

Berardi, Franco "Bifo." 2009. *The Soul at Work: From Alienation to Autonomy*. Los Angeles: Semiotext(e).

Bergeron, Suzanne. 2003. "Challenging the World Bank's Narrative of Inclusion." In *World Bank Literature*, edited by Amitava Kumar. Minneapolis: University of Minnesota Press.

Berlant, Lauren. 1991. "National Brands/National Body: Imitation of Life." In *Comparative American Identities: Race, Sex, and Nationality in the Modern Text*, edited by Hortense J. Spillers. New York: Routledge.

———. 1997. *The Queen of America Goes to Washington City: Essays on Sex and Citizenship*. Durham, N.C.: Duke University Press.

———. 2007a. "Cruel Optimism: On Marx, Loss and the Senses." *New Formations* 63 (1): 33–51.

———. 2007b. "Slow Death (Sovereignty, Obesity, Lateral Agency)." *Critical Inquiry* 33 (4): 754–80.

———. 2011. *Cruel Optimism*. Durham, N.C.: Duke University Press.

Beverungen, Armin, and Stephen Dunne. 2007. "'I'd Prefer Not To': Bartleby and the Excesses of Interpretation." *Culture and Organization* 13 (2): 171–83.

Bitti, Mary Teresa. 2011. "Are Women More Rational Investors?" *Calgary Herald*, October 5. http://www2.canada.com/calgaryherald.

Bousquet, Marc. 2008. *How the University Works: Higher Education and the Low-Wage Nation.* New York: New York University Press.

Braithwaite, John. 2002. *Restorative Justice and Responsive Regulation.* Oxford: Oxford University Press.

Brown, Paul B. 2006. "How to Invest, Times Three." *New York Times,* January 8. http://www.nytimes.com.

Brown, Wendy. 1995. "Rights and Losses." In *States of Injury: Power and Freedom in Late Modernity.* Princeton, N.J.: Princeton University Press.

———. 2001. *Politics out of History.* Princeton, N.J.: Princeton University Press.

———. 2003. "Neo-liberalism and the End of Liberal Democracy." *Theory & Event* 7 (1). http://muse.jhu.edu.

Browning, Lynnley. 2007. "The Subprime Loan Machine; Automated Underwriting Software Helped Fuel a Mortgage Boom." *New York Times,* March 23. http://www.nytimes.com.

Bryan, Dick, Randy Martin, and Mike Rafferty. 2009. "Financialization and Marx: Giving Labor and Capital a Financial Makeover." *Review of Radical Political Economics* 41 (4): 458–72.

Burchell, Graham, Colin Gordon, and Peter Miller, eds. 1991. *The Foucault Effect: Studies in Governmentality.* Chicago: University of Chicago Press.

Butler, Judith. 1993. *Bodies That Matter: On the Discursive Limits of "Sex."* New York: Routledge.

Cabrera, Nolan L., Jeffrey F. Milem, and Ron W. Marx. 2012. "An Empirical Analysis of the Effects of Mexican American Studies Participation on Student Achievement within Tucson Unified School District." Report to Special Master Dr. Willis D. Hawley on the Tucson Unified School District Desegregation Case, Tucson, Ariz.

California Department of Corrections and Rehabilitation. 2011. *CDCR Calculation Methodology.* Sacramento: California Department of Corrections and Rehabilitation. http://www.cdcr.ca.gov.

Carnegie Mellon University, Open Learning Initiative. 2012. "Probability & Statistics." http://oli.cmu.edu.

Chow, Rey. 2002. *The Protestant Ethic and the Spirit of Capitalism.* New York: Columbia University Press.

Cillario, L. 1996. *L'economia degli spettri: Forme del capitalismo contemporaneo.* Rome: Manifestolibri.

Clark, Gordon, Nigel Thrift, and Adam Tickell. 2004. "Performing Finance: The Industry, the Media and Its Image." *Review of International Political Economy* 11 (2): 289–310.

Clarke, James W. 1998. *The Lineaments of Wrath: Race, Violent Crime, and American Culture.* New Brunswick, N.J.: Transaction.

Clarke, John. 2004. "Dissolving the Public Realm? The Logics and Limits of Neo-liberalism." *Journal of Social Policy* 33 (1): 27–48.

———. 2007. "Citizen-Consumers and Public Service Reform: At the Limits of Neo-liberalism?" *Policy Futures in Education* 5 (2): 239–48.

Coates, J. M., and J. Herbert. 2008. "Endogenous Steroids and Financial Risk
    Taking on a London Trading Floor." *Proceedings of the National Academy
    of Sciences of the United States of America* 105 (16): 6167–72.

Coates, John. 2012. "The Biology of Bubble and Crash." *New York Times,* June 9.
    http://www.nytimes.com.

Cohen, Patricia Cline. 1982. *A Calculating People: The Spread of Numeracy in
    Early America.* Chicago: University of Chicago Press.

Coleman, Peter J. 1974. *Debtors and Creditors in America: Insolvency, Imprison-
    ment for Debt, and Bankruptcy, 1607–1900.* Madison: State Historical Society
    of Wisconsin.

Colvin, Mark. 1997. *Penitentiaries, Reformatories, and Chain Gangs: Social
    Theory and the History of Punishment in Nineteenth-Century America.*
    New York: St. Martin's Press.

Cooper, Christine, Phil Taylor, Newman Smith, and Lesley Catchpowle. 2005. "A
    Discussion of the Political Potential of Social Accounting." *Critical Perspectives
    on Accounting* 16: 951–74.

Cvetkovich, Ann. 1992. "Marx's *Capital* and the Mystery of the Commodity."
    In *Mixed Feelings: Feminism, Mass Culture, and Victorian Sensationalism.*
    New Brunswick, N.J.: Rutgers University Press.

———. 2012. *Depression: A Public Feeling.* Durham, N.C.: Duke University Press.

Daniels, Christine. 1995. "'Without Any Limitation of Time': Debt Servitude in
    Colonial America." *Labor History* 36 (2): 232–50.

Dash, Eric. 2006. "Looking Out for Yourself: Some Tips." *New York Times,*
    April 11. http://www.nytimes.com.

Davis, Angela Y. 1998. "Race and Criminalization: Black Americans and the
    Punishment Industry" (1997). In *The Angela Y. Davis Reader,* edited by Joy
    James. London: Blackwell.

———. 2003. *Are Prisons Obsolete?* New York: Seven Stories Press.

Dean, Mitchell. 1997. "Sociology after Society." In *Sociology after Postmodernism,*
    edited by David Owen. London: Sage.

De Angelis, Massimo, and David Harvie. 2009. "'Cognitive Capitalism' and the
    Rat-Race: How Capital Measures Immaterial Labour in British Universities."
    Historical Materialism 17 (3): 3–30.

de Goede, Marieke. 2005. *Virtue, Fortune, and Faith: A Genealogy of Finance.*
    Minneapolis: University of Minnesota Press.

———. 2011. "How to Fight a Derivative." *Environment and Planning D: Society
    and Space.* http://societyandspace.com.

Deleuze, Gilles. 1995. *Negotiations, 1972–1990.* New York: Columbia University
    Press.

Delgado, Richard. 2000. "Goodbye to Hammurabi: Analyzing the Atavistic
    Appeal of Restorative Justice." *Stanford Law Review* 52: 751–75.

Derrida, Jacques. 1992. "Force of Law: The 'Mystical Foundation of Authority.'"
    In *Deconstruction and the Possibility of Justice,* edited by Drucilla Cornell,
    Michel Rosenfeld, and David Gray Carlson. New York: Routledge.

Deutsch, Tracey. 2010. *Building a Housewife's Paradise: Gender, Politics, and American Grocery Stores in the Twentieth Century*. Chapel Hill: University of North Carolina Press.

DiCosmo, LouAnn. 2008. "Warren Buffett Invests like a Girl." Motley Fool, March 20. http://www.fool.com.

Dowling, Emma, Rodrigo Nunes, and Ben Trott, eds. 2007. "Immaterial and Affective Labour: Explored." Special issue. *ephemera: theory & politics in organization* 7 (1).

Dudley, Kathryn. 2000. *Debt and Dispossession: Farm Loss in America's Heartland*. Chicago: University of Chicago Press.

Duggan, Lisa. 2003. *The Twilight of Equality? Neoliberalism, Cultural Politics, and the Attack on Democracy*. Boston: Beacon Press.

Dunleavey, M. P. 2005. "Basic Instincts: Debunking the Myths of Budgeting." *New York Times*, October 22. http://www.nytimes.com.

———. 2006. "The Inflation of Our Expectations." *New York Times*, January 14. http://www.nytimes.com.

Dymski, Gary A. 2009. "Racial Exclusion and the Political Economy of the Subprime Crisis." *Historical Materialism* 17 (2): 149–79.

Ebert, Teresa L. 2009. *The Task of Cultural Critique*. Urbana: University of Illinois Press.

Eckholm, Erik. 2006. "Plight Deepens for Black Men, Studies Warn." *New York Times*, March 20. http://www.nytimes.com.

Edelman, Lee. 2004. *No Future: Queer Theory and the Death Drive*. Durham, N.C.: Duke University Press.

———. 2013. "Occupy Wall Street: 'Bartleby' against the Humanities." *History of the Present* 3 (1): 99–118.

Ehrenberg, Alain. 2010. *The Weariness of the Self: Diagnosing the History of Depression in the Contemporary Age*. Montreal: McGill-Queen's University Press.

Ehrenreich, Barbara. 2007. "Smashing Capitalism." *The Nation*, August 20. http://www.thenation.com.

Ezzamel, Mahmood, and Keith Robson. 1995. "Accounting in Time: Organization Time-Reckoning and Accounting Practice." *Critical Perspectives on Accounting* 6: 149–70.

Fessenden, Ford. 2007. "College Towns Escape the Pain." *New York Times*, November 4. http://www.nytimes.com.

Fine, Michelle, María Elena Torre, Kathy Boudin, Iris Bowen, Judith Clark, Donna Hylton, Migdalia "Missy" Martinez, Rosemarie A. Roberts, Pamela Smart, and Debora Upegui. 2003. "Participatory Action Research: Within and Beyond Bars." In *Qualitative Research in Psychology: Expanding Perspectives in Methodology and Design*, edited by Paul M. Camic, Jean E. Rhodes, and Lucy Yardley. Washington, D.C.: American Psychological Association.

Finelli, R. 1987. *Astrazione e dialettica dal romanticismo al capitalismo (saggio su Marx)*. Rome: Bulzoni Editore.

Fishbein, Allen J., and Patrick Woodall. 2006. *Women Are Prime Targets for Subprime Lending: Women Are Disproportionately Represented in High-Cost Mortgage Market.* Washington, D.C.: Consumer Federation of America.

Fisher, Melissa S. 2012. *Wall Street Women.* Durham, N.C.: Duke University Press.

Fisher, Thomas A. 2009. "Does Testosterone Explain Investment Behavior in Men and Women?" *Fisher Financial Strategies, FFS Blog,* August 25. http://ffscambridge.com.

Fleischman, Richard K., David Oldroyd, and Thomas N. Tyson. 2011. "The Efficacy/Inefficacy of Accounting in Controlling Labour during the Transition from Slavery in the United States and British West Indies." *Accounting, Auditing & Accountability Journal* 24 (6): 751–80.

Fleischman, Richard K., and Vaughan S. Radcliffe. 2005. "The Roaring Nineties: Accounting History Comes of Age." *Accounting Historians Journal* 32 (1): 61–109.

Flint, John. 2003. "Housing and Ethopolitics: Constructing Identities of Active Consumption and Responsible Community." *Economy and Society* 32 (3): 611–29.

Floyd, Kevin. 2009. *The Reification of Desire: Toward a Queer Marxism.* Minneapolis: University of Minnesota Press.

Foucault, Michel. 1977. *Discipline and Punish: The Birth of the Prison.* Translated by Alan Sheridan. New York: Vintage Books.

———. 1978. *The History of Sexuality.* Vol. 1. New York: Vintage Books.

———. 2008. *The Birth of Biopolitics: Lectures at the Collège de France, 1978–79.* Edited by Michel Senellart, translated by Graham Burchell. Basingstoke: Palgrave Macmillan.

Freeman, Elizabeth. 2010. *Time Binds: Queer Temporalities, Queer Histories.* Durham, N.C.: Duke University Press.

Fukuyama, Francis. 1994. *Trust: The Social Virtues and the Creation of Prosperity.* New York: Free Press.

Fuller, Rex, D. Patrick Morton, and Ann Korschgen. 2005. "Incentive-Based Budgeting: Lessons from Public Higher Education." In *On Becoming a Productive University: Strategies for Reducing Cost and Increasing Quality in Higher Education,* edited by James E. Groccia and Judith E. Miller. San Francisco: Jossey-Bass.

Gallhofer, Sonja, and Jim Haslam. 2003. *Accounting and Emancipation: Some Critical Interventions.* New York: Routledge.

Garland, David. 1990. *Punishment and Modern Society: A Study in Social Theory.* Chicago: University of Chicago Press.

———. 2001. *The Culture of Control: Crime and Social Order in Contemporary Society.* Oxford: Oxford University Press.

Geronimus, Arline T., and J. Phillip Thompson. 2004. "To Denigrate, Ignore, or Disrupt: Racial Inequality in Health and the Impact of a Policy-Induced Breakdown of African American Communities." *Du Bois Review* 1 (2): 247–79.

Gersen, Hannah. 2011. "Bartleby's Occupation of Wall Street." The Millions, October 11. http://www.themillions.com.

Gilmore, Ruth Wilson. 2002. "Fatal Couplings of Power and Difference: Notes on Racism and Geography." *Professional Geographer* 54 (1): 15–24.

———. 2007. *Golden Gulag: Prisons, Surplus, Crisis, and Opposition in Globalizing California.* Berkeley: University of California Press.

Goode, Judith. 2002. "From New Deal to Bad Deal: Racial and Political Implications of U.S. Welfare Reform." In *Western Welfare in Decline: Globalization and Women's Poverty,* edited by Catherine Kingfisher. Philadelphia: University of Pennsylvania Press.

Gordon, Avery F. 1997. *Ghostly Matters: Haunting and the Sociological Imagination.* Minneapolis: University of Minnesota Press.

Gordon, Colin. 1991. "Governmental Rationality: An Introduction." In *The Foucault Effect: Studies in Governmentality,* edited by Graham Burchell, Colin Gordon, and Peter Miller. Chicago: University of Chicago Press.

Graeber, David. 2004. *Fragments of an Anarchist Anthropology.* Chicago: Prickly Paradigm Press.

———. 2011. *Debt: The First 5,000 Years.* Brooklyn, N.Y.: Melville House.

Gronewold, Laura. 2012. "Chick Lit and Its Canonical Forefathers: Anxieties about Female Subjectivity in Contemporary Women's Fiction." Ph.D. diss., University of Arizona.

Grow, Brian, and Keith Epstein. 2007. "The Poverty Business." *Bloomberg Businessweek,* May 20. http://www.businessweek.com.

Gubar, Susan. 1998."What Ails Feminist Criticism?" *Critical Inquiry* 24: 878–902.

Hall, Sarah. 2011. "Geographies of Money and Finance II: Financialization and Financial Subjects." *Progress in Human Geography* 36 (3): 403–11.

Hall, Stuart. 1990. "The Emergence of Cultural Studies and the Crisis of the Humanities." *October* 53 (Summer): 11–23.

———. 2003. "Marx's Notes on Method: A 'Reading' of the '1857 Introduction.'" *Cultural Studies* 17 (2): 113–49.

Hann, Chris. 2012. "CSSH Notes." Review of *Debt: The First 5,000 Years,* by David Graeber. *Comparative Studies in Society and History* 54 (2): 447–61.

Haraway, Donna. 1997. *Modest_Witness@Second_Millennium.FemaleMan©_ Meets_OncoMouse™: Feminism and Technoscience.* New York: Routledge.

Harcourt, Bernard E. 2007. *Against Prediction: Profiling, Policing, and Punishing in an Actuarial Age.* Chicago: University of Chicago Press.

———. 2008. *Neoliberal Penality: The Birth of Natural Order, the Illusion of Free Markets.* John M. Olin Law & Economics Working Paper No. 433 (2nd series). Chicago: University of Chicago Law School. http://ssrn.com.

Hardesty, Michele. 2011. "I Would Prefer Not To." Occupy Wall Street Library, October 26. http://peopleslibrary.wordpress.com.

Hardt, Michael, and Antonio Negri. 2000. *Empire.* Cambridge, Mass.: Harvard University Press.

Harney, Stefano, and Fred Moten. 2013. *The Undercommons: Fugitive Planning and Black Study.* Brooklyn, N.Y.: Minor Compositions.

Hartman, Saidiya. 1997. *Scenes of Subjection: Terror, Slavery, and Self-Making in Nineteenth-Century America.* New York: Oxford University Press.

———. 2007. *Lose Your Mother: A Journey along the Atlantic Slave Route.* New York: Farrar, Straus and Giroux.

Harvey, David. 1974. "Class-Monopoly Rent, Finance Capital and the Urban Revolution." *Regional Studies* 8 (3): 239–55.

———. 1990. *The Condition of Postmodernity: An Enquiry into the Origins of Cultural Change.* Oxford: Blackwell.

———. 2003. *The New Imperialism.* Oxford: Oxford University Press.

———. 2005. *A Brief History of Neoliberalism.* Oxford: Oxford University Press.

Hearn, James C., Darrell R. Lewis, Lincoln Kallsen, Janet M. Holdsworth, and Lisa M. Jones. 2006. "'Incentives for Managed Growth': A Case Study of Incentives-Based Planning and Budgeting in a Large Public Research University." *Journal of Higher Education* 77 (2): 286–316.

Heintz, James, and Radhika Balakrishnan. 2012. "Debt, Power, and Crisis: Social Stratification and the Inequitable Governance of Financial Markets." *American Quarterly* 64 (3): 387–409.

Hennessy, Rosemary. 2000. *Profit and Pleasure: Sexual Identities in Late Capitalism.* New York: Routledge.

———. 2003. "Class." In *A Concise Companion to Feminist Theory,* edited by Mary Eagleton. Oxford: Blackwell.

Herbert, Bob. 2006. "A Triumph of Felons and Failure." *New York Times,* August 24. http://www.nytimes.com.

Hilferding, Rudolf. 1981. *Finance Capital: A Study of the Latest Phase of Capitalist Development.* Edited by Tom Bottomore, translated by Morris Watnick and Sam Gordon. London: Routledge & Kegan Paul.

Ho, Karen. 2009. *Liquidated: An Ethnography of Wall Street.* Durham, N.C.: Duke University Press.

Hoskin, Keith W., and Richard Macve. 1988. "The Genesis of Accountability: The West Point Connections." *Accounting, Organizations and Society* 13 (1): 37–73.

———. 1994. "Writing, Examining, Disciplining: The Genesis of Accounting's Modern Power." In *Accounting as Social and Institutional Practice,* edited by Anthony G. Hopwood and Peter Miller. Cambridge: Cambridge University Press.

———. 2000. "Knowing More as Knowing Less? Alternative Histories of Cost and Management Accounting in the U.S. and the U.K." *Accounting Historians Journal* 27 (1): 91–149.

Hudson, Barbara. 1998. "Restorative Justice: The Challenge of Sexual and Racial Violence." *Journal of Law and Society* 25 (2): 237–56.

Jones, T. Colwyn. 1995. *Accounting and the Enterprise: A Social Analysis.* New York: Routledge.

Jones, T. Colwyn, and David Dugdale. 2001. "The Concept of an Accounting Regime." *Critical Perspectives on Accounting* 12: 35–63.

Joseph, Miranda. 2002. *Against the Romance of Community*. Minneapolis: University of Minnesota Press.

———. 2006. "A Debt to Society." In *The Seductions of Community: Emancipations, Oppressions, Quandaries*, edited by Gerald W. Creed. Santa Fe, N.M.: School of American Research Press.

———. 2010. "Accounting for Interdisciplinarity." In *Interdisciplinarity and Social Justice: Revisioning Academic Accountability*, edited by Joe Parker, Ranu Samantrai, and Mary Romero. Albany: State University of New York Press.

Kear, Mark. 2011. Review of *The Bonds of Debt: Borrowing against the Common Good*, by Richard Dienst, and *Debt: The First 5,000 Years*, by David Graeber. *Environment and Planning D: Society and Space*. http://societyandspace.com.

King, Martin Luther, Jr. 1963. "I Have a Dream." Address delivered at the March on Washington for Jobs and Freedom, August 28. King Papers Project. http://mlk-kpp01.stanford.edu.

Kingfisher, Catherine. 2002a. "Neoliberalism I: Discourses of Personhood and Welfare Reform." In *Western Welfare in Decline: Globalization and Women's Poverty*, edited by Catherine Kingfisher. Philadelphia: University of Pennsylvania Press.

———, ed. 2002b. *Western Welfare in Decline: Globalization and Women's Poverty*. Philadelphia: University of Pennsylvania Press.

Kinsella, Sophie. 2001. *Confessions of a Shopaholic*. New York: Bantam Dell.

Klein, Lauren. 2011. "What Bartleby Can Teach Us about Occupy Wall Street." Arcade, November 21. http://arcade.stanford.edu.

Kochhar, Rakesh, Richard Fry, and Paul Taylor. 2011. *Wealth Gaps Rise to Record Highs between Whites, Blacks and Hispanics*. Washington, D.C.: Pew Research Center.

Koeppel, David. 2008. "Single Women Slammed by Housing Mess." MSN Money, August 25. http://money.msn.com.

Kristeva, Julia. 1981. "Women's Time." *Signs: A Journal of Women in Culture and Society* 7 (1): 13–35.

Kristof, Nicholas D. 2005. "The Larger Shame." *New York Times*, September 6. http://www.nytimes.com.

Lacey, Nicola, and Lucia Zedner. 1995. "Discourses of Community in Criminal Justice." *Journal of Law and Society* 22 (3): 301–25.

Langenohl, Andreas. 2008. "'In the Long Run We Are All Dead': Imaginary Time in Financial Market Narratives." *Cultural Critique* 70: 3–31.

Langley, Paul. 2008. "Financialization and the Consumer Credit Boom." *Competition & Change* 12 (2): 133–47.

———. 2010. *The Everyday Life of Global Finance: Saving and Borrowing in Anglo-America*. Oxford: Oxford University Press.

Lapavitsas, Costas. 2009. "Financialised Capitalism: Crisis and Financial Expropriation." *Historical Materialism* 17 (2): 114–48.

Larner, Wendy. 2000. "Post–Welfare State Governance: Towards a Code of Social and Family Responsibility." *Social Politics* 7 (2): 244–65.

Lattman, Peter. 2012. "Former Citigroup Manager Cleared in Mortgage Securities Case." *New York Times,* July 31. http://www.nytimes.com.

Lauer, Josh. 2008. "From Rumor to Written Record: Credit Reporting and the Invention of Financial Identity in Nineteenth-Century America." *Technology and Culture* 49 (2): 301–24.

Lazzarato, Maurizio. 2012. *The Making of the Indebted Man: An Essay on the Neoliberal Condition.* Translated by Joshua D. Jordan. Los Angeles: Semiotext(e).

Leland, John. 2008. "Baltimore Finds Subprime Crisis Snags Women." *New York Times,* January 15. http://www.nytimes.com.

Leonhardt, David. 2006. "On Their Own: Save Yourself." *New York Times,* April 11. http://www.nytimes.com.

Leps, Marie-Christine. 1990. *Apprehending the Criminal: The Production of Deviance in Nineteenth-Century Discourse.* Durham, N.C.: Duke University Press.

Lewis, Michael. 1989. *Liar's Poker: Rising through the Wreckage on Wall Street.* New York: Norton.

Leyshon, Andrew, Nigel Thrift, and Jonathan Pratt. 1998. "Reading Financial Services: Texts, Consumers and Financial Literacy." *Environment and Planning D: Society and Space* 16 (1): 29–55.

Lieber, Ron. 2011. "For the Recently Widowed, Some Big Financial Pitfalls to Avoid." *New York Times,* September 2. http://www.nytimes.com.

Livingston, Ira. 2006. *Between Science and Literature: An Introduction to Autopoetics.* Urbana: University of Illinois Press.

Lofton, LouAnn. 2011. *Warren Buffett Invests Like a Girl: And Why You Should Too.* New York: HarperBusiness.

Lorenz, Chris. 2012. "If You're So Smart, Why Are You under Surveillance? Universities, Neoliberalism, and New Public Management." *Critical Inquiry* 38 (3): 599–629.

Luban, Daniel. 2012. "Indebted." *Dissent* 59 (2): 102–6.

Lubiano, Wahneema. 1992. "Black Ladies, Welfare Queens, and State Minstrels: Ideological War by Narrative Means." In *Race-ing Justice, En-gendering Power: Essays on Anita Hill, Clarence Thomas, and the Construction of Social Reality,* edited by Toni Morrison. New York: Pantheon.

Luciano, Dana. 2007. "Coming around Again: The Queer Momentum of *Far from Heaven.*" *GLQ* 13 (2–3): 249–72.

Luhmann, Niklas. 1979. *Trust and Power.* Chichester, England: Wiley.

Lukács, Georg. 1971. *History and Class Consciousness: Studies in Marxist Dialectics.* Cambridge: MIT Press.

Luken, Paul C., and Suzanne Vaughan. 2005. "'. . . Be a Genuine Homemaker in

Your Own Home': Gender and Familial Relations in State Housing Practices, 1917–1922." *Social Forces* 83 (4): 1603–26.

MacDonald, Scott B., and Albert L. Gastman. 2001. *A History of Credit and Power in the Western World*. New Brunswick, N.J.: Transaction.

Mahmood, Saba. 2005. *Politics of Piety: The Islamic Revival and the Feminist Subject*. Princeton, N.J.: Princeton University Press.

Mahmud, Tayyab. 2012. "Debt and Discipline." *American Quarterly* 64 (3): 469–94.

Mann, Bruce H. 2002. *A Republic of Debtors: Bankruptcy in the Age of American Independence*. Cambridge, Mass.: Harvard University Press.

Marron, Donncha. 2009. *Consumer Credit in the United States: A Sociological Perspective from the 19th Century to the Present*. New York: Palgrave Macmillan.

———. 2010. "Over-indebtedness, Consumption and the Self." Lecture presented at the Centre for Research on Socio-cultural Change conference "Finance in Question/Finance in Crisis," University of Manchester, April 12–14.

Martin, Andrew. 2011. "Judge Allows Redlining Suits to Proceed." *New York Times*, May 5. http://www.nytimes.com.

Martin, Randy. 2002. *Financialization of Daily Life*. Philadelphia: Temple University Press.

———. 2011a. "Taking an Administrative Turn: Derivative Logics for a Recharged Humanities." *Representations* 116 (1): 156–76.

———. 2011b. *Under New Management: Universities, Administrative Labor, and the Professional Turn*. Philadelphia: Temple University Press.

Marx, Karl. 1973. *Grundrisse*. Translated by Martin Nicolaus. New York: Random House.

———. 1977. *Capital*. Vol. 1. Translated by Ben Fowkes. New York: Random House.

———. 1990. *Capital: A Critique of Political Economy*. Vol. 3. Translated by David Fernbach. London: Penguin Books.

———. 1978. "On the Jewish Question." In *The Marx-Engels Reader*. 2nd ed. Edited by Robert C. Tucker. New York: Norton.

McDowell, Linda. 2010. "Capital Culture Revisited: Sex, Testosterone and the City." *International Journal of Urban and Regional Research* 34 (3): 652–58.

McLafferty, Sara L. 1995. "Counting Women." *Professional Geographer* 47 (4): 436–42.

McLaney, Eddie, and Peter Atrill. 2005. *Accounting: An Introduction*. 3rd ed. New York: Financial Times/Prentice Hall.

Meagher, Thomas F. *The Commercial Agency "System" of the United States and Canada Exposed*. New York, 1876.

Meaney, Thomas. 2011. "Anarchist Anthropology." *New York Times*, December 8. http://www.nytimes.com.

Meranze, Michael. 1996. *Laboratories of Virtue: Punishment, Revolution, and Authority, 1760–1835*. Chapel Hill: University of North Carolina Press.

Messer-Davidow, Ellen. 2002. *Disciplining Feminism: From Social Activism to Academic Discourse*. Durham, N.C.: Duke University Press.

Meyerhoff, Eli, Elizabeth Johnson, and Bruce Braun. 2011. "Time and the University." *ACME: An International E-Journal for Critical Geographies* 10 (3): 483–507.

Miller, Peter. 1994. "Accounting as Social and Institutional Practice: An Introduction." In *Accounting as Social and Institutional Practice*, edited by Anthony G. Hopwood and Peter Miller. Cambridge: Cambridge University Press.

Miller, Peter, and Ted O'Leary. 1987. "Accounting and the Construction of the Governable Person." *Accounting, Organizations and Society* 12 (3): 235–65.

Mitchell, Dan. 2008. "At Last, Buffett's Key to Success." *New York Times*, April 5. http://www.nytimes.com.

Moynihan, Daniel Patrick. 1965. *The Negro Family: The Case for National Action*. Washington, D.C.: U.S. Department of Labor, Office of Policy Planning and Research.

Muldrew, Craig. 1998. *The Economy of Obligation: The Culture of Credit and Social Relations in Early Modern England*. New York: St. Martin's Press.

Muñoz, José Esteban. 2007. "Cruising the Toilet: LeRoi Jones, Amiri Baraka, Radical Black Traditions, and Queer Futurity." *GLQ* 13 (2–3): 353–67.

National Research Council. 2011. *A Data-Based Assessment of Research-Doctorate Programs in the United States*. Washington, D.C.: National Academies Press.

Nature. 2007. "The University of the Future." Vol. 446 (April 26).

Nelson, Julie A. 1996. *Feminism, Objectivity and Economics*. London: Routledge.

———. 2012. *Would Women Leaders Have Prevented the Global Financial Crisis? Implications for Teaching about Gender, Behavior, and Economics*. INET Research Note 014 (Revision of Global Development and Environment Institute Working Paper No. 11-03). Rochester, N.Y.: Social Science Research Network.

Newfield, Christopher. 2008. *Unmaking the Public University: The Forty-Year Assault on the Middle Class*. Cambridge, Mass.: Harvard University Press.

Newman, Jane. 2002. "The Present in Our Past: Presentism in the Genealogy of Feminism." In *Women's Studies on Its Own*, edited by Robyn Wiegman. Durham, N.C.: Duke University Press.

Nietzsche, Friedrich. 1989. *On the Genealogy of Morals*. Translated by Walter Kaufman and R. J. Hollingdale. New York: Vintage Books.

Norris, Floyd. 2007. "Solving the Mortgage Crisis May Require a Guardian Angel." *New York Times*, December 21. http://www.nytimes.com.

Olegario, Rowena. 2006. *A Culture of Credit: Embedding Trust and Transparency in American Business*. Cambridge, Mass.: Harvard University Press.

Omi, Michael, and Howard Winant. 1994. *Racial Formation in the United States: From the 1960s to the 1990s*. New York: Routledge.

Orman, Suze. 2007. *Women and Money: Owning the Power to Control Your Destiny*. New York: Spiegel & Grau.

Parker, Joe, Ranu Samantrai, and Mary Romero, eds. 2010. *Interdisciplinarity and Social Justice: Revisioning Academic Accountability*. Albany: State University of New York Press.

Pavlich, George. 2001. "The Force of Community." In *Restorative Justice and Civil Society*, edited by Heather Strang and John Braithwaite. Cambridge: Cambridge University Press.

Pollitt, Christopher. 1995. "Justification by Works or by Faith? Evaluating the New Public Management." *Evaluation* 1 (2): 133–54.

Poovey, Mary. 1995. *Making a Social Body: British Cultural Formation, 1830–1864*. Chicago: University of Chicago Press.

———. 1998. *A History of the Modern Fact: Problems of Knowledge in the Sciences of Wealth and Society*. Chicago: University of Chicago Press.

———. 2001a. "For Everything Else, There's . . ." *Social Research* 68 (2): 397–426.

———. 2001b. "The Twenty-First-Century University and the Market: What Price Economic Viability?" *differences: A Journal of Feminist Cultural Studies* 12 (1): 1–16.

———. 2003. "Can Numbers Ensure Honesty? Unrealistic Expectations and the U.S. Accounting Scandal." *Notices of the American Mathematical Society* 50 (1): 27–35.

Postone, Moishe. 1993. *Time, Labor, and Social Domination: A Reinterpretation of Marx's Critical Theory*. Cambridge: Cambridge University Press.

Powell, Michael. 2010. "Blacks in Memphis Lose Decades of Economic Gains." *New York Times*, May 30. http://www.nytimes.com.

Power, Michael. 1997. *The Audit Society: Rituals of Verification*. Oxford: Oxford University Press.

Pranis, Kay. 1998. *Engaging the Community in Restorative Justice*. Balanced and Restorative Justice Project (Grant 95-JN-FX-0024). Washington, D.C.: U.S. Department of Justice, Office of Juvenile Justice and Delinquency Prevention.

———. 2001. *Building Justice on a Foundation of Democracy, Caring and Mutual Responsibility*. Saint Paul: Minnesota Department of Corrections, Community and Juvenile Services Division.

Prebble, Lucy. 2009. *Enron*. London: Methuen Drama.

Previts, Gary John, and Barbara Dubis Merino. 1998. *A History of Accountancy in the United States: The Cultural Significance of Accounting*. Columbus: Ohio State University Press.

Prudential Financial. 2012. *Financial Experience and Behaviors among Women: 2012–2013 Prudential Research Study*. Newark, N.J.: Prudential Financial. http://research.prudential.com.

Purdue University. 2008. "New Synergies: Strategic Plan: 2008–2013 (Draft 4/21/08)." West Lafayette, Indiana.

Pyle, Kevin, Susan Willmarth, Sabrina Jones, Ellen Miller-Mack, Craig Gilmore, and Lois Ahrens. 2008. *Prison Town: Paying the Price*. Oakland, Calif.: PM Press.

Quattrone, Paolo. 2005. "Is Time Spent, Passed or Counted? The Missing Link between Time and Accounting History." *Accounting Historians Journal* 32 (1): 185–208.

Rancière, Jacques. 1989. "The Concept of 'Critique' and the 'Critique of Political Economy.'" In *Ideology, Method and Marx: Essays from Economy and Society,* edited by Ali Rattansi. London: Routledge.

Readings, Bill. 1996. *The University in Ruins.* Cambridge, Mass.: Harvard University Press.

Rees, John. 1998. *The Algebra of Revolution: The Dialectic and the Classical Marxist Tradition.* New York: Routledge.

Rhoades, Gary. 1998. *Managed Professionals: Unionized Faculty and Restructuring Academic Labor.* Albany: State University of New York Press.

Ricciardi, Victor. 2008. *The Financial Psychology of Worry and Women.* Rochester, N.Y.: Social Science Research Network.

Rifkin, Glenn. 2006. "Financial Advice for the 'Mass Affluent.'" *New York Times,* April 6. http://www.nytimes.com.

Roberts, Mary Louise. 1998. "Gender, Consumption, and Commodity Culture." *American Historical Review* 103 (3): 817–44.

Roitman, Janet. 2003. "Unsanctioned Wealth; or the Productivity of Debt in Northern Cameroon." *Public Culture* 15 (2): 211–37.

Rose, Nikolas. 1999. *Powers of Freedom: Reframing Political Thought.* New York: Cambridge University Press.

Roth, Louise M. 2006. *Selling Women Short: Gender Inequality on Wall Street.* Princeton, N.J.: Princeton University Press.

Rubin, Gayle. 1975. "The Traffic in Women: Notes on the 'Political Economy' of Sex." In *Toward an Anthropology of Women,* edited by Rayna R. Reiter. New York: Monthly Review Press.

Rubin, Lillian B. 1992. *Worlds of Pain: Life in the Working-Class Family.* New York: Basic Books.

Saegert, Susan, Desiree Fields, and Kimberly Libman. 2009. "Deflating the Dream: Radical Risk and the Neoliberalization of Homeownership." *Journal of Urban Affairs* 31 (3): 297–317.

Scannell, Kara. 2009. "FASB Eases Mark-to-Market Rules." *Wall Street Journal,* April 3, C1.

Schor, Julia. 1991. *The Overworked American: The Unexpected Decline of Leisure.* New York: Basic Books.

———. 1998. *The Overspent American: Upscaling, Downshifting, and the New Consumer.* New York: Basic Books.

Schultz, Sally M., and Joan Hollister. 2004. "Single-Entry Accounting in Early America: The Accounts of the Hasbrouck Family." *Accounting Historians Journal* 31 (1): 141–74.

Scobey, David. 2009. "Meanings and Metrics." Inside Higher Ed, March 19. http://www.insidehighered.com.

Scott, Joan W. 1986. "Gender: A Useful Category of Historical Analysis." *American Historical Review* 91 (5): 1053–75.

Scott, Joan Wallach, ed. 1997. "Women's Studies on the Edge." Special issue. *differences: A Journal of Feminist Cultural Studies* 9 (3).

Seligson, Hannah. 2010. "The Shopaholic Myth." Slate, November 10. http://www.slate.com.

Sennett, Richard. 2006. *Culture of the New Capitalism.* New Haven, Conn.: Yale University Press.

Serido, Joyce, Soyeon Shim, Anubha Mishra, and Chuanyi Tang. 2010. "Financial Parenting, Financial Coping Behaviors, and Well-Being of Emerging Adults." *Family Relations* 59: 453–64.

Sherman, Lawrence W. 2003. "Reason for Emotion: Reinventing Justice with Theories, Innovations, and Research—The American Society of Criminology 2002 Presidential Address." *Criminology* 41 (1): 1–38.

Shim, Soyeon, Bonnie L. Barber, Noel A. Card, Jing Jian Xiao, and Joyce Serido. 2010. "Financial Socialization of First-Year College Students: The Roles of Parents, Work, and Education." *Journal of Youth and Adolescence* 39 (12): 1457–70.

Shim, Soyeon, and Joyce Serido. 2010a. *Arizona Pathways to Life Success for University Students: Wave 1.5 Economic Impact Study—Financial Well-Being, Coping Behaviors and Trust among Young Adults.* Tucson: University of Arizona.

———. 2010b. *Transitioning into Adulthood during Economic Uncertainty: APLUS Wave 1.5.* Tucson: University of Arizona.

———. 2011. *Young Adults' Financial Capability: Arizona Pathways to Life Success for University Students Wave 2.* Tucson: University of Arizona.

Shore, Cris, and Susan Wright. 2000. "Coercive Accountability: The Rise of Audit Culture in Higher Education." In *Audit Cultures: Anthropological Studies in Accountability, Ethics, and the Academy,* edited by Marilyn Strathern. London: Routledge.

———. 2004. "Whose Accountability? Governmentality and the Auditing of Universities." *Parallax* 10 (2): 100–116.

Silva, Denise Ferreira da. 2007. *Toward a Global Idea of Race.* Minneapolis: University of Minnesota Press.

Silver-Greenberg, Jessica. 2012. "Perfect 10? Never Mind That. Ask Her for Her Credit Score." *New York Times,* December 25. http://www.nytimes.com.

Slaughter, Sheila, and Larry L. Leslie. 1997. *Academic Capitalism: Politics, Policies, and the Entrepreneurial University.* Baltimore: Johns Hopkins University Press.

Slaughter, Sheila, and Gary Rhoades. 2004. *Academic Capitalism and the New Economy: Markets, State, and Higher Education.* Baltimore: Johns Hopkins University Press.

Smith, Andrea. 2010a. "Decolonizing Anti-rape Law and Strategizing Accountability in Native American Communities." *Social Justice* 37 (4): 36–43.

————. 2010b. "Queer Theory and Native Studies: The Heteronormativity of Settler Colonialism." *GLQ* 16 (1–2): 42–68.

Smith, Anna Marie. 2002. "The Sexual Regulation Dimension of Contemporary Welfare Law: A Fifty State Overview." *Michigan Journal of Gender and Law* 8 (2): 121–218.

Smith, Susan J. 2008. "Owner-Occupation: At Home with a Hybrid of Money and Materials." *Environment and Planning A* 40 (3): 520–35.

Sohn-Rethel, Alfred. 1978. *Intellectual and Manual Labour: A Critique of Epistemology.* London: Macmillan.

Solinger, Rickie. 2000. *Wake Up Little Susie: Single Pregnancy and Race before Roe v. Wade.* 2nd ed. New York: Routledge.

————. 2007. "Interrupted Life: Incarcerated Mothers in the United States: A Traveling Public Art Exhibition." *Meridians: Feminism, Race, Transnationalism* 7 (2): 63–70.

Sommer, Jeff. 2010. "How Men's Overconfidence Hurts Them as Investors." *New York Times,* March 14. http://www.nytimes.com.

Soss, Joe, Richard C. Fording, and Sanford F. Schram. 2011. *Disciplining the Poor: Neoliberal Paternalism and the Persistent Power of Race.* Chicago: University of Chicago Press.

Spence, Crawford. 2009. "Social Accounting's Emancipatory Potential: A Gramscian Critique." *Critical Perspectives on Accounting* 20: 205–27.

Spivak, Gayatri Chakravorty. 1999. *A Critique of Postcolonial Reason: Toward a History of the Vanishing Present.* Cambridge, Mass.: Harvard University Press.

————. 2003. *Death of a Discipline.* New York: Columbia University Press.

Stein, Ben. 2005. "O.K., Freshmen, It's Time to Study the Real World." *New York Times,* August 28. http://www.nytimes.com.

Suskind, Ron. 2004. "Faith, Certainty and the Presidency of George W. Bush." *New York Times,* October 17. http://www.nytimes.com.

Swan, Scott. 2011. "Research Shows Women Invest Better than Men." WHTR, September 29. http://www.wthr.com.

Taylor, Avram. 2002. *Working Class Credit and Community since 1918.* New York: Palgrave Macmillan.

Thompson, E. P. 1967. "Time, Work-Discipline, and Industrial Capitalism." *Past and Present* 38: 56–97.

Thompson, Grahame. 1994. "Early Double-Entry Bookkeeping and the Rhetoric of Accounting Calculation." In *Accounting as Social and Institutional Practice,* edited by Anthony G. Hopwood and Peter Miller. Cambridge: Cambridge University Press.

Thorne, Deborah K. 2001. "Personal Bankruptcy through the Eyes of the Stigmatized: Insight into Issues of Shame, Gender, and Marital Discord." Ph.D. diss., Washington State University.

Tinker, Tony. 1985. *Paper Prophets: A Social Critique of Accounting.* New York: Praeger.

Tonry, Michael. 1999. *Reconsidering Indeterminate and Structured Sentencing.* Sentencing and Corrections: Issues for the 21st Century, Papers from the Executive Sessions on Sentencing and Corrections, no. 2, September. Washington, D.C.: U.S. Department of Justice, Office of Justice Programs, National Institute of Justice.

Torre, María Elena, Michelle Fine, Kathy Boudin, Iris Bowen, Judith Clark, Donna Hylton, Migdalia "Missy" Martinez, Rosamarie A. Roberts, Pamela Smart, and Debora Upegui. 2001. "A Space for Co-constructing Counter Stories under Surveillance." *Critical Psychology* 4: 149–66.

Toscano, Alberto. 2008. "The Open Secret of Real Abstraction." *Rethinking Marxism* 20 (2): 273–87.

Tyson, Thomas. 1990. "Accounting for Labor in the Early 19th Century: The U.S. Arms Making Experience." *Accounting Historians Journal* 17 (1): 47–59.

University of Minnesota, Office of the President. 2007. *Transforming the U for the 21st Century: Strategic Positioning Report to the Board of Regents.* Minneapolis: University of Minnesota.

University of North Carolina at Chapel Hill. 2003. *Academic Plan.* Chapel Hill: University of North Carolina.

———. 2004. *Progress Report on the Academic Plan* (Robert N. Shelton, Executive Vice Chancellor and Provost). Chapel Hill: University of North Carolina.

U.S. Department of Education. 2006. *A Test of Leadership: Charting the Future of U.S. Higher Education.* Washington, D.C.: U.S. Department of Education.

Valverde, Mariana. 1999. "Derrida's Justice and Foucault's Freedom: Ethics, History, and Social Movements." *Law & Social Inquiry* 24 (3): 655–76.

Virno, Paolo. 2004. *A Grammar of the Multitude: For an Analysis of Contemporary Forms of Life.* Cambridge, Mass.: Semiotext(e).

Vobejda, Barbara. 1996. "Clinton Signs Welfare Bill amid Division." *Washington Post,* August 23. http://www.washingtonpost.com.

Wacquant, Loïc. 2005. "Race as Civic Felony." *International Social Science Journal* 57 (183): 127–42.

Walker, Stephen P. 2005. "Accounting in History." *Accounting Historians Journal* 32 (2): 233–59.

Warren, Elizabeth, and Amelia Warren Tyagi. 2003. *The Two-Income Trap: Why Middle-Class Parents Are Going Broke.* New York: Basic Books.

Weber, Max. 2000. *The Protestant Ethic and the Spirit of Capitalism.* Translated by Talcott Parsons. London: Routledge.

Wellman, Jane V., Donna M. Desrochers, and Colleen M. Lenihan. 2008. *The Growing Imbalance: Recent Trends in U.S. Postsecondary Education Finance.* Washington, D.C.: Delta Cost Project.

White, Brent T. 2009. *Underwater and Not Walking Away: Shame, Fear and the Social Management of the Housing Crisis.* Arizona Legal Studies Discussion Paper No. 09-35. Tucson: University of Arizona, James E. Rogers College of Law.

Wiegman, Robyn. 2000. "Feminism's Apocalyptic Futures." *New Literary History* 31: 805–25.

———. 2002a. "Introduction: On Location." In *Women's Studies on Its Own*, edited by Robyn Wiegman. Durham, N.C.: Duke University Press.

———. 2002b. "Academic Feminism against Itself." *NWSA Journal* 14 (2): 18–37.

———. 2004. "On Being in Time with Feminism." *Modern Language Quarterly* 65 (1): 161–76.

Williams, Brett. 1994. "Babies and Banks: The 'Reproductive Underclass' and the Raced, Gendered Masking of Debt." In *Race,* edited by Steven Gregory and Roger Sanjek. New Brunswick, N.J.: Rutgers University Press.

Williams, Juan. 2006. "Getting Past Katrina." *New York Times,* September 1. http://www.nytimes.com.

Woodward, Kathleen M. 1999. "Statistical Panic." *differences: A Journal of Feminist Cultural Studies* 11 (2): 177–203.

———. 2009. *Statistical Panic: Cultural Politics and Poetics of the Emotions.* Durham, N.C.: Duke University Press.

Wootton, Charles W., and Mary Virginia Moore. 2000. "The Legal Status of Account Books in Colonial America." *Accounting History* 5 (1): 33–58.

Yin, Maryann. 2011. "'Bartleby, the Scrivener' Reading at Occupy Wall Street." GalleyCat, November 11. http://www.mediabistro.com/galleycat.

Zehr, Howard. 1990. *Changing Lenses: A New Focus for Crime and Justice.* Scottdale, Pa.: Herald Press.

Zelizer, Viviana A. 1997. *The Social Meaning of Money: Pin Money, Paychecks, Poor Relief, and Other Currencies.* Princeton, N.J.: Princeton University Press.

Zeman, Thomas E. 1982. "Order, Crime, and Punishment: The American Criminological Tradition." PhD diss., University of California, Santa Cruz.

Žižek, Slavoj. 1989. *The Sublime Object of Ideology.* London: Verso.

———. 2006. *The Parallax View.* Cambridge: MIT Press.

INDEX

abstraction: Berlant on dialectic between embodiment and, 156n12; critical, xx, 125–26; generative role of, 9, 14–16; Gilmore on, 10–11; Graeber on, 10, 15, 157n8; Marx on, 9, 11–14, 15; Poovey on, xviii–xix; as process rather than product, recognizing, 10–11, 13–15; "real," 11–14; violences attributed to, xvii–xx, 10–11

abstraction/particularity dialectic, xi, xiv, xxi, 3, 6, 55; the concrete as product of abstract social processes and relations, 13–14; of credit reporting system, 45; double-entry bookkeeping and, 26–28; in exchange of women, 16–17; Gordon's "haunting," 15; intervening directly in articulation of, 147–48; new communality and, 42; predatory lending and articulation of, 25; in slave trade, 16, 17–18; technologies of articulation of, 25–28

Academic Capitalism (Slaughter and Leslie), 123

Academic Capitalism and the New Economy (Slaughter and Rhoades), 123

academic knowledge production. *See* knowledge production

academy, contesting value in, 119–49; "culture wars" attacks on universities and, 143; discourse of "excellence" as rationale of bureaucratic accounting, 124; downsizing and reorganization, 128–30; genesis of accountability in universities, 142; impact of measurement and rankings, 135–39; interdisciplinarity to solve "societal grand challenges," 126–27; modes of accountability in, 130–45; response to quantitative accounting, 139–49; sets of metrics, 133–35, 136, 137, 168n12; sets of metrics, values embodied in, 134–35

accountability: accounting for purpose of public, 26; conjunctures of accounting practices and regimes of, xvi–xvii; connotations of, xii–xiii; of criminal to society, under social contract, 47–49; divergence in regimes of, xiii–xiv; of elected officials, 144; for financial crisis (2008), debate over, xii–xiv; Foucault on,

MIRANDA JOSEPH is professor of gender and women's studies at the University of Arizona. She is the author of *Against the Romance of Community* (Minnesota, 2002) and coauthor (with Sandra K. Soto) of "Neoliberalism and the Battle over Ethnic Studies in Arizona," in *Thought and Action: The NEA Higher Education Journal,* which received the National Education Association Excellence in the Academy Award: Democracy in Higher Education. She served as chair of the University of Arizona Strategic Planning and Budget Advisory Committee, 2007–2009.